a call to # Prayer

for the
Children,
Teens, and
Young Adults
of the
10/40 Window

Beverly Pegues and Nancy Huff

YWAM
PUBLISHING

P.O. BOX 55787   SEATTLE, WA 98155

YWAM Publishing is the publishing ministry of Youth With A Mission. Youth With A Mission (YWAM) is an international missionary organization of Christians from many denominations dedicated to presenting Jesus Christ to this generation. To this end, YWAM has focused its efforts in three main areas: 1) training and equipping believers for their part in fulfilling the Great Commission (Matthew 28:19); 2) personal evangelism; 3) mercy ministry (medical and relief work).

For a free catalog of books and materials, contact:
YWAM Publishing
P.O. Box 55787, Seattle, WA 98155
(425) 771-1153 or (800) 922-2143
www.ywampublishing.com

A Call to Prayer for the Children, Teens,
and Young Adults of the 10/40 Window

Copyright © 2002 by Beverly Pegues and Nancy Huff

10 09 08 07 06 05 04 03 02   10 9 8 7 6 5 4 3 2 1

Published by YWAM Publishing
P.O. Box 55787, Seattle, WA 98155

ISBN 1-57658-255-8

Printed in the United States of America.

To the modern-day Heroes of the Faith who are laboring in the field without recognition but are being used powerfully by God to impact the children, teens, and young adults in the 10/40 Window for Christ.

Special Tribute

This is a special tribute to my dearly beloved husband, Leonard, who went home to be with the Lord on Monday, November 19, 2001. We had been married nearly 27 years.

We began our journey in the 10/40 Window together in 1992. He was such an important part of impacting the 10/40 Window with the gospel. He loved ministering to those living in our beloved Window and strongly believed that believers in this generation will reach the Window with the gospel.

Leonard was a man of valor and wisdom, a man of God, an encourager, my love, and my very best friend. LaTonya, family members, and I miss his beautiful dimpled smile and lovely demeanor.

A year ago Leonard told me he had completed everything God had called him to do on the planet. Of course, I wasn't ready to let him go. A good friend said it best: "Leonard is now an honored guest at the King's table!"

BEVERLY PEGUES

Acknowledgments

Many of us have traveled to areas where there is no hope for the children outside of a miracle from God. We have viewed the world through the eyes of a suffering child, and the love of God compels us to speak up for them, tell their story, and urge those who know Jesus Christ as a personal Savior to pray and intercede on their behalf.

For each one who helped in this project, we are grateful. We give recognition in this world to those who volunteered, but the God who keeps records knows the time and effort put into this project, and our prayer is that what they have done in secret, He will reward openly.

Each country in the *10/40 Window* required many hours of research before its story could be told. Thank you to our volunteer research team. We deeply appreciate the excellent work of Cristine Crowe and her team of researchers: Dianna Williams, Stephanie Cousins, Cindy Golden, Annette Hammond, Stacey Humphrey, Jeanine Mackenzie, Sharon Manning, Susan Waddell, Amy Williams, and Jean Wulf. Cheryl Chamberlain and Jo Heck also worked on the research in the office of Teach the Children International.

We are extremely appreciative of the WINDOW INTERNATIONAL NETWORK staff, Casey Collins and Jackie Shepherd, who worked diligently on this project. Thank you for finishing the race with us.

We are very thankful to our faithful volunteer editor, Sue Henderson. Sue turned 71 years old last year, and it was difficult for us to keep up with her! She held our feet to the fire and worked long hours to see this book to completion. We appreciate you, Sue. Our thanks also to Stephana Colbert for proofreading with a fresh eye and for her suggestions.

We also realize the vital role that our adult children, LaTonya Pegues and Amanda and Jonathan Huff, played in this book. Thank you, LaTonya, Amanda, and Jonathan, for giving us eyes to see the children of the world. We bless you, our special treasures from heaven.

We are particularly grateful for the important role played by our wonderful husbands, Leonard Pegues and Keith Huff. Leonard's and Keith's constant encouragement and loving support were vital to the completion of the book. It's amazing how our husbands are always cheering for us, no matter how many projects we take on! Thank you, men of God.

Contents

Introduction

Speak up for those who cannot speak for themselves, for the rights of all who are destitute. Speak up and judge fairly; defend the rights of the poor and needy (Proverbs 31:8–9).

Imagine that you, your children, or your grandchildren were born in the 10/40 Window. This would mean that any or all of a score of social ills—abject poverty, starvation, famine, illiteracy, ethnic wars, martyrdom, female genital mutilation, child prostitution, pedophilia, poor health, AIDS, and many others—would plague your lives.

The 10/40 Window is a geographic location where nearly four billion people live, 70 percent of whom are under the age of 35. The Window spans the globe from 10 degrees to 40 degrees north of the equator, including North Africa, West Africa, the Middle East, and the Far East. Within this area, comprising 65 nations where the poorest of the poor eke out a living, lie the headquarters of three major non-Christian religions—Islam, Buddhism, and Hinduism—as well as many indigenous religions. Children are being raised under tyrannical governments in the midst of political upheaval with very little chance of ever hearing the gospel.

It is disheartening that in this supertechnological age nearly 38 percent of the world's population still have not heard the gospel even once in a culturally sensitive way and in their own language. The majority of them live in the 10/40 Window.

Children are being conscripted into the armies of many of these countries, sometimes at the tender age of six or seven, and methodically trained to kill. They are systematically programmed to hate and massacre certain people groups; therefore, they have no respect for and do not value the sanctity of life. Ungodly governments and radical factions are deliberately searing the consciences of these precious little ones who, if they are not reached with the gospel, will become the tyrants of the next generation.

Many of the social ills that are plaguing people in the 10/40 Window have long been resolved in developed nations. It is an established fact that education is the single most important factor in combating poverty, child labor, high rates of infant mortality, and exploitation of children. Nevertheless, more than 130 million children of primary-school age, most of whom live in the 10/40 Window, have not had an opportunity to attend school.

God has given the church financial resources, manpower, and knowledge to overcome the social ills that are prevalent in these nations. Many times He commands us in the Bible to minister to those less fortunate than ourselves and to take the gospel to those who have not heard His transforming message. This especially includes those living in the dreadful conditions of the 10/40 Window.

We must be proactive in our approach to this international problem. It will negatively affect the lives of future generations unless we, as God's people, rise up and seek His plans for reaching the 10/40 Window with the gospel. Our marching orders from the Lord will come through prayer. Ask God to impress on your heart to pray for the children, teens, and young adults in the Window. You as a Christian have been called to shepherd the nations, battle against the forces of darkness, and ask God's blessings on the nations in your prayer closet.

When God wants to change a country, He moves on the hearts of His people to pray—prayer is the beginning of the change process. Christians don't go on prayer journeys in the 10/40 Window because it's a nice vacation spot. They usually go because they started praying during one of the prayer initiatives—Praying Through the Window I, II, III, IV, or V— and God prompted them to prayerwalk the land. We have been called by Jesus Christ to go into all the world and preach the gospel.

It may be that you don't know how to start. The first step is prayer, which leads to giving, which leads to going—one step at a time. As you pray, God will give you insight into how you fit into His great plan. He will reveal how you are to use your training, profession, talents, finances, and gifts to rescue the children, teens, and young adults in the 10/40 Window. One of the greatest acts of faith is offering a simple prayer for a child, teen, or young adult you have never seen, in a land where you have never been, for things about which you may never know God's answer in this life.

Unless we respond to their cries for help, these young ones face a bleak future. The task may seem overwhelming, but as together we seek God, He will release His sovereign plan to reach these precious ones. Our responsibility is to pray and obey once God has revealed our personal responsibility. Some are called to go; some are called to pray. God will show us where we fit in—through prayer, planning, time, or finances.

It is shocking that 87 percent of the U.S.$207 billion given by Christians in 1999 to the church was spent inside the walls of the church,

12 percent on "retelling the told" (those who have heard the gospel many times but rejected it), and 1 percent on missions. Only 1/20 of the 1 percent spent on missions is spent in the 10/40 Window, where nearly 1.6 billion people have yet to hear the gospel for the first time. In the perspective of God's revealed plan, it is difficult to understand these figures.

Allocation of Global Church Income

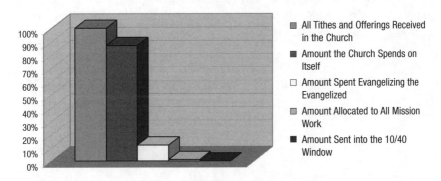

- All Tithes and Offerings Received in the Church
- Amount the Church Spends on Itself
- Amount Spent Evangelizing the Evangelized
- Amount Allocated to All Mission Work
- Amount Sent into the 10/40 Window

According to the researchers and authors of *World Christian Encyclopedia,* Dr. David Barrett et al., for every American dollar spent reaching a person in the West with the gospel, we could reach 100 people (and in some ethnolinguistic groups, 1,000 people) in the 10/40 Window. What would the Lord consider the best investment into His kingdom? The reality is, we can spend time *now* to pray, go, and invest the finances needed to reach these people with the gospel, or we can spend time and billions of dollars later to defend ourselves against the tyrannical dictators and evil fanatics that we help to create by doing nothing.

God is calling Great Commission Christians who will see beyond the four walls of their churches and look realistically at the cold, hard facts. There is a part of the world where children are starving, enslaved in bonded labor, sold into prostitution, dying of childhood diseases, being orphaned by the tens of thousands in the growing AIDS epidemic, and growing up in abject poverty with no way of escape because they have not heard the transforming message of the gospel of Jesus Christ.

It is our prayer that this book will be a wake-up call to bring the church to a new level of awareness so that God can use His people as informed intercessors who pray targeted prayers that will bring a new generation of young people out of darkness into his marvelous light.

Is God speaking to you about a specific nation or an at-risk group within the 10/40 Window—Thailand's child prostitutes, Sri Lanka's young boys falling prey to a growing number of pedophiles, or Sudan's war-ravaged, starving, undereducated children? Whatever He has put on your heart, we have broken down these huge problems into prayers that can be prayed in a few moments. Now is the time to join the millions who will pray for the children, teens, and young adults of the 10/40 Window.

Co-author Nancy Huff, our research and editorial teams, and I believe that as the children, teens, and young adults are prayed for and exposed to the gospel, they will be part of one of the greatest revivals ever known to mankind.

BEVERLY PEGUES, President and Founder
WINDOW INTERNATIONAL NETWORK
Colorado Springs, Colorado
USA

The World of Children at a Glance *

There are approximately 50 million uprooted people around the world—refugees who have sought safety in another country and people displaced within their own country. Around half of this displaced population is children.

The United Nations High Commissioner for Refugees cares for 22.3 million of these people. An estimated 10 million are children under the age of 18.

The majority of people flee their homes because of war. It is estimated that more than two million children were killed in conflict in the last decade. Another six million are believed to have been wounded and one million orphaned.

In recent decades the proportion of war victims who are civilians rather than combatants has leaped from 5 percent to more than 90 percent.

Children in 87 countries live among 60 million land mines. As many as 10,000 children per year continue to become victims of mines.

More than 300,000 boys and girls currently are serving as child soldiers around the world. Many are less than 10 years old. Many girl soldiers are forced into different forms of sexual slavery.

The 1989 Convention on the Rights of the Child is the most important legal framework for the protection of children. The Convention has the highest number of state parties of any human-rights treaty, being ratified by all countries except the United States and Somalia.

Last year the U.N. General Assembly approved two Optional Protocols to the convention, one on the sale of children and child pornography and another establishing 18 as the minimum age for participation of children in hostilities.

UNHCR [United Nations High Commissioner for Refugees] has recognized the special needs of refugee children and youngsters uprooted in their own countries. In the last few years, the agency has introduced many new programs, expanded others, and attempted to incorporate all of them into its operations.

---

* Permission given to reprint. "Refugees" (United Nations High Commissioner for Refugees, UNHCR, 2001), vol. 1, no. 122, p. 7.

Children, whether accompanied by parents or on their own, account for as many as half of all asylum seekers in the industrialized world. In 1996 Canada became the first country with a refugee determination system to issue specific guidelines on children seeking asylum.

At any one time there may be up to 100,000 separated children in Western Europe alone. As many as 20,000 separated children lodge asylum applications every year in Europe, North America, and Oceania.

Between 1994 and 1999 the U.N. requested $13.5 billion in emergency relief funding, much of it for children. It received less than $9 billion.

The amount of assistance varied dramatically by region. Donors provided the equivalent of 59 U.S. cents per person per day for 3.5 million people in Kosovo and Southeastern Europe in 1999, compared with 13 cents per person per day for 12 million African victims.

AIDS has killed more than 3.8 million children and orphaned another 13 million. In the last five years HIV/AIDS has become the greatest threat to children, especially in countries ravaged by war. In the worst affected countries, it is estimated that as many as half of today's 15-year-olds will die from the disease.

In 1998 donor countries allocated $300 million to combat AIDS, though an estimated $3 billion was needed.

More than 67,000 children were reunited with their families in Africa's Great Lakes region between 1994 and 2000, thanks to a global tracing program organized by humanitarian organizations.

An estimated 45,000 households in Rwanda today are headed by children, 90 percent of them girls.

School buildings, like teachers and children, have become deliberate targets in war. During the Mozambique conflict in the 1980s and '90s, for instance, 45 percent of schools were destroyed.

If developed countries met an agreed aid target of 0.7 percent of their gross national product, an extra $100 billion would be available to help the world's poorest nations.

Ten million children under the age of five die each year, the majority from preventable diseases and malnutrition.

Around 40 million children each year are not registered at birth, depriving them of a nationality and a legal name.

Afghanistan

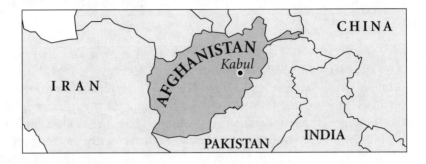

Major Languages: Pashtu, Afghan Persian (Dari)
Total Population: 25,889,000
Population 0–34: 19,795,000
Life Expectancy: 46 years
Religion: Muslim 97.89%, Parsee 1.50%, Hindu 0.35%, traditional ethnic
  0.10%, Baha'i 0.10%, Christian 0.02%, Sikh 0.02%, non-religious 0.01%,
  unknown 0.01%
Literacy Rate: male 46%, female 16%

*L*ate into the night 10-year-old Ismael listened to the sound of tanks
and truck engines as Taliban fighters fled his city of Mazar-e-Sharif.
Fear gripped him, and he couldn't sleep. He kept thinking, *What will hap-*
pen to my family? My father is dead, and I am the one who must protect my mother
and sister. How can I make sure they are safe? What if the soldiers come to take us
away? His stomach ached from hunger, and he couldn't stop worrying.

That morning his mother told him that the Taliban was gone and
American soldiers now occupied the city. At midday he heard shouting
in the streets and ventured outside to see what was causing the commo-
tion. He watched in amazement as the people of his city danced in the
marketplace. Men had cut off their beards, and women walked freely
without being covered from head to toe in their *burqas*. He realized there
was nothing here to fear. His people were free.

Later his friend came with enough paper and string to make a kite.
For five years kite flying and playing games had been forbidden by the
Taliban. He had almost forgotten how to make a kite, but with some
help they managed to put one together. He listened as his mother chat-
ted endlessly about the possibility of his sister going to school and how
she could now return to teaching and earn a living for the family.

Outside, with his friend and his new kite, Ismael dug his heels in as
he ran across the sandy ground. He glanced over his shoulder to watch

his new toy catch a draft and soar into the sky. Suddenly he felt the string tighten. He stopped and watched the kite rise above his head and flutter in the wind. This was indeed a new day for Ismael and for Afghanistan.

*F*or well over two decades Afghanistan has experienced civil war. In 1978 left-wing military leaders and civilians revolted and killed the prime minister, Muhammad Daoud Khan. The revolting faction then set up a government that favored the Soviet Union. Many Afghanis opposed this new government because they did not like the Soviets and they believed the new government policies conflicted with the teachings of Islam. Widespread fighting broke out between the government and rebel forces. The rebels called themselves *mujaheddin,* or holy warriors. In 1994 a faction of fighters called the Taliban rose to the forefront of the fighting and began to take over the country, enforcing strict Islamic law. By 1998 they occupied 90 percent of the country. Because of this prolonged civil strife, the country suffers from enormous poverty, a crumbling infrastructure, and live land mines throughout the countryside. Following the terrorist attack of September 11, 2001, instigated by one of the Taliban's most notorious leaders, Osama bin Laden, the United States and allied forces waged war on the militant Taliban in Afghanistan.

Today a different battle for the country's future looms on the horizon. The question of whether a girl should attend school is no longer asked; now the question is how to build new schools and restructure the few existing ones so that girls can attend. One no longer asks whether a woman can go to the market unaccompanied by her nearest unmarriageable male relative and without being clad in her burqa. The question is whether there will be food in the market to purchase. Though no longer ruled by the Department of Virtue and Vice, and though an interim government is in place, the Afghanis remain in limbo. The defeat of the Taliban and hopefully the end of the war will mark the beginning of the rebuilding of a nation that has known little but war for a long time.

The problems that face the children of Afghanistan run the gamut for children at risk. They not only know the horrors of war in a very real and intense way, but many of the young boys took up arms in the recent intense fighting. Only the love of Jesus can banish the trauma and hate that has saturated their lives.

Education held a low priority long before the conflicts of the past 20 years. In some sections of the country, the literacy rate for males is as low as 10 percent. For national, state, and local governments to reformulate with such a low level of education could prove to be extremely difficult. Currently there are only a few schools in the whole country, and those in operation are often run by foreign nongovernmental organizations. It could take years to build an educational system that will raise the literacy rate so that the majority of children will be able to read.

Malnutrition is also a major problem. The mainstay of a child's diet may be bread and tea. The results of poor nutrition—disease, birth defects, low birth weight, and high mortality rates—have taken a heavy toll on the children.

The conditions in Afghanistan have been so harsh that Afghanis have constituted the largest single refugee group in the world. In refugee camps in surrounding countries, Afghan children die daily of disease and suffer lack of food, medicine, clean water, and protection from the elements.

Afghanistan needs much prayer as the country is being rebuilt. The children need to know the love of God, who will heal the wounds of the past and give them hope and a future.

Prayer Points

- Pray for the eradication of childhood diseases afflicting Afghan children.
- Pray for the children in the mountainous regions to receive food, medical attention, and proper education.
- Pray for God to raise up leaders who fear Him and have a love for their people.
- Pray for the girl child who is devoid of any sense of self-worth and believes she has no value.
- Pray for this generation, that the hatred and violence of their countrymen will cease.
- Pray for a new government in Afghanistan that will value children.
- Pray that as Afghanistan is rebuilt, Christians will be allowed to provide services to children that will make a difference in their lives physically and spiritually.
- Pray for the girls and women, that God would restore the youthful years spent in oppression.
- Pray for God to raise up those who will educate the children.

Quick Reference

Ethnic Breakdown: Pashtun 47.5%, Tajik 17.9%, Uzbek 8.0%, Hazara 8.1%, minor ethnic groups (Aimaks, Turkmen, Balock, other) 18.5%
Type of Government: Interim government
Economy: Agriculture 53%, Industry 28.5%, Services 18.5%
Per capita income: U.S.$599

National debt: U.S.$5.5 billion
Economic conditions: Extremely poor

Education

Quality of education: There are only a few schools and teachers.
Gender discrimination against girls: The educational system is being restructured and may include girls. In the past, girls over eight were denied an education.

Religion

Religious concerns: Evangelism is prohibited. Afghanistan is one of the least-reached nations. Conversion to Christianity is punishable by death.
Status of the church: There are only a few secret national believers.
Are Christians being persecuted? Yes

Societal Viewpoint Toward Children

Are they viewed as precious? No
Are there street children? Yes
Is there a large population of orphans? Yes
Are there child soldiers? Yes
Is child labor a problem? Yes. There is no evidence that authorities enforce labor laws.

Albania

Major Languages: Albanian, Greek
Total Population: 3,490,000
Population 0–34: 2,212,000
Life Expectancy: 72 years
Religion: Christian 41.48%, Muslim 38.79%, nonreligious/other 19.54%,
   Baha'i 0.18%, Jewish 0.01%
Literacy Rate: male 95%, female 88%

Gwen nervously eyed the blinking brake light on the van's dashboard, but the driver didn't seem to notice. Gwen tried to leave the maneuvering of the sharp mountain curves to him by concentrating on the beautiful green mountains and the low-lying clouds they were driving through.

Because of the huge potholes and washed-out sections of road, the trip that should have taken three hours lasted over six. Tired and hungry, Gwen wondered how she would manage once they reached the mountain village.

The van rounded the last curve, and Gwen was surprised to see a sprawling city nestled in a lush green valley, complete with olive groves and high-rise buildings. They drove into town past huge steel mills. Inactive since the early '90s, the mills appeared to be rusting from the inside out. The city reflected its lack of jobs. It was the middle of the day, but the streets were vacant except for children playing there. Only a few shops were open, and the fountain in the middle of the city needed repair.

After a successful children's service for over 700 children, the local pastor talked to Gwen. "Will you help us?" he pleaded. "Just show us what to do and we will do it. We want to learn how to minister to our children. We just don't know how." Never in all her years as a youth minister had Gwen seen such openness to children's ministry.

19

"I didn't really come prepared," she tried to explain. "I only came to stay two days, and all I have is enough for five children's services, but I can do that." She thought of the meager amount of curriculum tucked away in her suitcase and prayed that the stories, prizes, and toys would help this pastor with his desire to reach children.

"Maybe you can help us with training," he suggested. "Would you be willing to talk this afternoon at 2:00 to some people who want to do children's ministry?"

At 2:00 Gwen was at the church, ready to talk to three or four children's ministers. Instead, over 30 men, women, and young adults showed up. Gwen taught them how to make flannelgraph figures, manipulate puppets, and teach children to act out a Bible story. Eager learners, they tried everything that was suggested. The next couple of days were a blur, taking these new "ministers" on outreaches to homes of migrant workers and apartment complex clubrooms. Children came from everywhere and readily soaked up the Bible lessons and special attention they were given.

While most Albanians are Muslims, many don't know why and are often soft in their beliefs. The church has experienced some major breakthroughs as large denominations have made inroads into the country. Much still needs to be done, but reaching the children in Albania is rich with possibilities.

Albania has workers, national ministers, who are doing a wonderful job with "Miracle Clubs," which are much like backyard Bible clubs. Another effective outreach to Albanian children is summer camps. For most of the children it is the nearest thing to a vacation they will ever see.

Because of poor soil and drought, Albania cannot produce enough food to feed its people, and the country is almost totally dependent on humanitarian efforts. Many children are malnourished. They are also undereducated. Educational opportunities are cut short, as many leave school early so that they can work to support their families. Albania is rich with promise for the future of the children, and pastors are asking for help. They need prayer and resources.

The infrastructure is in such disrepair that roads are often next to impossible to travel. Power blackouts are common, equipment repair is difficult, and telephones frequently do not work. Trying to minister under these conditions can be frustrating, and many give up. Pray for Albania. The people have an open door for the gospel, and this may be their hour to receive a visitation of God.

Prayer Points

~· Pray for God to bless the "Miracle Clubs" and every Christian effort to reach the children of Albania. Thank God for strategies and activities to help Muslim children see His great love for them.

~· Pray for the leaders in Albania as they struggle with problems of severe unemployment, crime, and lack of infrastructure.

~· Pray for protection of children who are being sold into sodomy and prostitution rings. Pray that God will expose this evil, protect the children, and emotionally heal these precious ones.

~· Pray for Albanians to find real friendship and love from Christians. Thank God for the hospitable and welcoming nature of the Albanian people.

~· Pray for stronger enforcement of laws meant to protect women. Because of its strategic location, Albania is a transit point for illegal drugs and trafficking of women and girls for the purpose of forced prostitution. Many times the women and girls are raped, beaten, and injected with heroin.

~· Pray for Christians to make an impact on the mainstream of Albanian government, education, business, agriculture, politics, and arts.

~· Pray that entire Albanian families will come to know Jesus Christ.

~· Pray for the unity of local Christian churches to work strategically to reach children, teens, and young adults, including those who are refugees from Kosovo.

~· Pray for the 25 percent of the population who are without homes, that the international church community will come alongside the local church to resolve this problem.

~· Pray for the Romany (Gypsy) children in Albania to be reached with the gospel of Jesus Christ.

Quick Reference

Ethnic Breakdown: Albanian 95%, Greeks 3%, Vlachs, Romany, Serbs, and Bulgarians 2%

Type of Government: Emerging democracy

Economy: Agriculture 54%, Industry 25%, Services 21%

Per capita income: U.S.$670

National debt: U.S.$820 million

Economic conditions: Extremely poor

Education

Quality of education: Eight years of education are required by law, although in rural areas, children leave school early to help their parents.

Gender discrimination against girls: Girls are being educated.

Religion

Religious concerns: Society is largely secular.

Status of the church: The church has grown steadily since the 1990s and needs discipleship and leadership training.

Are Christians being persecuted? No, but church leaders are encountering difficulty getting permits to build churches.

Societal Viewpoint Toward Children

Are they viewed as precious? No

Are there street children? Romany children beg on the streets.

Is there a large population of orphans? No specific data available.

Are there child soldiers? There are reports of young boys fighting with the ethnic Albanian Kosovars against Yugoslavia.

Is child labor a problem? Children are used in the labor force. Trafficking children for the purpose of prostitution is a problem.

Algeria

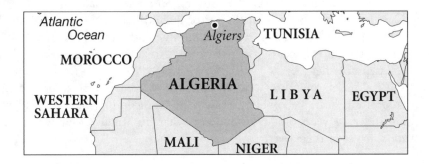

Major Languages: Arabic, French
Total Population: 31,194,000
Population 0–34: 23,067,000
Life Expectancy: 70 years
Religion: Muslim 96.68%, nonreligious 3.02%, Christian 0.29%, Baha'i 0.01%
Literacy Rate: male 73%, female 54%

Night settled over the desert, and sand blew in Kahmal's face as he waited for the new troops to come into camp. At the age of 26, Kahmal had achieved the status of *jihad* (holy war) commander and served the Armed Islamic Group (AIG—a militant Muslim offensive) for over 14 years. He and his devoted men had been involved in many skirmishes.

As new recruits came in every month, Kahmal drilled them to understand that anyone who was not a Muslim was an infidel and fit for death. He couldn't remember how many men, women, and children he'd killed. He should have kept count. After all, this would be his reward in the afterlife, and if he were killed in his redemption of others, so be it. Then he would have a glorious reward awaiting him in heaven.

Kahmal's first village raid was particularly difficult. For months afterward he woke up during the night with thoughts of the old woman who begged for the life of her daughter as the soldiers brutally raped the young girl.

That first malicious rape of a little girl the age of his sister made him sick to his stomach. He remembered vomiting for days and having horrendous nightmares. In retrospect, he realized that he had lived in torment every night for 14 years. Kahmal covered his ears because he could still hear the little girl scream as her mother begged the jihad soldiers not to abuse her daughter.

After training these new recruits, Kahmal would go with them into the small villages and perform raids. One little village at a time—that's how they would take over the country. So far they had seen whole villages abandoned because of the terror he and his troops inflicted on the "small people." Christians were the ones he hated most, and it would be Christians he trained his men to hate. Anyone who believed in Jesus Christ must die.

Kahmal's thoughts were interrupted with the arrival of the new troops. His heart sank when he saw that the incoming jihad soldiers were all under 15 years old! He wondered what nightmares they would have for the rest of their lives.

S eventy-four percent of Algeria's population is under the age of 35. They are looking for solutions to the problems in their country, and in their youthful zeal some of them have joined the AIG. In 1994 the AIG started a campaign to install an Islamic republic similar to those found in Iran and Saudi Arabia. One of its major focuses was to eliminate Jews, Christians, and polytheists from Algeria. In December 1997 these Islamic extremists killed 400 people in isolated villages in the Relizane region in one weekend. The BBC reported that over 100 were killed in other incidents that same weekend.

In July 1999 the U.N. Human Rights Committee declared that it was "appalled at the widespread massacre of men, women, and children in a great number of villages and towns, and at the sexual violence directed against women." The committee urged independent investigations into abuses, among which was the 1994 *fatwa* forbidding all children from going to school. Many obeyed that order for fear that violent acts might otherwise be committed against them.

Another concern of the U.N. committee was the high mortality rate among girls from ages one to ten because better care was provided for boys.

The government of Algeria initiated programs to assist children traumatized by violence. Over 150,000 children have been orphaned in Algeria as a result of the upheaval there. In May 1998 a UNICEF-appointed representative started activities to address the situation of children and women in the country.

Today Algeria constitutes yet another humanitarian crisis to which the West remains overtly indifferent. Tens of thousands of children have been affected by a decade of ongoing violence since the conflict within Algeria began. Hundreds of babies, children, and other vulnerable civilians have been seriously traumatized as a result of seeing family members shot, cut to pieces, or burned alive, and of witnessing bomb explosions and brutal military operations by security forces and armed groups.

Prayer Points

~· Pray for God to send dreams and visions of Jesus Christ, the one and only true God, to the young jihad soldiers so that they will be reached with the gospel and be discipled.

~· Pray for exposure of the lie that if a jihad soldier kills an infidel, the murderer is assured a place in heaven and seven virgins.

~· Pray for God's love to saturate the hatred and hardness of heart of those causing the human-rights violations against Algerian citizens.

~· Pray for UNICEF as it endeavors to improve the quality of life for the children.

~· Pray for the people displaced by terrorists, especially the 150,000 orphaned children. Pray that they will know the love of Christ and will be cared for.

~· Pray for the doors of the gospel to be open wide to the children, as the government has now made English the second language and English is being taught in the schools.

~· Pray for the West to become concerned about the ongoing violence and how it affects the children.

~· Pray for the protection of Christians from fierce terrorist insurgents.

Quick Reference

Ethnic Breakdown: Algerian Arab 59.1%, Hamyan Bedouin 6.9%, Greater Kabyle 6.1%, Shawlya 5.2%, Tajakant Bedouin 4.1%, other 18.6%

Type of Government: Republic, developing into an Islamic socialist state

Economy: Industry 51%, Services 37%, Agriculture 12%

Per capita income: U.S.$1,600

National debt: U.S.$30 billion

Economic conditions: Poor

Education

Quality of education: Instruction includes mandatory Koranic curriculum.

Gender discrimination against girls: Not much importance is placed on education for girls.

Religion

Religious concerns: Evangelism is prohibited. In 1994 the Armed Islamic Group declared its intention to eliminate Christians from Algeria.

Status of the church: The number of Christians is growing. Christians quietly practice their faith. The church needs discipleship and leadership training.

Are Christians being persecuted? Yes

Societal Viewpoint Toward Children

Are they viewed as precious? Boys are, girls are not.

Are there street children? Yes, it is a growing problem.

Is there a large population of orphans? There are 150,000 orphans in Algeria.
Are there child soldiers? Yes
Is child labor a problem? The government prohibits compulsory child labor.

Azerbaijan

Major Languages: Azerbaijani, Russian, Armenian
Total Population: 7,748,000
Population 0–34: 3,378,000
Life Expectancy: 63 years
Religion: Muslim 83.67%, nonreligious 11.31%, Christian 4.63%,
   Jewish 0.37%, Baha'i 0.02%
Literacy Rate: male 100%, female 99%

When Ann followed her husband to Azerbaijan so that he could pursue his successful career in geophysical engineering, she knew it was going to be a challenge. They secured a hotel room where the faucet dripped brown water and the bed could not possibly have been changed from the last guests. Ann shuddered at the thought of spending the night in the run-down hotel. She could see that the country ran on foreign currency, because the only money the merchants or the hotel desk clerk would accept was American dollars, and each bill had to be clean, unwrinkled, and preferably $100.

After a fitful night's sleep, Ann felt that her mission here had something to do with the children in the land. Her husband could work here, but since the government would not give work permits to the wives of foreign employees, most women in Ann's situation learned to play bridge or tennis at the local foreign health spa. Ann wanted to touch the people, especially the children.

On her second day in town Ann visited the children's cancer wing of a local hospital, where all the rooms accommodated at least four children. Some children were in the last stages of leukemia. Her heart ached as she looked at the outdated medical equipment and lack of sanitary conditions. This was one of the largest hospitals for children in the city, where whole families came for treatment. The rooms were hot, and no breeze ventured through the open windows, even in the intensive care unit.

27

Ann's translator apologized, "I'm so sorry, Mrs. Langley. We have so few resources in Azerbaijan." She went on to explain that a lot of diseases the children had were a direct result of poor quality tap water.

Ann's visit to a local orphanage wasn't much better—too many children in too little space with far too few workers. The situation looked dismal. On the streets child beggars accosted her. The schools were the most inspiring, with children who sat in neat rows, often sharing desks. The spartan classrooms sported few textbooks, but the children looked as though they enjoyed learning.

Ann set about mobilizing the women from the local Petroleum Women's Guild. With over 200 women from Australia, Great Britain, the United States, and Spain, Ann had a lot of good raw material with which to work. She fully intended to liberate these women from their bridge games and afternoon teas. On the first Saturday of every month the women "adopted" a child from the local orphanage for the day. Regular hospital visits were set up with a person designated to coordinate the efforts. In all, Ann managed to get over 75 women involved in making the lives of the children more comfortable, and she hoped the lives of the women were also enriched.

*R*ich in oil reserves, Azerbaijan hosts petroleum employees from all over the world. Many women who are married to foreign employees fall into the same trap as Ann's friends, enjoying a life of ease among poverty and suffering. Pray that Christians who accept jobs in countries like Azerbaijan will see themselves as ambassadors for Christ and will become involved in improving the lives of those around them. Pray they will find favor and foster good relationships between the West and the struggling countries. They may not be able to openly proclaim the gospel, but they are able to show the love of Christ by the acts of kindness they do for the children of the world.

Local scientists consider the region around the Caspian Sea to be the most ecologically devastated area in the world. The region suffers severe air, water, and soil pollution, due in part to the use of DDT as a pesticide and the use of toxic defoliants in the production of cotton.

Azerbaijan is Muslim and not open to the sharing of the gospel. Christians have been harassed and arrested for meeting in house churches. The authorities state that Azerbaijan is a Muslim country.

Prayer Points

- Pray for leaders to have compassion, love, and the best interest of the people in mind in all of the decisions they make.

⌣· Pray for Christians working in Azerbaijan to make the most of every opportunity to tell the children, teens, and young adults about Jesus Christ and to have a lifestyle that mirrors Christ.

⌣· Pray for safe water and sanitation systems to prevent disease for the sake of future generations.

⌣· Pray for the leaders to utilize Azerbaijan's vast oil reserves to benefit the masses.

⌣· Pray for God to provide viable job opportunities for young women and girls who otherwise turn to prostitution to survive.

⌣· Pray for Christians to be mindful that God has given them an open door to reach the Azeris through literature distribution.

⌣· Pray for Christians to develop literature, especially Christian material, that is relevant to children, teens, and young adults.

⌣· Pray for God to raise up Christian organizations to reach the battered, abused, and raped. Pray that they will be emotionally healed and will know the love Christ has for them. They are precious to Him!

Quick Reference

Ethnic Breakdown: Azerbaijani 85.6%, Armenian 3.2%, Russian 3.0%, Talyah 1.9%, other 6.3%

Type of Government: Federal multiparty republic

Economy: Services 60%, Agriculture 22%, Industry 18%

Per capita income: U.S.$480

National debt: U.S.$684 million

Economic conditions: Extremely poor

Education

Quality of education: Education is compulsory.

Gender discrimination against girls: Girls are being educated.

Religion

Religious concerns: Evangelism is restricted.

Status of the church: The Christian population is almost entirely Armenian and Russian. Many Christians fled the country following a massacre in 1989. The church needs discipleship and leadership training.

Are Christians being persecuted? Yes

Societal Viewpoint Toward Children

Are they viewed as precious? Yes

Are there street children? Yes

Is there a large population of orphans? Yes. More than 108,000 orphans are children under five.

Are there child soldiers? No specific data available.

Is child labor a problem? There are no reports of child labor.

Bahrain

Major Languages: Arabic, English, Farsi
Total Population: 634,000
Population 0–34: 396,461
Life Expectancy: 73 years
Religion: Muslim 82.31%, Christian 10.36%, Hindu 6.25%, nonreligious 0.69%, Baha'i 0.22%, Jewish 0.10%, Buddhist 0.07%
Literacy Rate: male 89%, female 79%

W hat will you do? Where will you go?" Mifti asked her son. She nervously twisted the end of her *hijab,* her veiled head covering. For the first time in her life, a man in her family was facing the likelihood of not being able to find a well-paying job in Bahrain, and she was afraid. Mifti's husband had had a good job with an oil company, and they'd had a wonderful life. When the oil reserves in Bahrain began to diminish, her husband was forced into early retirement from his position as a geophysical engineer. The job loss caused his health to deteriorate until he suffered a stroke. Now her son was facing a similar situation with his position at the local bank.

"It's okay, Mother." Muhammad tried to soothe his mother's fears. "I'll find a job in Saudi Arabia. The causeway to the mainland is only 16 miles long."

Mifti looked at her son. He had been so sheltered in this small country. He refused to be involved with the Shiite Muslims and their radical ways. Brought up as a proper man, he loved Allah and his country. "Your father would be so proud of you, even though you are not an engineer."

Muhammad laughed. "I am a measly accountant, but I'm sure Father would approve, especially knowing how much he loved money. I see how hard he worked and what he provided for all of us children, but things are changing in this country. The oil reserves here are not as plentiful as they were 10 years ago, and the banking industry is not as good as it has been in the past. The case is clear. I must go somewhere else to look for a job."

Mifti's family was close, enjoying outings together at the parks and weekends at one of the many natural mineral baths in the country. Mifti could trust Muhammad to come home often and to let the family choose a wife for him. Once the family decided on a girl for him to marry and the girl's father approved, Mifti knew that would be settled. After all, no self-respecting girl would go against her father's wishes. Mifti just didn't want her son to marry someone from another country, not even a Saudi. She had watched over the years as the Saudis came to Bahrain to vacation. Sometimes they even came to buy Bibles from the bookstore in town. You just couldn't trust them.

Muhammad looked at his mother with that twinkle in his eye she had learned to love when he was a child. She smiled, and he knew what she was thinking. "Don't worry, Mother. I will marry the girl of your choice. I will not marry a foreigner."

They both laughed.

*M*ifti and Muhammad are in the middle of change. Their country, Bahrain, is undergoing economic changes that will affect the next generation. The vast oil reserves that were discovered in the country in 1934 are being depleted. The country has set itself up as a banking center and is known as the Singapore of the Middle East because of its great financial institutions, but the changes in the oil industry have negatively impacted the banking institutions. The country is working to shift its economy to other bases, such as aluminum processing and tourism. Natural mineral springs make Bahrain one of the most desirable vacation spots in the Middle East.

While a large number of expatriate Christians live in the country, only a handful of national believers live there. The believers may meet freely, but they must not proselytize Muslims. The first school in Bahrain was founded in 1899 by the National Evangelical Church. As a result of the foundation of this school and a subsequent hospital, the church has gained favor with the emir. It has been reported that he grants $40,000 a year to the hospital and has also donated $30,000 to remodel the church.

The tiny island nation maintains a high literacy rate, especially among the younger generation, and girls are treated equally with boys with regard to education.

Prayer Points

⌐· Pray for national believers to have a burning desire to reach the children, teens, and young adults in their nation.
⌐· Pray for Christian satellite programs to impact the youth.
⌐· Pray that the young people will seek God for His purpose for their lives and that their search will bring them to Jesus Christ, the Son of the living God!
⌐· Pray for God to give the church cutting-edge strategies to reach Bahrain with the gospel.
⌐· Pray that Bibles and Christian children's books will be distributed and read.
⌐· Pray that as the economy is changing in Bahrain, people will begin to put their faith in God and not the oil industry.
⌐· Pray that Bahraini believers will pray for and take the gospel to children, teens, and young adults in other 10/40 Window countries.
⌐· Pray that the youth in Bahrain will be attracted to Christian music.

Quick Reference

Ethnic Breakdown: Bahraini Arab 63.9%, Persian 13.0%, Filipino 4.5%, Urdu 4.5%, Malayali 3.5%, other 10.6%
Type of Government: Traditional monarchy
Economy: Services 53%, Industry 46%, Agriculture 1%
Per capita income: U.S.$7,840
National debt: U.S.$2 billion
Economic conditions: Oil reserves are being depleted and the economy is shifting toward aluminum processing and tourism.

Education
Quality of education: Instruction includes mandatory Koranic curriculum. The school system is well organized.
Gender discrimination against girls: Girls are being educated.

Religion
Religious concerns: Evangelism is restricted.
Status of the church: No national church exists, although there is a thriving expatriate church.
Are Christians being persecuted? No

Societal Viewpoint Toward Children
Are they viewed as precious? Yes
Are there street children? Street children are not a noted problem.
Is there a large population of orphans? No specific data available.
Are there child soldiers? None noted.
Is child labor a problem? There are no reports of child labor.

Bangladesh

Major Languages: Bengali, English
Total Population: 129,194,000
Population 0–34: 95,837,000
Life Expectancy: 60 years
Religion: Muslim 85.63%, Hindu 12.38%, Christian 0.72%, Buddhist 0.62%,
traditional ethnic 0.57%, nonreligious/other 0.08%
Literacy Rate: male 63%, female 48%

*R*aj, what are you doing here? You know this is dangerous." Raj's sister Ahmedi took him by the arm and pulled him through the doorway. Raj couldn't see anything, and for a moment he thought he, his sister, and an older woman were the only ones in the room. When his eyes adjusted, he saw five, maybe six, women sitting on the floor in a circle.

"Ahmedi, our mother has been arrested," Raj said. "You must come quickly." He tried to focus on Ahmedi's face to see her reaction. She seemed to have such peace. Maybe she didn't realize the seriousness of the situation.

"What is the charge?" Ahmedi asked.

"She went out of the house without wearing her *burqa.*"

"That is no crime," Ahmedi responded. "It is pouring down rain, and the burqa would hinder her from shopping."

"This morning the *mullah* issued a *fatwa* saying that every woman should wear the burqa, even when going to the market." Raj was talking so fast he had to stop to catch his breath.

Ahmedi threw up her hands. "What are we women to do if every time we see daylight we must cover ourselves from head to toe? It is so hot, and this garment is stifling. We have no father to shop for us. Where did they take her?"

"She is at the police station. We must go quickly, or you know what will happen to her."

"Yes, I know. We will hurry, but first we will pray." Ahmedi turned to face the women. Immediately the older woman who had met Raj at the door began to pray for his mother.

Once at the police station, Raj and Ahmedi waited in a crowded room for three hours before they were allowed to talk to anyone. Even though the police officer was nice, he gave them no information other than the fact that their mother had been caught disobeying a fatwa. They waited another hour.

The police officer motioned for them to come to the desk. "Your mother will be released in a few moments. Please meet her at the exit."

Ahmedi stood in front of the desk like a stubborn calf. "Why did you arrest my mother and then let her go?" She threw up her hands to emphasize her question.

The man stopped shuffling the papers on his desk and looked up at Ahmedi. "Your mother disobeyed the order of the local mullah, but things have changed. You may have your mother back. Maybe we will release her to you in time to celebrate the new year with her family. It is December 31, you know."

"Yes, and I am grateful to you." Raj watched as Ahmedi subdued her anger and stepped back from the man's desk. Evidently their mother was not the only one being released. They watched as many women were reunited with their families. Later they learned that there had been a high court decision to ban fatwas issued by local mullahs.

On December 31, 2000, two high court judges handed down a verdict banning any fatwa or legal opinion not delivered by a court. The judgment also asked Parliament to enact a law to severely punish any-body issuing a fatwa. Muslim clerics frequently issue fatwas based on *sharia* (Islamic law), which often victimizes women in issues such as dress, marriage, and divorce. The extremist Islamic Unity Alliance immediately denounced the judges as apostates and threatened to launch a nationwide campaign against the verdict.

Bangladesh is over 88 percent Muslim. Although Bangladesh law allows for religious freedom, Christians are persecuted. For the most part, the Muslims are peaceable and are tolerant of others' religious beliefs, but the militant Muslim faction has been fueled in recent years by money from Islamic nations that have rich oil reserves.

Bangladesh is one of the world's most densely populated and poorest countries. With a per capita income of less than U.S.$250 per year, well over a third of the population lives below the poverty line, and slightly more than half of the children are considered malnourished. With an annual rainfall between 66 and 200 inches, a third of the country floods every year during monsoon season, leaving most of the population with polluted water. More than six million children between the ages of 5 and 14 are required, at the expense of an education, to work to support their families.

Bangladesh needs our prayers.

Prayer Points

- ⌣· Pray for equality for girls in educational opportunities. Higher female literacy rates will enable women to increase their chances for employment, improve their quality of life, and understand their rights.
- ⌣· Pray for the physical needs of the children to be met.
- ⌣· Pray for clean water. Many of the diseases are caused by lack of potable water.
- ⌣· Pray for creative ways for parents to provide for their children without having to resort to child slavery, trafficking, and prostitution.
- ⌣· Pray for an end to the evil practices of dowry-related killings and other abusive attacks on girls and women. Pray that the government will be successful in punishing those involved in these deplorable crimes.
- ⌣· Pray for God to give Christians fresh compassion and courage that will empower them to reach out to even the most extreme Muslims with the good news of the gospel and that He will protect them as they testify of His love.
- ⌣· Pray for Christian laborers—especially doctors, engineers, and teachers—to go to Bangladesh and use every opportunity given them to share the gospel with their friends and neighbors. Medical providers and equipment are desperately needed.
- ⌣· Pray for girls and boys to have an opportunity to go to school.

Quick Reference

Ethnic Breakdown: Bengali 79.0%, Hindu 11.7%, Sylhetti Bengali 4.6%, Bihar 1.5%, Urdu 0.6%, other 2.6%
Type of Government: Republic
Economy: Services 53%, Agriculture 30%, Industry 17%
Per capita income: U.S.$240
National debt: U.S.$16.5 billion
Economic conditions: Extremely poor

Education

Quality of education: The government lacks the resources to implement compulsory education.

Gender discrimination against girls: Not much importance is placed on education for girls.

Religion

Religious concerns: The government allows various religions to establish places of worship and train clergy, although it restricts evangelism.

Status of the church: Slow, steady growth. Although the Christians in Bangladesh make up a small minority, the churches are quite active.

Are Christians being persecuted? Yes

Societal Viewpoint Toward Children

Are they viewed as precious? No

Are there street children? Children work as street vendors, selling small items.

Is there a large population of orphans? No specific data available.

Are there child soldiers? No specific data available.

Is child labor a problem? Children are used in the labor force. They are trafficked for prostitution, which is a serious problem.

Benin

Major Languages: Fon, Yoruba, Bariba
Total Population: 6,396,000
Population 0–34: 5,184,000
Life Expectancy: 50 years
Religion: traditional ethnic 47.70%, Christian 31.78%, Muslim 20.03%, nonreligious/other 0.29%, Baha'i 0.20%
Literacy Rate: male 43%, female 19%

*M*ondu kicked the sand with her bare feet and balanced a chicken wrapped in a red rag on top of her head. It looked as if she were wearing a red hat with a live chicken peeping out, but she didn't care. If she and her sister sold the chicken at the market today, they would get to go to school next month.

Her sister Silka urged her to hurry. "Quit dragging your feet. We need to get the best spot at the market. We have to sell this chicken."

"I'm trying," Mondu said as she walked faster.

"If you can't keep up, then I'll go ahead." With that, Silka sped up and soon was out of sight. When Mondu arrived at the market, an older man who was selling cigarettes had taken the prime spot. Mondu and Silka took a place near a small restaurant and hoped the restaurant owner would come out and buy their chicken, but he acted as though he didn't know they were there.

At the end of the day, they still had the chicken in their possession. "We'd better go home before it gets dark," Silka said, trying not to sound discouraged. Mondu knew how important school was to her sister. The girls trudged home, this time with the chicken on top of Silka's head. They walked in silence until they reached the clearing where their compound was situated. Mama sat in front of the fire stirring a pot.

"I see you didn't sell the chicken," she said as she looked at the tired girls.

"No, but we can try tomorrow," Silka said.

"There won't be a tomorrow," Mama said.

Mondu was the first to speak. "What does that mean?"

"That means tomorrow I will become a *videmegon,*" Silka replied.

"Silka, how do you know that? Mama hasn't said anything about sending you off." Mondu tried hard to keep back the tears. She felt she couldn't live without her sister.

"Mondu, we don't have any money. How can Mama keep both of the little ones and us? I heard her talking with the man from Cotonou. He said he could find me work in a family that would send me to school instead of paying my wages. At least I would get to go to school."

Mondu yelled at her sister. "That's a lie, and you know it! The teacher said they send us off to work and we end up as slaves. We never get to go to school, and we have to work in the hot fields all day long."

"Maybe the teacher is wrong. Maybe," said Silka, sticking out her lower lip at her sister.

"Maybe I sold a chicken today," Mondu said. "You know that isn't true. All kinds of bad things happen to girls who are sold off to help families." Hot tears ran down her face.

Silka spoke with resignation in her voice. "At least I can read and write. That's a lot more than most girls can do. So maybe I won't be sold off to someone who will take me to another country, like Cameroon or Nigeria. I have no choice, Mondu. If Mama says so, I must go. I'm afraid my fate is sealed."

*P*oor families in Benin, like that of Mondu and Silka, participate in a tradition called videmegon, where a child is placed with a wealthy family in exchange for wages or an education. According to a recent UNICEF report, approximately 400,000 videmegons are employed in Benin. Twenty percent are less than 10 years of age, and 90 percent have never been to school. Many of the girls are transported to nearby countries to work as field laborers or domestic helpers, being promised wages or an education in exchange for their work. More often than not, however, the promises made to them and their families are not fulfilled. In reality the girls are forced into a form of slavery. They face poor working and living conditions, earn little or no income, and are highly vulnerable to sexual harassment, physical violence, early pregnancies, secret abortions, and abandonment. The government is trying to discourage this practice by educating the children and their parents concerning their rights.

Matthew Kerekou, the former Marxist dictator of Benin, was eventually elected president after becoming a born-again Christian. On his inauguration he dedicated his country to Christ and asked Christians to come and help invest in the lives of the people. Benin may have turned a corner, but much progress is needed to help the people out of traditions that mix Christianity with traditional indigenous beliefs.

Prayer Points

- Pray that the government will continue to expose the evils of videmegon and that families will be able to feed and educate their children so that they will not fall victim to this practice.
- Pray that President Kerekou, government officials, and the citizens of Benin will seek God for strategies to meet the needs of the nation.
- Pray that God will raise up churches and ministries that will partner to build a strong infrastructure for the agricultural, educational, medical, and financial sectors of Benin.
- Pray that the literacy rate will be drastically increased and girls will be educated.
- Pray that the government will continue to combat child abuse and trafficking of children. Ask God to use media campaigns and ongoing programs to eradicate these evil practices.
- Pray that there will be a better quality of life for the young people.
- Pray that the government will continue in its efforts to bring awareness of the dangers of female genital mutilation (FGM), which is widely practiced. Pray that the Beninese will stop this practice.
- Pray that families will cease the inhumane practice of killing deformed babies, breech babies, or one of newborn twins, thought in some rural areas to be sorcerers.
- Pray that the practice of a groom abducting and raping his prospective "child bride" will cease.

Quick Reference

Ethnic Breakdown: African 99%, French 0.3%, other 0.7%
Type of Government: Republic under multiparty democratic rule
Economy: Services 52%, Agriculture 34%, Industry 14%
Per capita income: U.S.$370
National debt: U.S.$1.6 billion
Economic conditions: Extremely poor

Education
Quality of education: There is a severe shortage of schools and teachers.

Gender discrimination against girls: In some parts of the country, girls receive no formal education.

Religion
Religious concerns: Open to evangelism. People often practice Christianity, Islam, traditional indigenous religions, or combinations of all. Believers need discipleship and leadership training.
Status of the church: Lack of discipleship
Are Christians being persecuted? There have been instances of persecution, although the government is working to reduce tension between Muslims, Christians, and those who practice tribal religions.

Societal Viewpoint Toward Children
Are they viewed as precious? No
Are there street children? Children commonly work as street vendors.
Is there a large population of orphans? No specific data available.
Are there child soldiers? No specific data available.
Is child labor a problem? Yes

Bhutan

Major Languages: Dzongkha, Bhotes, Nepalese
Total Population: 2,005,000
Population 0–34: 1,463,000
Life Expectancy: 63 years
Religion: Buddhist 72.04%, Hindu 23.00%, Muslim 4.00%,
    traditional ethnic 0.50%, Christian 0.46%
Literacy Rate: male 56%, female 28%

*H*urry, Sangla, hurry. You are going on a holiday." Sangla's mother busied herself about the kitchen, packing some tomatoes, cucumbers, and bread to eat on the train.

For Sangla, this was one of the most exciting times of her life. She had never been out of her small village, and now she was actually getting to go on a holiday with her father. She asked her mother, "Should I take my sleeping mat?"

"No, you won't need it. Take nothing with you." Sangla's mother turned away from her as she spoke.

Sangla thought about the many times she had heard her father complain about how poor they were and wondered how they could afford a holiday in Thimphu. She decided not to worry. She would go and have fun.

Sangla and her father registered at the hotel in Thimphu. The next morning when she awoke, her father was gone and she was alone. All day long Sangla sat next to the window and watched for him to come back.

It was late afternoon when he returned. He pointed at Sangla. "You come with me," he demanded.

They took a taxi to a tall building with huge doors that her father said was a hotel. As they walked inside, a man dressed in a blue suit held the door open for them. Sangla felt funny inside. Was it fear? They walked silently toward a door at the end of the hallway. Her father knocked, and a strange man answered.

"Come in," the man said and motioned for them to sit down on a green sofa. Sangla sat next to her father.

The man gave her father an envelope, and Sangla watched in horror as her father got up to leave. She felt her heart race. She tried to run after him, but the man next to her held her arm. She began to scream, "Father, please, please don't leave me here." Her father never looked back at her but walked to the door, opened it, and left. Sangla is now a statistic. She is a child who has been sold into prostitution.

Sangla belongs to a group of ethnic Nepalese who live in Bhutan. As the poorest of the poor, they often take drastic measures to provide for their children. A child may be sold into bonded labor or prostitution simply because the family cannot afford the expense of another mouth to feed. There are reports of Bhutanese who sell their children for the price of a television set or a VCR. Once sold, these children live in adverse circumstances with no hope of a better life.

Bhutan is predominately Buddhist and intolerant of other religions. No religious literature is allowed to enter the country, and preaching is forbidden. One pastor who proclaimed the gospel in his mountain village was captured and put to death.

The country was closed to all foreigners until 1974. Although it is now possible to obtain a visa to Bhutan, the government is reluctant to grant entry. About 4,000 visas are issued per year, and a tourist may be assessed U.S.$250 per day—a fee that goes directly to the government.

The Bhutanese government has tried for years to purge the country of the ethnic Nepalese who flooded the country in the early 1900s. Over 97,000 Nepalese who for generations had lived in Bhutan have been forced to leave and have been put into refugee camps in Nepal. If persons of Nepalese origin can prove their Bhutanese citizenship (not an easy task), they are allowed to stay in Bhutan. The conditions under which they remain in the country, however, are substandard. Often the children are denied basic education, and it is difficult for the parents to find work.

Factors that contribute to the country's high mortality rate include the severe climate, less-than-hygienic living conditions, and smoke inhalation from inadequately ventilated cooking equipment. The lack of potable water causes many gastrointestinal problems.

The children of Bhutan have a low literacy rate. Only 60 percent of those entering elementary school complete seven years of academic training. A young boy may be given to a Buddhist monastery for life. He will then be supported by the government and expected to perform the temple rituals as his life work.

Bhutan needs our prayers.

Prayer Points

⌇· Pray that there will be increased opportunities for ethnic Nepalese children to attend school and have the same rights as other Bhutanese children.

⌇· Pray that restrictions concerning entry to Bhutan and freedom to witness will be relaxed. Pray that Christian laborers will demonstrate God's character by their truthfulness, integrity, and love.

⌇· Pray that the Christian relief organizations currently working in Bhutan will be effective. Pray that the people of Bhutan will be attracted to the Christ they see in His followers and will want to follow Jesus.

⌇· Pray that children will be considered precious gifts from God and the practice of selling them into slavery and prostitution will be abolished.

⌇· Pray that the government will enforce existing laws for the punishment of sexual abuse against women and children.

⌇· Pray that Christians with influence and wisdom in the areas of business, education, health care, and finance will be used by God to make an impact on this nation.

Quick Reference

Ethnic Breakdown: Bhotia 43.0%, Nepalese 12.0%, Sangla 7.1%, other indigenous or migrant tribes 37.9%

Type of Government: Constitutional monarchy

Economy: Agriculture 38%, Industry 37%, Services 25%

Per capita income: U.S.$420

National debt: U.S.$120 million

Economic conditions: Extremely poor

Education

Quality of education: There is a shortage of schools and teachers.

Gender discrimination against girls: Not much importance is placed on education for girls.

Religion

Religious concerns: Evangelism is prohibited.

Status of the church: There is only one Christian church building in the country. Many believers worship at home. There is a need for discipleship and leadership training.

Are Christians being persecuted? Yes. In 1997, a pastor was thrown in prison and tortured, causing severe head injuries. He died 10 days after his release.

Societal Viewpoint Toward Children

Are they viewed as precious? Yes

Are there street children? Street children are not a noted problem.

Is there a large population of orphans? No specific data available.

Are there child soldiers? No specific data available.

Is child labor a problem? Children are being sold into bonded labor and prostitution.

Brunei

Major Languages: Malay, English, Chinese
Total Population: 336,000
Population 0–34: 225,628
Life Expectancy: 74 years
Religion: Muslim 64.39%, Christian 11.25%, Buddhist 9.09%, traditional ethnic 7.60%, Chinese 5.31%, nonreligious 1.22%, Hindu 0.84%, Baha'i 0.30%
Literacy Rate: male 93%, female 85%

Your daddy is a traitor. Your daddy belongs to a cult." The children pointed their fingers at seven-year-old Tokching and sang in unison, "Your daddy is a traitor. Your daddy belongs to a cult."

Tokching put his hands over his ears until he passed the playground and the mocking children. Then he began to run as fast as he could to his home.

"Mama, Mama," he called as he bounded through the door. "Tell them, Mama. Tell them that my daddy doesn't belong to a cult and that he loves Brunei. Please, Mama, tell them." He tried to hold back the tears, but he couldn't. He began to sob uncontrollably.

Mary knelt down to look her son in the face. "Your daddy stood up for what he believed. He isn't a traitor to his country. As a matter of fact, your daddy loves this country very much."

"Why do the kids at school make fun of him? Every day they laugh and point fingers at me."

"I know this is very hard for you, and you may not understand. Your daddy is a Christian. He found Jesus Christ and asked him into his life. For many in Brunei, this is considered a dangerous act. You see, Tokching, they are afraid of what they do not understand. For them religion is an external form of worship. Every day they pray five times facing Mecca and they fast during Ramadan, but they do not understand how people can accept someone like Jesus Christ, who shows us how to change on the inside so we can become children of God and live a good life."

Mary smoothed Tokching's hair and held him close to her. This was also a very difficult time for her. Her husband, Muhammad, had been arrested last week. His arrest and subsequent detainment cost him his job, and already Mary didn't know where the next meal was coming from. It would be even harder to explain to Tokching when there was no food in the house.

It had started out as an ordinary day. Mary had walked Tokching to the corner and watched him run off in the direction of his school. Muhammad had gone to his job as an auditor at the bank. At noon Mary had received a call from a friend who worked at the same bank. Muhammad, along with five others, had been arrested for being in a cult. He was being questioned at the local police station, and if she didn't want to be arrested also, she should stay home.

Mary stayed away, anxiously waiting for news. Three days later Muhammad was released, more determined than ever to make his conversion from Islam to Christianity publicly known. How would she ever explain this to their son? Muhammad had told her to trust God, and even though she knew that was the only thing she could do at this point, it would not be an easy road.

*I*n December 2000 and January 2001, according to the news reporting agency Compass Direct, five Christians were arrested and detained because of their participation in a well-organized prayer program. They were also suspected of evangelizing, which is forbidden in this Muslim country. Any converts to Christianity from Islam have to go through Islamic rehabilitation. The government considers Christian groups cults that must be extinguished. While adults may understand why they are being arrested and such persecution may strengthen their beliefs, their children may find it difficult to understand why they also must suffer at the hands of their friends and teachers.

The constitution of Brunei guarantees the free practice of religion, but that freedom shows signs of erosion. In 1991 the government banned Christian literature from the country and the following year outlawed the celebration of Christmas. At present there are no known missionaries working in the country.

Brunei is one of the wealthiest countries in the world, with an annual per capita income of over U.S.$25,000. This is due to the large export of oil and natural gas. The government provides all medical services for the people and subsidizes food and housing. The sultan of Brunei is one of the wealthiest men in the world. Because of this immense wealth, the country enjoys a high standard of living. The government provides programs promoting health care for children and progressive education.

Prayer Points

⌐· Pray for female domestic servants, who are often beaten and confined. Ask God not only to protect them but also to give them courage to bring complaints to the embassies of their governments.

⌐· Pray for Christian schools to emerge as alternatives to Islamic schools for Filipino, European, and Chinese Christians living in Brunei.

⌐· Pray for opportunity and boldness for Christians to evangelize. Pray for their protection.

⌐· Pray for God to creatively bring missionaries into the country through business, tourism, and international student exchange programs.

⌐· Pray for the continued freedom of religion, which seems to be eroding. Pray for the Lord to reveal Himself to the sultan.

⌐· Pray for young adults not to become materialistic and to have a desire to care for others who are poor.

⌐· Pray for this generation to be touched by the Lord in an extraordinary way and be used by God to fulfill His divine purpose for their nation.

⌐· Pray for protection of believers and their families.

⌐· Pray for young people, that they will be dissatisfied with things money can buy and begin to search for God.

Quick Reference

Ethnic Breakdown: Orang Bukit 44.9%, Dusun 6.9%, Southern Bisaya 6.4%, Bisayan 5.7%, Han Chinese 5.6%, other indigenous 30.5%
Type of Government: Constitutional sultanate
Economy: Services 49%, Industry 46%, Agriculture 5%
Per capita income: U.S.$25,160
National debt: No debt
Economic conditions: Thriving economy

Education
Quality of education: School system is well organized. Instruction includes mandatory Koranic instruction.
Gender discrimination against girls: Girls receive the same type of education as boys.

Religion
Religious concerns: Evangelism is restricted, since it is illegal to evangelize Muslims. There are no known missionaries working in the country.

Status of the church: There are expatriate Christian churches. No national church exists.

Are Christians being persecuted? Yes

Societal Viewpoint Toward Children

Are they viewed as precious? Yes

Are there street children? Street children are not a noted problem.

Is there a large population of orphans? No

Are there child soldiers? No

Is child labor a problem? Forced and bonded labor by children is prohibited and is not practiced.

Burkina Faso

Major Languages: Mossi, French, Bobo
Total Population: 11,946,000
Population 0–34: 9,670,000
Life Expectancy: 47 years
Religion: Muslim 50.00%, traditional ethnic 30.96%, Christian 18.36%, nonreligious 0.66%, Baha'i 0.02%
Literacy Rate: male 29%, female 10%

Sandel peeped around the corner of the hut to watch the strange white people. He wanted to see what they were doing with the black box they brought with them. He ducked back behind the door when the woman looked at him. His heart raced as he saw her come through the door toward him.

"What are you doing out here?" Her perfect French and kind smile made him feel better immediately. He couldn't take his eyes from her face. She had blonde hair and glasses that made her eyes look larger than they were. "Won't you come in?" she asked.

Slowly Sandel slipped into the dark hut and hunched down close to the box.

"My name is Elsa," the woman said. "What is your name?"

"Sandel," he whispered.

"Sandel, would you like to see what we are doing?" she asked.

He nodded his head. By now he could hear familiar sounds coming from the box. The black box was talking to him in his tribal tongue of Samogho.

"Would you like to hear a story from the box?"

"Yes," he nodded.

The story was one his grandfather, the great family storyteller, had told him long ago about a man called Moses, who led many people across a great sea. When it was finished, she asked him, "Do you know this story?"

"My grandfather is a great *imam,* and he tells me stories from the Book."

"So you are Muslim?" she asked.

"Yes, all my family worships Allah. But we know stories from the Book."

"You mean the Bible, don't you?" she asked.

He nodded.

"Can you bring some friends tomorrow to listen?"

"No, madam. We cannot meet with strangers when there are more than two of us, but maybe I could bring my grandfather and we could listen to the stories."

"Yes, Sandel. Come tomorrow and bring your grandfather. That would be fine."

Sandel rushed out of the hut and hurried toward his family's compound to find his grandfather. Tomorrow was going to be a good day. He just knew it.

With 60 different ethnic groups in Burkina Faso, crossing the language barrier presents a major challenge. Recently over 80 Old Testament Bible stories were translated into the Samogho language. Normally the Burkinabe will not meet in large groups with someone of a religion other than their own (they are predominately Muslim), but Christians have been able to play cassette recordings of the Bible translations at some small gatherings.

Burkina Faso is one of the poorest countries in the world. The people eke out a living from the mineral-depleted soil and cattle herding. Frequent droughts make it even more difficult to survive, often leaving many children orphaned. A large number of the adults migrate south every year to Cote d'Ivoire and Ghana to work. Forty-five percent of the population remains poor, and more than two-fifths live in extreme poverty. More than 40 percent of the children suffer from malnutrition.

The educational system in Burkina Faso is in a downward spiral. Presently about 40 percent of the children attend primary school, with just 9 percent continuing through secondary school. Parents must provide school supplies, but many of them cannot afford to feed their children, let alone purchase textbooks.

The AIDS epidemic exacerbates poverty because of an increased number of children losing one or both parents to this deadly disease. Children with only one parent have less than a 50 percent chance of being schooled, and those orphaned have only a 10 percent chance of attending school.

The future for girls in Burkina Faso is dismal. The years of their youth are cut short, as they are encouraged to marry young and have many children. Domestic violence is common and often goes unreported because of the stigma attached to it. Female genital mutilation (FGM) is practiced widely in rural areas, with an estimated 70 percent of girls having undergone this procedure.

Prayer Points

- Pray that more schools will be established and that the existing schools will be improved. Burkina Faso has the lowest literacy rate in the world.
- Pray that the government will make literacy a national concern and that open invitations will be made for Christian educators to teach the children.
- Pray that Bible translation and literacy work being done in Burkina Faso will have a powerful impact on the nation, especially among the young people.
- Pray that believers will seek God for creative ways to reach this generation with the gospel.
- Pray that believers will be properly discipled and will stop mixing other religions with Christianity.
- Pray that the physical needs of the children will be met. Christians must do their part to feed the more than 40 percent of the children who are malnourished.
- Pray that there will be Christian health-care teams working with AIDS victims. Ask God to encourage and strengthen the teams as they endeavor to care for those with this deadly disease.
- Pray that God will work through Christian health-care workers to supernaturally heal those who have AIDS.
- Pray that the practice of FGM will be eliminated.

Quick Reference

Ethnic Breakdown: Mossi 46.3%, Bissa 3.8%, Liptako Fula 3.4%, Gurma 3.3%, Black Bobo 2.7%, other 40.5%

Type of Government: Multiparty republic

Economy: Services 44%, Agriculture 36%, Industry 20%

Per capita income: U.S.$230

National debt: U.S.$1.3 billion

Economic conditions: Extremely poor

Education

Quality of education: There is a severe shortage of schools and teachers. Education has little value in this society.

Gender discrimination against girls: Girls are often encouraged to stay home to work and tend to younger siblings.

Religion

Religious concerns: Christians are involved with syncretism, a result of failure to break with tribal religions. This practice plagues the church.

Status of the church: The church is in great need of discipleship. A strong national team in the capital city of Ouagadougou has been committed to church planting.

Are Christians being persecuted? No

Societal Viewpoint Toward Children

Are they viewed as precious? No

Are there street children? Street children are not a noted problem.

Is there a large population of orphans? Yes

Are there child soldiers? No specific data available.

Is child labor a problem? Children often work to help their parents.

Cambodia

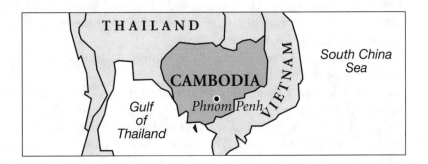

Major Languages: Khmer, French, English
Total Population: 12,212,000
Population 0–34: 9,260,000
Life Expectancy: 57 years
Religion: Buddhist 82.57%, Chinese 4.69%, traditional ethnic 4.35%,
    Muslim 3.90%, nonreligious/other 2.92%, Christian 1.19%, Hindu 0.26%,
    Baha'i 0.12%
Literacy Rate: male 79%, female 58%

"What made you take in all these beautiful children?" the tall man asked Norene.

Norene thought for a moment, then answered the visitor. "First of all, I am a believer in Jesus Christ, and I love children because He loved them. Second, I give homeless children a chance because I remember my children in their youth and their potential. Who knows, one of these lovely children could be my grandchild. You see, sir, I had two precious daughters. One I have not seen in 20 years, and the other is waiting for me in heaven."

The man nodded as though he heard but did not fully understand. "How did you lose contact with your daughter?"

Even though Norene had related the story many times, it still brought tears to her eyes. How could this visitor possibly understand war and heartache that had stretched out over the decades and torn families apart?

"You see, sir, I was a schoolteacher in Phnom Penh, the capital city of Cambodia, and my husband was a civil engineer. When the country was taken over by Pol Pot, professional persons like my husband and me were ordered to go into camps to be retrained for work in the fields. Those working in the fields were given our positions. It was an exchange the government thought would better our country. I was sent to one camp with my two small children, and my husband was sent to another. I never saw him again. My two-year-old child died of dysentery in my arms, and my four-year-old child was separated from me while I was in the fields working. I never saw her again."

The man attempted to change the subject. "You have many lovely children now, don't you?"

"Yes, I do. I take them from the streets when they have been deserted by their families and must beg for food. I give them a home." She motioned to the compound of several buildings that surrounded a small garden. "We now have over 200 children and a waiting list of many more."

The man looked at her and said, "I am very impressed. Mrs. Lamm, I do understand a little about the trauma of separating families. You see, my family was separated in the Holocaust when Hitler was in power. I know the effect of a godless ruler."

"Yes, you do understand. Then you realize the importance of what we are trying to do here. So many of the Cambodian young people have no hope. Many are sold into prostitution by their families because there is no food. Others, especially girls, are not educated and must begin working when they are very young. We bring them to our home and teach them about Jesus Christ."

"I notice that your girls are well cared for, and the dances they perform are exquisite."

Norene laughed. "Thank you for the compliment. The dances are what Cambodians are famous for. We have beautiful national dances, and each one tells a story. Our history is passed down from generation to generation through the storytelling dance. I decided to use the dances to tell the story of the gospel to the people of Cambodia. Today we go to many places and dance to spread the gospel."

The tall German man led the way to the practice area to watch the girls. As he and Norene walked, he asked her another question. "What do you see as the hope of Cambodia? Is it in these children?"

"Sir, our only hope is that our children have a good foundation in knowing Jesus Christ. Therein lies the hope for Cambodia."

*C*ambodia suffered much from the effects of the godless Communist government that came to power in the 1970s. Over one million people were executed or died as a result of enforced hardships. Today the country is filled with land mines left over from the conflict and as a result has one of the highest numbers of amputees in the world. Children

are the most vulnerable to the explosives, which have injured an estimated 20 percent of Cambodia's children. Those who survive an explo-
sion are likely to be more seriously injured than adults because their
bones grow faster than the surrounding tissue. Therefore a wound may
require repeated amputation and a new artificial limb as often as every
six months.

Street children pose a major problem in Cambodia, and an inadequate education system does not give them tools to combat poverty.

Cambodia is open to the gospel, and the young people in particular
are interested in learning about God.

Prayer Points

- Pray that the government will make the removal of land mines a top
  priority.
- Pray for an end to the most recent political infighting and civil violence in Cambodia, which have slowed economic progress and foreign
  investment.
- Pray that Cambodian medical personnel living abroad will return to
  their land to immunize and care for the children.
- Pray that God will send Christian engineers, influential business people, finances, and industry to Cambodia. The population lacks productive skills.
- Pray for the looting, killing, raping, and other atrocities committed
  by the Khmer Rouge to stop and for the apprehension of those
  involved in this renegade army.
- Pray that new believers will mature in their walk and be properly
  discipled. Pray that they will forgive those who committed horrible
  atrocities against them and their families.
- Pray that the educational sector in Cambodia will continue to be
  restored. An estimated 75 percent to 80 percent of teachers fled or
  were killed during the 1970s and 1980s.
- Pray that the youth of Cambodia will continue to show interest in
  the gospel, that their eyes will be opened to see Jesus Christ as the
  answer to their deepest needs, and that they will come to know Him
  as their Savior.

Quick Reference

Ethnic Breakdown: Khmer 85.1%, Vietnamese 3%, Han Chinese 2.5%,
other 9.4%

Type of Government: Multiparty liberal democracy under a constitutional
monarchy

Economy: Agriculture 43%, Services 37%, Industry 20%
Per capita income: U.S.$260
National debt: U.S.$829 million
Economic conditions: Extremely poor, coming out of 30 years of war

Education

Quality of education: Education has little or no value in this society.
Gender discrimination against girls: The government does not deny girls equal access to education, but families with limited resources often give priority to educating boys.

Religion

Religious concerns: The Christian church in Cambodia has had relative freedom.
Status of the church: Today there is much interest in the gospel, particularly among the youth, though the Christian community is still small.
Are Christians being persecuted? Yes

Societal Viewpoint Toward Children

Are they viewed as precious? No
Are there street children? It is estimated there are over 20,000.
Is there a large population of orphans? Yes
Are there child soldiers? The Khmer Rouge, still active today as a guerrilla force, uses children as soldiers.
Is child labor a problem? Children are routinely used in the labor force. Child prostitution and the trafficking of children are common. Half of the teen prostitutes are sold into prostitution by their families. There are reports of children being kidnapped and forced to work in the illegal sex trade.

Chad

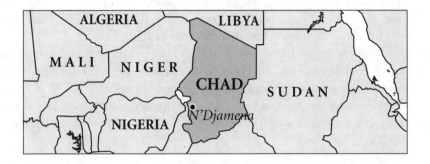

Major Languages: French, Arabic, Sara
Total Population: 8,425,000
Population 0–34: 6,703,000
Life Expectancy: 51 years
Religion: Muslim 55.00%, Christian 27.78%, traditional ethnic 16.00%, Baha'i
    1.05%, nonreligious/other 0.17%
Literacy Rate: male 44%, female 22%

*M*y sister died before my eyes at the hands of a Massa soldier. My father is dead and my mother is very sick. My two brothers, along with many of my friends, died in the civil war under President Habre. I am ashamed to admit that I sometimes cry. This is not good for a man to have such emotions. I am always crying for God to bring my family back together, but it is impossible." Eighteen-year-old Bui talked about his experiences as a child soldier during the civil war in Chad. He recently emigrated to Canada, where he now receives post-traumatic stress counseling.

Sad to say, he is one of the few young men from Chad who are being helped to deal with a horrific past where they witnessed friends and family members die. Many children and youths have no access to counseling and do not know how to interpret the symptoms of trauma, such as flashbacks, bed-wetting, night sweats, and nightmares. The civil war in Chad (1965–1990) created a generation of young people with deep emotional scars, which may be why ethnic fighting continues 12 years after peace was declared.

Others describe events they witnessed at young ages that only the power of God can heal. One young girl watched her mother and younger sister starve to death during the drought and subsequent famine that occurred in 1990. "Every day I watched as my three-year-old sister cried for food and my mother cried because she had none to give her. After many days my sister didn't cry anymore but just lay on the ground and stared at nothing. When we got a little food, she couldn't eat. It was too late. She died. My mother didn't eat because she gave any food she had to us children. I still cry when I think of those days."

One young man who served in the Chadian army told why he became a soldier at the age of 14. "I was separated from my family. I didn't know where they were and thought they were probably all dead. A group of soldiers came to the camp where I was staying and adopted me. I served for 10 years, killing my own people. Now I am sorry for what I have done. Will God help me?"

*D*uring the civil war, Chad was the scene of some of the worst human-rights abuses in Africa. Although the new government under President Idriss Deby has stopped the war, there are still reports of ethnic conflict. Forty-four percent of the population is 15 years old or younger, and many of these young people have lived for years in extreme poverty and war, far from any kind of professional help. It is almost impossible for those who have not known civil war to understand its impact on children and young people. Most carry the scars of deep trauma yet are expected to mend the current ethnic conflict and repair a government that has been divided. These expectations are coupled with lack of education and vocational skills because money designated to provide education, food, and health care for children is being used to support an army of over 50,000 soldiers.

Chad is one of the poorest countries in Africa. With the current government policies, many do not believe that Chad will be able to rise above its present level for many years to come. A bright ray of hope is the recent discovery of oil in the south and north. There are over 300 oil wells in the Doba region of southern Chad. If the country receives income from oil reserves and uses the money to build the country and develop its youth, it has a chance to recover economically in spite of the divisive past.

The prevailing desire of the population seems to be for Muslims and Christians to coexist as a nation—a nation that has survived long years of civil war.

Prayer Points

- Pray for God to heal deep emotional scars caused by the war, especially for the children, teens, and young adults.

⌣· Pray that all sides will honor the peace agreement and that God will give the people a desire to end ethnic skirmishes for the sake of future generations.

⌣· Pray that God will raise up leaders to rebuild the infrastructure of the country on Christlike principles.

⌣· Pray that the church will be emotionally healed, given resources, and trained to be an effective tool in the hand of God to bring healing to the land.

⌣· Pray that FGM will end. This custom is deeply rooted in the culture, with about 60 percent of the girls being subjected to this barbaric procedure.

⌣· Pray for young girls who are married as soon as they reach puberty.

⌣· Pray that the recent discovery of oil will be used by God to bring this nation out of poverty. Pray that this blessing will benefit all the people and the money it produces will not corrupt Chad's leaders.

⌣· Pray that children, teens, and young adults will be properly educated so that they will be able to run their country with excellence.

⌣· Pray for an increase in the literacy rate and that Christian teaching will be available on cassettes and videos to train this upcoming generation in the principles of God.

⌣· Pray that God will give this generation hope and a future as He is established in the hearts of the people.

Quick Reference

Ethnic Breakdown: Sara 28%, Arab 12%, Mayo Kebbi 12%, Kanem Bornou 9%, Ouaddai 9%, Tandjile 7%, Hadjara 7%, Gorane 6%, other 10%

Type of Government: Republic

Economy: Agriculture 85%, other 15%

Per capita income: U.S.$180

National debt: U.S.$1 billion

Economic conditions: Extremely poor. Landlocked, Chad's economic development suffers from its geographic remoteness, drought, political turmoil, and lack of infrastructure.

Education

Quality of education: There is a severe shortage of resources, schools, and teachers. The civil war diverted funds from education to support the military.

Gender discrimination against girls: Girls may be removed from school at puberty. Not much importance is placed on education for girls.

Religion

Religious concerns: Lack of Christian teaching material and inability of people to read make discipleship and leadership training extremely difficult. Tribalism, syncretic lifestyle, and petty legalisms cripple many congregations. Christian witness to Muslims is rare. Huge cultural, historical, and emotional barriers must be overcome.

Status of the church: The church needs emotional healing from the war so that it can minister effectively to an emotionally traumatized nation. Many Christians fear Islamic persecution, while others feel burdened to witness to Muslims.

Are Christians being persecuted? Yes

Societal Viewpoint Toward Children

Are they viewed as precious? No

Are there street children? No specific data available.

Is there a large population of orphans? Yes

Are there child soldiers? Yes

Is child labor a problem? Children are actively involved in the labor force in agriculture and herding.

China

Major Languages: Mandarin, English
Total Population: 1,271,832,482
Population 0–34: 760,149,000
Life Expectancy: 69 years
Religion: nonreligious/other 49.58%, Chinese 28.50%, Buddhist 8.38%,
  Christian 7.25%, traditional ethnic 4.29%, Muslim 2.00%
Literacy Rate: male 90%, female 73%

A young female preacher stands before a packed underground house church in the Zhenping district in Henan, China. "We can see that God is already working," she exclaims. All around her, young people sit on the floor of the packed room and look up at her attentively. "The time has come—we must preach the gospel. We must rise up and make spiritual warfare for the Lord. We have to go forth in the name of the Lord and heal the sick. We must now rise up and cause the gospel to catch fire in the hearts of our people throughout this land!"

The crowd bursts into singing but is not led by a choir or worship leader. People from the congregation take turns leading the singing. The worship and praise lasts for over an hour. This meeting is part of China's house church movement. There are now tens of thousands of unregistered churches like this one throughout the People's Republic of China. These Christians are often young and have an intense love for the Lord and each other. House meetings are usually packed, sometimes throughout several rooms. The time is spent taking the Lord's Supper, preaching, and singing psalms, hymns, and praise songs. The house churches exist without denominations, divisions, or ministry positions. The believers meet from house to house, district to district, and they see themselves as one church.

The stories that have come out of these meetings are right out of the book of Acts, with miraculous physical healings—a baby raised from the dead, a woman with leprosy healed, a long-term paralysis victim restored to complete mobility overnight. Young and old alike spend time in intercession for their country's leaders and for the authorities who would gladly imprison them if they were ever discovered at a house church meeting. The house churches have no legal rights in China. Unlike the Three-Self Patriotic Movement and the Catholic Patriotic Association, these churches are not registered and are considered by the government to be cults that are dangerous to society.

Despite persecution, the zeal of God burns brightly in the lives of new converts in China. Many Christians who attend house church meetings have been blacklisted as fugitives or forced to live under some form of police probation. More than half of them have spent time in prison. As a result of this massive revival, the Bible has become the best seller in China and ranks second only to the works of former leader Deng Xiao Ping.

Evangelicals estimate that 20,000 to 30,000 people come to Christ daily in China.

According to some estimates, well over 75 percent of the world's youth live in Asian countries, of which China has the highest number. Asian youth are not unlike those in Western countries. They like cell phones, pagers, trendy clothes, and the Internet. They watch American films and TV shows and listen to music from the West. Now, more than ever, is the time for the church to rise up and use new methods of evangelism available through technological advances.

With over 1.2 billion people, China's strong market economy gives the young people jobs and training opportunities, especially in the field of technology. Because of their close contact with the West and their ability to afford modern gadgets, young people discover a world outside of China. Many experts feel that because of this generation's new way of thinking, the old policies of isolationism may be a way of the past. The young people are hungry for God and are seeking viable answers to life's problems.

China's one-child policy has forced many families to abort children to comply with the law, but that is not the only cause of the high abortion rate. Some mothers wanting a male child will abort a female fetus. Currently, as a result of the abortions, the male population outnumbers the female population. There are also reports of female children and those with physical and mental handicaps being abandoned.

Prayer Points

- Pray for the underground house church in China to have courage and endurance in the midst of persecution.

⌣· Pray for God to continue to draw the Chinese people to Himself. Praise God that 20,000 to 30,000 people come to Christ each day in China.

⌣· Pray for God to give Christians creative and effective ways to use technology to reach the youth culture so that young people will have a hunger to find the one true God.

⌣· Pray for a drastic change of the deplorable conditions in which orphans live. Pray for increased government funds for orphanages and that the additional funds will be properly used to provide for the needs of the children.

⌣· Pray for female children to be viewed as precious. Pray for an end to female infanticide, abandonment, neglect, and gender-selective termination of pregnancies.

⌣· Pray for greater enforcement of laws targeting the lucrative sex trade in China. Ask God to provide avenues of escape for the young women trapped in cycles of crime, exploitation, disease, and abuse.

⌣· Pray for increased access to Bibles and sound teaching materials in all Chinese dialects. Pray that there will be a dramatic turning of the nation to Christ.

Quick Reference

Ethnic Breakdown: Han Chinese 91.9%, Zhuang, Uygur, Hui, Yi, Tibetan, Miao, Manchu, Mongol, Buyi, Korean, other 8.1%
Type of Government: Communist
Economy: Industry 46%, Agriculture 41%, Services 13%
Per capita income: U.S.$620
National debt: U.S.$159 billion
Economic conditions: Recovering from economic depression

Education
Quality of education: Children are pressured to do well in school, which may result in undue stress.
Gender discrimination against girls: Girls are being educated.

Religion
Religious concerns: Evangelism is prohibited. Only Christian churches affiliated with the Catholic Patriotic Association or the Three-Self Patriotic Movement are allowed to operate openly.
Status of the church: Authorities closely monitor the activities of underground churches. At least 80 percent of the pastors are women. The church is growing.
Are Christians being persecuted? Yes. Christians are being jailed and tortured.

Societal Viewpoint Toward Children
Are they viewed as precious? The male child is; the female child is not.

Are there street children? Yes

Is there a large population of orphans? Yes, approximately 1.7 million.

Are there child soldiers? No specific data available.

Is child labor a problem? The Chinese government prohibits the forced and bonded labor of children.

Djibouti

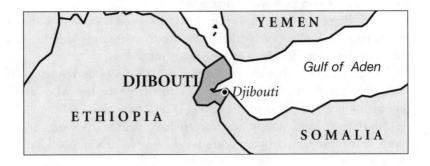

Major Languages: French, Arabic
Total Population: 451,000
Population 0–34: 335,709
Life Expectancy: 51 years
Religion: Muslim 93.90%, Christian 4.67%, nonreligious/other 1.32%,
   Baha'i 0.09%, Hindu 0.02%
Literacy Rate: male 60%, female 33%

*E*very day shortly after noon a plane approaches and the cry goes up that the *khat* is here. Vendors race to receive the precious bundles that will be hurled at them over the wire fence. The rush is on. Those who move the fastest make the most money, a powerful incentive in a country with 80 percent unemployment and a cost of living much higher than anywhere else in the Horn of Africa.

Hundreds of cars and mopeds shatter the calm of the city as, horns blaring, they race each other from the airport. For the next hour they tear along the city's main roads and down its narrow, dusty side streets, selling and distributing thousands of parcels of bright green leaves to screaming street traders in a burst of manic activity. At the same time, government offices and private businesses shut down and Djibouti's men make one last, vital purchase before heading home or finding a tree to sit under. Then the city goes quiet, dramatically quiet, for the rest of the day. It's time to chew khat.

The leaf, which comes from a plant of the same name, is a natural stimulant with the qualities of a mild amphetamine, and chewing it is a daily ritual for almost all men in this tiny Muslim nation. Sheltered from the afternoon sun, the men sit in small groups, methodically stripping the leaves from the stalks and chewing them into a wad that bulges inside their cheeks. Chewers take the edge off khat's bitter taste with sweet tea, water, or soda as they chat and joke through long afternoons. After an early surge of euphoria and energy, many later feel lethargic and sleep badly, waking up with a hangover.

"We don't drink alcohol, but this is like our beer. It is our way of relaxing, of talking to each other," says Abdi, a 30-year-old father of four who says he chews for three or four hours most days.

Khat is widely popular in Yemen and Somalia and in pockets of Ethiopia, Kenya, and Egypt. It tends to dominate life wherever it is chewed. Once restricted to the affluent, it is now chewed by men of all social classes. More and more women have started chewing in recent years, but most family budgets are barely able to sustain one khat habit, let alone two.

"We can't afford to let our women chew khat," said Omar, a government worker who hasn't been paid his salary in five months but still manages to scrape together enough cash to chew most days. It is by far the most used consumer item in the country, accounting for between 25 percent and 40 percent of household spending.

The leaf is not even produced in Djibouti. It is imported, a further drain on the resources of a country of just over 450,000 people that has virtually no agriculture or industry.

Government officials admit khat hinders productivity, but only a brave man would call for a campaign against it. Even Djibouti's economic minister, who does not chew, uses distorted logic to say it helps people work longer hours.*

D jibouti is an impoverished nation with almost no natural resources, scanty rainfall, and little industry. The country produces few consumer goods, and much of the food supply must be imported. Famine and malnutrition have created reliance on foreign aid for food. The people live in poverty, as unemployment rates have soared to 80 percent. Illiteracy is high, with only a 33 percent literacy rate for females.

Schools are run-down and in need of upgrading. Disease is rampant, with very poor health care. Generally, girls are considered less valuable than boys and are revered only because of their ability to bear children. It is estimated that as many as 98 percent of females age seven or older have undergone FGM.

Because of the custom of chewing khat, the poor economic conditions, the deterioration of the educational system, and the lack of access

---

* Adapted from an article by Reuters News Service and several other sources found in the bibliography.

to the gospel of Jesus Christ, the children of Djibouti have little chance of combating poverty and gaining a better life for themselves and their country.

Prayer Points

- Pray for God to reveal the hidden treasures He has placed in Djibouti so that this nation can financially sustain itself. Pray that God will send rain on the crops so that the people will have sufficient food.
- Pray for the church to rise up and take responsibility to reach the children of the nation with the gospel and to improve the living conditions of the people. Large numbers of people are dying of malnutrition, sickness, and disease.
- Pray for an end to the domination that the stimulant drug khat has on the lives of the Djibouti people and that future generations will not be addicted to khat.
- Pray for elimination of the barbaric practice of FGM.
- Pray for God to give Christians in Djibouti strategies to reach children, teens, and young adults with the love and saving knowledge of Jesus Christ.
- Pray for discipleship of new believers, that they will grow in faith, love, and understanding of the Lord and the power God has given them to transform their nation.
- Pray for God to raise up national young people to become missionaries to take the gospel to neighboring countries.
- Pray for more teachers and schools so that the literacy rate will improve and positively impact the nation.

Quick Reference

Ethnic Breakdown: Somali 60%, Afar 35%, French, Arab, other 5%
Type of Government: Republic
Economy: Services 77%, Industry 20%, Agriculture 3%
Per capita income: U.S.$475
National debt: U.S.$350 million
Economic conditions: Extremely poor

Education
Quality of education: There is a severe shortage of teachers and schools. Instruction includes mandatory Koranic curriculum.
Gender discrimination against girls: Not much importance is placed on education for girls.

Religion

Religious concerns: Evangelism is prohibited.

Status of the church: Severe lack of discipleship.

Are Christians being persecuted? Yes

Societal Viewpoint Toward Children

Are they viewed as precious? Yes

Are there street children? No specific data available.

Is there a large population of orphans? No specific data available.

Are there child soldiers? Yes

Is child labor a problem? There are no reports of forced child labor.

Egypt

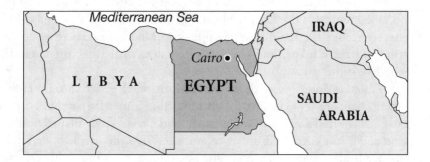

Major Languages: Arabic, English, French
Total Population: 68,360,000
Population 0–34: 48,504,000
Life Expectancy: 63 years
Religion: Muslim 86.52%, Christian 12.98%, nonreligious/other 0.50%
Literacy Rate: male 64%, female 38%

*M*oqattam, a city of squalor and sorrow, lies sprawled beneath the shadow of a large limestone mountain. On the rough, narrow streets a passerby can look inside the shops through doorways that open directly off the narrow passageway. Children as young as six years old can be seen working at lathes, covered with oil from head to toe, or sorting through mounds of plastic garbage bags to glean what is recyclable. The stench of burning debris makes one's eyes burn and water. Dirt and blatant poverty are everywhere, from the butcher who has just slit a pig's throat and let the blood run down the hillside to the dogs, cats, and donkeys that roam the streets and nose through piles of garbage for food.

This city of over 130,000 residents is predominately Christian. Past all the squalor is a beautiful church carved in the side of a mountain. This is St. Stephen's Catholic Church, dedicated to the man who led the Christians to this part of the city hundreds of years ago as the Muslims were chasing them. The church building, blasted out of the side of the mountain, has amphitheater-style seating. The platform and pulpit are flanked by massive rock walls that have beautifully carved scenes of Jesus Christ and His disciples. The church has grown, and God has truly visited His people—in the garbage dump of Cairo.

Eight-year-old Immanuel lives in Moqattam with his mother, father, four brothers, and three sisters. All of his life he has collected old newspapers and plastic from the garbage that comes daily into the city on donkey carts and run-down trucks. He has never been to school because there is too much work to do, and his father needs him to help provide money for the family. He and his family live in a green building that overlooks the main road coming into Moqattam. There is no electricity in their home, and they share a toilet with three other families who live in the same building.

Thursdays are special days because Immanuel gets to attend church, where there are services just for children like him. His parents go regularly to hear Father Saman preach and have seen many healings. Immanuel has witnessed only one miracle. Two months ago a friend of his was healed from polio, and now he no longer has to use his crutches, which now hang from one of the rock walls, just below the picture etched in stone of Jesus Christ and His disciples. Immanuel has hope because he is learning about Jesus.

While Muslims are the majority, Egypt has more Christians than any other Middle Eastern country. The Coptic Church comprises about 90 percent of the Christian population.

A girl in Egypt has more educational opportunities and less chance of abuse if she lives in Cairo. In rural areas, to minimize her interaction with boys, she is usually withdrawn from school as she reaches puberty. Many girls have no chance to get an education because their fathers feel it would be money wasted, since a girl will leave home at marriage to become the property of her husband's family.

Education is often expensive because of the bribes a student is expected to pay the teacher. Teachers' salaries are often less than $200 per month, and the difference is made up by taking "tutoring fees" to help students pass their tests.

There are few youth programs that cater to the needs of the children and youths of Egypt. One of the leading pastors in Cairo feels that this is an opportunity for Christians to step in and provide Christian music, videos, and activities that are relevant to the culture.

Prayer Points

- Pray for the school curriculum and educational programs.
- Pray for children who are poor, orphaned, abused, or living on the streets.
- Pray for poor children who are usually deprived of an education because they have to work to bring income into the family.

- Pray for the end of professional begging, where gangs use children for begging and mutilate them to gain sympathy.
- Pray for young girls who are forced to marry as early as 11 to bring income into the family.
- Pray for an end to the inhumane practice of FGM. A 1997 survey of Egyptian adolescents stated that 86 percent of the girls between 13 and 19 had undergone FGM.
- Pray for elimination of drugs in the schools.
- Pray for revival among the 700 to 900 children who live in an orphanage in Upper Egypt.
- Pray for teenagers, who are at the age of questioning their beliefs, to recognize the deception of Islam. Pray that they will turn to Jesus Christ, the true and living God.
- Pray for young evangelists to rise up and overcome their fears of sharing the gospel. Pray the protection of Psalm 91 over them.
- Pray for an improved economy. The current economic crisis seriously affects young people and breeds fatalism and fanaticism. Young men believe that if they become stronger in their religion, Allah will solve their problems. This belief can pave the way to terrorism.

Quick Reference

Ethnic Breakdown: Egyptian Arab 84.1%, Sudanese 5.5%, Arabized Berber 2.0%, Bedouin 2.0%, Halebi Gypsy 1.6%, French and Italian 1.0%, other 3.8%

Type of Government: Republic

Economy: Services 51%, Industry 32%, Agriculture 17%

Per capita income: U.S.$790

National debt: U.S.$30 billion

Economic conditions: Poor

Education

Quality of education: Quality of education is questionable. Instruction includes mandatory Koranic curriculum.

Gender discrimination against girls: Some families have a tendency to withdraw girls from school when they reach puberty.

Religion

Religious concerns: Evangelism is restricted, although there is a renewed openness to the gospel.

Status of the church: Egypt has the Middle East's largest Christian community. The evangelical church is growing and is very active in reaching the nation for Christ.

Are Christians being persecuted? Yes

Societal Viewpoint Toward Children

Are they viewed as precious? Yes

Are there street children? There are many children who live on the streets.

Is there a large population of orphans? No specific data available.

Are there child soldiers? No specific data available.

Is child labor a problem? Yes. An estimated 1.3 million children between the ages of 6 and 14 are in the labor force. Many of them are abused and overworked by their employers.

Eritrea

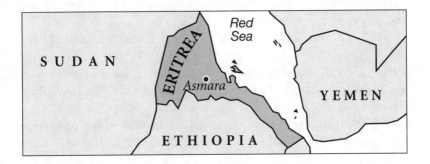

Major Languages: Tigray, Tigre, Afar
Total Population: 4,136,000
Population 0–34: 3,220,000
Life Expectancy: 52 years
Religion: Muslim 47.97%, Christian 47.43%, nonreligious/other 4.00%,
    traditional ethnic 0.60%
Literacy Rate: male 30%, female 10%

*E*ighteen-year-old Halie remembers well the time he became a man. The day started uneventfully. He had gone outside the village to where his father kept the family livestock. The makeshift pens made of salvaged wire, old car parts, and discarded building materials held four camels, proof of the family wealth—above average for the Danakil tribe, as most clansmen own no camels. The goats and sheep the women of the tribe tended didn't count; it was the number of camels a man possessed that showed the extent of his prosperity.

Halie found the gate to the pen open and the camels gone. He returned to his village to get his father, and together they tracked through the hot sand on a hunch that the camels had been taken by the new caravan of workers recently spotted at the nearby salt mines. The extremely hot temperatures and hard work in the mines attracted only a few men, who usually came in on caravans from as far away as Sudan and stayed for two months before returning to their homeland. These weary workers frequently "borrowed" from local villagers.

After a day of searching, Halie and his father found their animals under the care of three miners. At first Halie thought he could reason with the man who was feeding them, but the man insisted the camels were his and had been brought in from Sudan. The confrontation lasted only a few moments. Halie plunged his knife into the man's stomach and stood back to watch him die. The significance of the event excited him. In the Danakil tribe a man is not really a man until he has killed another man. Watching the thief die at his hands gave Halie a sense of strength and power he had never known.

The village celebration over the event lasted two days. Now Halie could marry and become a member of the Danakil tribal council. His father called all the tribal elders together to start the arrangements to find a wife for him. Before the sun set, the elders decided Halie would wed at the next full moon.

With all the excitement of the day, Halie wished it would never end. He slept peacefully that night and dreamed of the days ahead as a true leader of his clan. He was brave, and he would help lead his people wisely—he knew it.

The Danakil tribe is also known as the Afar. It makes its home in the desert mountains and along the coast of the Red Sea. As Muslims the Danakil may have four wives but usually are monogamous. They live in one of the most rugged parts of the world, in camps surrounded by thorn barricades. They are considered one of the unreached peoples of the world.

*E*ritrea's president, Isaias Afworki, has adopted a no-nonsense approach to building a strong central government. He has managed to maintain a balance of religious freedom and peaceful coexistence between the Muslims and Christians. The people have made great strides in rebuilding the country after 30 years (1961–1991) of civil war with Ethiopia.

In 1991 Eritrea gained the right of self-determination, and in 1993 the people voted to become a country separate from Ethiopian rule. Since that time Eritrea has experienced relative peace with its neighbors, with the exception of border clashes with Sudan and Ethiopia.

The major needs of the children are for education and food. Only about 50 percent of the children attend school, and the resulting average literacy rate for the country is only 20 percent. Many of the schools destroyed during the war have not been rebuilt. Even if schools are available, there is a severe shortage of teachers. The huge national debt hinders the building of schools and hospitals. Eritrea has a high infant mortality rate and a high incidence of disease and poverty, and it depends heavily on external aid for its food supply.

Prayer Points

-· Pray that the Danakil (Afar) will banish the idea that a male has to kill another male before he becomes a man.

- ✑· Pray that the newly formed nation will have a Christian government and will successfully develop its infrastructure.
- ✑· Pray that God will move in the hearts of the 75,000 Eritreans living abroad to be born again and return as missionaries or investors to build a godly infrastructure in their nation.
- ✑· Pray that children, teens, and young adults will be properly educated.
- ✑· Pray that Christian ministries will come and invest in this country by teaching the people in the areas of education, nutrition, business, and health care.
- ✑· Pray for total reconciliation between Eritrea and Ethiopia for the sake of future generations.
- ✑· Pray that Christians and Muslims will continue to coexist peacefully.
- ✑· Pray that God will give Christians creative strategies to reach children, teens, and young adults.
- ✑· Pray for an end to the barbaric practice of FGM, which is widespread in the country. It is estimated that 95 percent of the girls and women have been subjected to this inhumane practice.

Quick Reference

Ethnic Breakdown: Tigrinya 50%, Tigre and Kunama 40%, Afar 4%, Saho 3%, other 3%
Type of Government: Transitional government
Economy: Subsistence Agriculture 80%, Industry and other 20%
Per capita income: U.S.$570
National debt: U.S.$10 billion
Economic conditions: Extremely poor, recovering from war

Education
Quality of education: Poor. There is a severe shortage of schools and teachers.
Gender discrimination against girls: Not much importance is placed on education for girls.

Religion
Religious concerns: There is a strong push by Islamic forces to convert Christians.
Status of the church: The church consists mainly of nominal Christians.
Are Christians being persecuted? No

Societal Viewpoint Toward Children
Are they viewed as precious? No
Are there street children? Street children are not a noted problem.
Is there a large population of orphans? No specific data available.
Are there child soldiers? No specific data available.
Is child labor a problem? Children work in the labor force.

Ethiopia

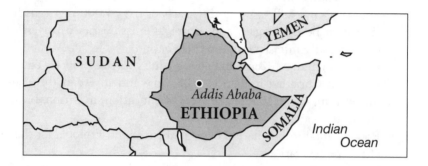

Major Languages: Amharic, Tigrinya, Orominga
Total Population: 64,117,000
Population 0–34: 50,731,000
Life Expectancy: 45 years
Religion: Christian 65.02%, Muslim 31.00%, traditional ethnic 2.98%,
    nonreligious/other 1.00 %
Literacy Rate: male 40%, female 27%

*F*ati held her frail baby in her arms. For days now she had had no milk to nurse the child, and if she couldn't find help soon, her baby had only a short time to live. She looked over at her mother lying on a mat in the middle of the dark hut. A small stream of light came through the door and streaked across her mother's face.

Fati bent over and whispered softly in her mother's ear. "In the morning, Mother, I will leave. My child will die if I don't get food, and you are too sick to walk. I go with great heaviness in my heart because I know I will never see you again." Tears ran down her face as she searched her mother for some type of response. There was none. The tired eyes only stared out into the distance. Fati knew her mother, at 47, was not old, but living through two major famines had taken its toll. Her mother would not live through this one. So many of the people in her village had died. Three years had come and gone with no rainfall. Last year they did not even have any seed to plant, which turned out to be a blessing because they'd had no rains in either the *belg* or the *mehr*, the short and long rainy seasons. Now there was no rain again.

Fati was just 10 years old when the last great famine hit Ethiopia in 1984. It had lasted for three years, and she would never forget how hungry she had felt during those days. After a while there was no hunger in her belly, just a tiredness that settled over her body and made her want to sit and sleep all the time. She must save her baby from the same misery that she suffered as a child.

Early the next morning Fati set out for a feeding station she'd heard about through her cousin, who had left the village in search of food. By her calculations, it would be a three-day walk to the town of Harer. There would be food there. She held her baby tight and said, "Don't worry, little Koret. Your mother will find you food." She covered the baby with her shawl to shield her sunken eyes from the relentless sun. She thought, *Maybe I waited too late to start this journey. Maybe my baby won't make it.* One thing she knew for sure—if she didn't make an effort, they would both die. She had to try.

The blazing sun had almost gone down when she reached the first huts along the road. The streets were crowded, and people sat in front of every store and along the side of the road. A little boy pointed the way to the feeding station. Fati joined the hundreds of other weary travelers at the end of a line that wound through town and ended at a large white sign.

Fati's baby was only one of 1,500 children at the feeding station that night suffering from malnutrition and dehydration. The workers gave Fati a high-protein porridge to feed Koret. Only time will tell whether the child will survive, but her chances are not good.

*E*thiopia is one of the poorest countries in the world. Plagued by drought and famine, the country is forced to depend on outside economic aid and loans from the World Bank to feed its people.

The needs of the children are great. There are not enough schools, and basic medical care is not in place for most of the population. Food, especially in rural areas, is scarce. An estimated 150,000 street children live in the urban areas. Schools are virtually nonexistent in rural areas. Girls marry young and are more likely than boys not to attend school, even if one is available.

Frequent border clashes with Sudan and Eritrea have drained the already poor economy and caused Ethiopia to be cited by the Human Rights Watch as a country that uses child soldiers, some as young as seven or eight years old.

The growing evangelical congregation in Ethiopia needs our prayers and financial support. The majority of national Christians may be so in name only. They need to know Jesus Christ in a personal relationship.

Prayer Points

- Pray for emotional healing of young refugees who carry scars as a result of being banished from their country.

⌣• Pray for the children of war. Pray for God to restore their innocence, that they will once again have the ability to love and trust and will be able to forgive.

⌣• Pray for the starving children to receive the food they need to survive.

⌣• Pray for God to heal the scars of the children who had to leave behind dying family members to search for food.

⌣• Pray for God to supernaturally send rain upon the land and give cutting-edge ideas for cultivating crops in the midst of drought.

⌣• Pray for Christians from other nations to set up feeding stations for those who are suffering from malnutrition.

⌣• Pray for the Lord to reveal Himself to this generation.

⌣• Pray for Damascus Road experiences for the country's leaders.

⌣• Pray for children to be protected from forced labor and prostitution.

Quick Reference

Ethnic Breakdown: Oromo 40%, Amhara and Tigre 32%, Sidamo 9%, Shankella 6%, Somali 6%, Afar 4%, Gurage 2%, other 1%
Type of Government: Federal republic
Economy: Agriculture 46%, Services 42%, Industry 12%
Per capita income: U.S.$100
National debt: U.S.$10 billion
Economic conditions: Extremely poor

Education
Quality of education: There is a severe shortage of teachers and schools.
Gender discrimination against girls: Not much importance is placed on education for girls.

Religion
Religious concerns: The church needs discipleship and leadership training.
Status of the church: Evangelism is allowed. Evangelical and Pentecostal churches are the fastest growing and now constitute more than 10 percent of the population.
Are Christians being persecuted? No

Societal Viewpoint Toward Children
Are they viewed as precious? No
Are there street children? Yes, approximately 150,000.
Is there a large population of orphans? Yes
Are there child soldiers? Yes, children as young as seven or eight are permitted to join the military.
Is child labor a problem? Thirty percent of workers on farms are between the ages of 7 and 14. Children typically work six days a week, receive no benefits, and earn less than U.S.$10 a month.

The Gambia

Major Languages: English, Mandenka, Wolof
Total Population: 1,367,000
Population 0–34: 1,060,000
Life Expectancy: 53 years
Religion: Muslim 88.80%, traditional ethnic 6.70%, Christian 4.10%,
Baha'i 0.40%
Literacy Rate: male 53%, female 25%

*T*en-year-old Watuba helped her mothers wash, cook, and pound rice, as well as care for her four younger siblings. She had more than one mother because her father, as a Muslim, could take more than one wife. As the oldest girl of seven children, she was responsible for tending to the compound while her two mothers worked in the rice fields or in the garden. Every day Watuba watched her two older brothers go off to a school that she was not allowed to attend. When she was six years old, she cried as they left their sleeping huts to go to the village for classes. She begged to go with them. Eventually she learned not to ask, and her life settled into a rhythm of cooking and tending to children.

She took her work seriously and tried hard to be a diligent worker. At times her mothers even bragged about her. Some days she carried six or seven heavy buckets of water from the village well in the morning and evening.

One of her mothers assured her that if Allah wanted her to learn, he would make the government build schools for girls and give her family the money to buy pencils and examination books. Watuba learned that fate willed that she would not learn to read.

As time passed, she busied herself with the chores assigned to her. When her body began to change, she felt more self-conscious about going to the village well if boys were there. At 13 she overheard her father and another man talking about her.

"It is time for us to find a husband for Watuba," her father said. "We want her to marry early while she is still afraid of men so that she may bring her family honor."

Watuba was afraid. She was so young, but she knew her father would choose a mate and she would do as he said. She had been trained to be a wife and mother, and even if she couldn't read, she was still smart. She would do a good job. Every day she went about her business, knowing that her fate was set by Allah and her father, and soon by her husband.

W atuba's story is not unique. Early marriage is the accepted norm in the Gambia. Girls marry early so that they will respect their husband as head of the household. Very little education is provided for girls, who are needed at home to tend to younger siblings and help with chores. This attitude is reflected in the low 25 percent female literacy rate.

In general, the government has not considered education a priority. During the 30 years from 1965 to 1995 not one hospital, high school, or university was built. Now, because of a growing awareness of the need for education, the government has shown some openness to those who will help educate the children. More and more parents are even beginning to see the necessity of sending their daughters to school.

The people of the Gambia believe that everything should be left to fate. This attitude has hindered their progress, preventing them from providing the means to combat disease and poverty. Although 90 percent of the population professes to be Muslim, the country is deeply steeped in animism and folk religion.

Although the government discourages the use of child labor, children commonly work as street vendors and employees in the marketplace. The income they produce is often necessary to sustain their families.

The Gambia needs our prayers. We must pray that doors will open wider than ever before for the gospel and that God will send intercessors into the country to break the spiritual bonds of witchcraft, slavery, and defeatism. The needs of the children are great, and without a breakthrough in the spiritual realm, the present generation could continue in the same bondage that has kept the people from being open to the gospel for hundreds of years. God is calling. Who will go?

Prayer Points

- Pray that the government's goal of free compulsory education for all children will become a reality.
- Pray for physical and psychological healing for girls and women who have undergone the barbaric practice of FGM. Some ethnic groups

perform this ungodly procedure on girls anytime between 3 months and 18 years of age.

◡· Pray that the government will renounce FGM, pass legislation against it, and consider it a crime.
◡· Praise God for the government's tough stand against prostitution.
◡· Pray for revival of the evangelical church, especially among children, teens, and young adults.
◡· Pray for powerful outreaches to the young people.
◡· Pray for continuing religious freedom to proclaim the gospel and that the church will rise to meet its responsibility to proclaim the gospel.

Quick Reference

Ethnic Breakdown: Mandinka 42%, Fula 18%, Wolof 16%, Jola 10%, Serahuli 9%, non-African 1%, other 4%
Type of Government: Republic under multiparty democratic rule
Economy: Services 64%, Agriculture 23%, Industry 13%
Per capita income: U.S.$320
National debt: U.S.$430 million
Economic conditions: Poor

Education
Quality of education: Instruction can include Christian and Koranic curriculum. There is a severe shortage of schools and teachers.
Gender discrimination against girls: Not much importance is placed on education for girls. While schools exist for girls, the enrollment remains low due to a combination of poverty and sociocultural factors that influence parents' decisions not to send girls to school. Domestic chores and early marriage take precedence over education.

Religion
Religious concerns: Islam has steadily grown in influence. Christian missionaries are restricted to development programs, but they have considerable opportunity to share their faith. Although Islam is dominant, the land remains open for the gospel.
Status of the church: The constitution provides for freedom of religion. There is a small but growing evangelical movement in the country. Believers need discipleship, leadership, and evangelism training.
Are Christians being persecuted? No

Societal Viewpoint Toward Children
Are they viewed as precious? Yes
Are there street children? No specific data available.
Is there a large population of orphans? No specific data available.
Are there child soldiers? No
Is child labor a problem? Children commonly work as street vendors and employees in the marketplace to help support their families.

Gaza Strip

Major Languages: Arabic, Hebrew, English
Total Population: 1,132,063
Population 0–34: 923,000
Life Expectancy: 71 years
Religion: Sunni Muslim 98.7%, Christian 0.7%, Jewish 0.6%
Literacy Rate: 70%

*T*his is a war between the children. They hate each other, and almost all boys have been involved in riots in the streets. What can we do? We are pushed into refugee camps with nothing to think about but our children's future, which doesn't look good right now." Saeba, a young Palestinian mother, tries to describe her frustration about living in the Gaza Strip with the continual threat of war and violence.

"My children have nightmares and show worry on their faces. They have lost their youth. My sons cannot go to school because of threats from other children. So now our children grow up without an education."

Jewish mothers make the same kinds of comments. "Our children are damaged. They have scars on the inside that may never heal. We don't like our children growing up in such a tense situation, but we don't have much choice. I worry day and night. Just last week a child was killed when some Palestinian boys threw rocks at him. You can't imagine the anxiety of raising children in this environment." Another mother commented, "This is a generation without a childhood. They are adults when they are 10 years old because they must work and learn to protect themselves on the streets."

Although the Gaza Strip and the West Bank are often considered together, the authors have chosen to stay with the directives of the original 10/40 Window prayer initiative, which does does not include the West Bank.

The Gaza Strip may be one of the most dangerous areas in the world for children. Continual fighting and terrorist attacks cause the children to take up the offenses of the generations that have preceded them, often fighting and shouting slurs at each other. Khulud, a 10-year-old Palestinian refugee, found it funny when she was asked if she had any Jewish friends. "They are people like us, but people cannot stand them—at least not me," she said. "They are somehow different, somehow unusual. I don't like them and don't intend to get to know anyone from their settlement. We can never be friends."

*I*n 1948, when Israel proclaimed its independence and the Arab states attacked, Israel won the war. The result was the confiscation of Palestinian land that forced tens of thousands of Palestinian refugees into the Gaza Strip area.

The Gaza Strip has remained a hotbed of violence because of the mixture of Palestinian refugees thrust into close quarters with Jewish settlers. Ninety-eight percent of those who live in the Gaza Strip are Palestinian refugees, with the other percentages made up of Jewish settlers and Christians. In all there are approximately 6,500 Israeli settlers and over 110,000 Palestinians. At Shati, a Palestinian refugee camp, there are 80,000 people living in less than one square mile. Sewage runs outside the doors of their thrown-together shacks, and the water is salty. As if these conditions aren't bad enough, most fathers have not been able to obtain jobs, and the unemployment rate is about 50 percent. The Palestinian men, with little to do, sit and talk of their hatred for the opposing group. Frequent clashes between Israelis and Palestinians lead to curfews and restrictions of free movement by the people, making it even more difficult for the men to find work. In retaliation, the Palestinians order frequent underground one-day strikes, further undermining the economy.

The Palestinians wait for the day when they can return to Jerusalem and their homeland. Many of the older people sit in their shanties and remember the land they still feel is theirs. They long for their orchards and yards with flowers that bloom in the spring. The Palestinians in Gaza hold the Israelis responsible for their loss of homes and land. Their desire is to return to Jerusalem, which would possibly mean the dissolution of the nation of Israel.

While there are no easy answers, jobs and a sense of belonging would help to ease the tensions. Most people can't get permission to go outside Gaza. Those who do get permission to travel outside the tiny territory's boundaries may find the border closed when they attempt to return, so many do not leave their families for fear they will never see them again. The whole situation makes Gaza like a prison camp.

Schools are in disrepair, and there is little or no medical care for the residents of the camps. This may account for the high dropout rate of Arab children.

Prayer Points

- Pray for a miraculous reconciliation between the descendants of Isaac and those of Ishmael for the sake of future generations.
- Pray for powerful Christian outreaches to minister to the spiritually, physically, and mentally wounded children, teens, and young adults.
- Pray for God to raise up an anointed Palestinian youth pastor to minister in this difficult place.
- Pray that the leaders in Gaza and Israel will come to an amicable agreement for the sake of the children, teens, and young adults.
- Pray for the needed resources for education, medicine, food, and business.
- Pray for Jesus Christ to appear to the teens and young adults in dreams and visions.
- Pray for God to give Christian radio and TV cutting-edge programming that will reach this generation with the gospel.
- Pray for this generation of children who have lost their innocence and childhood.
- Pray that this generation will break the cycle and leave the refugee camps and condensed areas where they live. Pray that they will be able to live in comfortable homes.
- Pray for God to raise up leaders who will seek His solution to the problems there.
- Pray for a lasting end to the violence.

Quick Reference

Ethnic Breakdown: Arab and other 99.4%, Jewish 0.6%
Type of Government: Palestinian-administered territory
Economy: Services 42%, Agriculture 33%, Industry 25%
Per capita income: U.S.$1,060
National debt: U.S.$108 million (includes West Bank)
Economic conditions: Poor

Education
Quality of education: There is a shortage of schools and teachers, and buildings are often in disrepair. Children may be kept home to avoid violence. Instruction includes mandatory Koranic curriculum.

Gender discrimination against girls: Because of early marriage, girls frequently do not finish the mandatory level of schooling.

Religion

Religious concerns: Evangelism is prohibited.

Status of the church: The fledgling church is in need of finances and discipleship training.

Are Christians being persecuted? Yes

Societal Viewpoint Toward Children

Are they viewed as precious? Yes

Are there street children? There are a growing number of street children.

Is there a large population of orphans? No specific data available.

Are there child soldiers? Children are engaged in conflicts, though not necessarily via the military.

Is child labor a problem? Children may be kept out of school to help with family chores and businesses. There are reports of children working in small manufacturing enterprises, such as shoe and textile factories.

Guinea

Major Languages: Fulani, Mandingo, French
Total Population: 7,466,000
Population 0–34: 5,866,000
Life Expectancy: 46 years
Religion: Muslim 85.41%, traditional ethnic 9.67%, Christian 4.72%, nonreligious/other 0.20%
Literacy Rate: male 50%, female 22%

Moulud has just celebrated his 20th birthday. In his country he is considered middle-aged, since his life expectancy is only 46 years. He has eked out a meager life through subsistence farming, barely able to provide for his wife and three children. He has heard stories about being a Christian and believing in Jesus Christ, who is claimed to be the Son of God.

He wonders, "How can God have a son?" A thought such as this is beyond his understanding. He has a Christian friend who talks about this God, but he's not sure what this Christianity is all about. His friend says it has to do with living forever with God when a person dies. That is also what the Koran teaches, so what is the difference?

Moulud can only think about Christianity. He knows he cannot say anything to anyone about becoming a Christian because the government forbids a Muslim to convert to another religion. He would be considered an apostate, and it would be an honor to spill his blood on the earth until he died.

Moulud's friend also told him about how God parted the Red Sea for a group of people to cross. The amazing part of the story was that the people did not have a boat or any way to cross over to the other side. These people walked over on the bed of the sea. It seemed impossible that they could walk on the ocean floor.

Moulud wishes he had someone he could speak with openly and ask questions about the Christian stories. There are many things he would like to know.

*P*lagued by civil war and turmoil caused by severe unrest in its neighboring countries, Guinea struggles to stay alive. A further drain on the economy is the huge refugee population. The United Nations High Commissioner for Refugees (UNHCR) estimates that there are 125,000 Liberian and 330,000 Sierra Leonean refugees in Guinea who have fled the brutal civil wars and gross human-rights violations in their countries. Of these refugees at least 57 percent are youths and children. In recent months, in violation of its international commitments, Guinea has intermittently closed its border to Sierra Leone. Fearful of incursions by Sierra Leonean rebels, the Guinean authorities closed the border in the summer of 2000 but later agreed to allow "vulnerable" refugees (pregnant and lactating women, children under the age of 18, and the elderly) to enter the country. In the fall the UNHCR confirmed reports that there were at least 10,000 refugees waiting to cross the border and many of them died because of the substandard living conditions.

Guinea, already a poor country with a per capita income of U.S.$510, can hardly absorb the new refugees, many of whom, particularly young girls, have been the victims of rape and beatings. Children and youths suffer the most because of the poverty and civil instability. Although Guinea is rich in natural resources, the country needs long-range economic planning to move out of poverty.

One Christian reported on a showing of the Jesus film in the Susu village. The people listened intently as they watched in amazement the miracles Jesus did, frequently making comments that showed their interest. As the story moved to the suffering and crucifixion of Jesus, they sat in utter silence. After it was over, the chief not only invited missionaries to return and show the film again but also said that other villages needed to see it and agreed to help arrange those showings. Thank God for speaking to this chief's heart.

Six out of seven Guineans are Muslim. The seventh may be Christian or animist. Guineans are open to the gospel through programs that center on health care, education, and youth involvement. In one village a Christian organization set up a well-baby clinic and has been able to introduce the gospel to the village through this venue.

A nurse who works at a clinic that provides basic care walks miles between families to visit those who need medical attention. She reports, "The people of Guinea are truly seeking God."

Prayer Points

⌣· Pray for a longer life span for the Guineans so that they will have an opportunity to know Jesus Christ.

⌣· Pray for the large population of Liberian and Sierra Leonean refugees to be reached with the gospel while they are in Guinea.

⌣· Pray for this generation to be the ones who will wholeheartedly follow God.

⌣· Pray that God will prosper this economically poor country.

⌣· Pray for the safety of young girls and women, who are in danger of rape.

⌣· Pray for these desperate people to know and accept Jesus as their Lord and Savior.

⌣· Pray for God to respond to the cry of these precious ones.

⌣· Pray for God to use this generation of young people to draw their nation to Him and that they will be properly discipled.

⌣· Pray for God to show us ways to touch Guinea's young people with His love.

Quick Reference

Ethnic Breakdown: Peuhl 40%, Malinke 30%, Soussou 20%, other 10%
Type of Government: Republic
Economy: Services 45%, Industry 31%, Agriculture 24%
Per capita income: U.S.$510
National debt: U.S.$3.15 billion
Economic conditions: Extremely poor

Education
Quality of education: Education has little or no value in this society.
Gender discrimination against girls: Not much importance is placed on education for girls.

Religion
Religious concerns: Evangelism is restricted.
Status of the church: Severe lack of discipleship and leadership training.
Are Christians being persecuted? No

Societal Viewpoint Toward Children
Are they viewed as precious? No
Are there street children? Children may work in the street markets but go home to their families at night.
Is there a large population of orphans? No
Are there child soldiers? No
Is child labor a problem? Children may be used in the labor force.

Guinea-Bissau

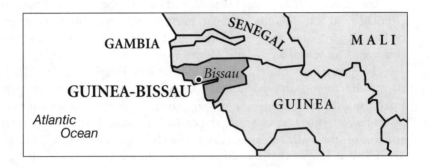

Major Languages: Portuguese, Crioulo, Portuguese Creole
Total Population: 1,286,000
Population 0–34: 986,000
Life Expectancy: 51 years
Religion: Muslim 43.00%, traditional ethnic 41.00%, Christian 14.32%, nonreligious/other 1.68%
Literacy Rate: male 67%, female 41%

Megan walked through the large market in Bissau, the capital of Guinea-Bissau. She made her way through eroded streets in search of the building that housed a clinic and the school where she would be teaching. The smell of burning garbage assaulted her nostrils and made her eyes water. Bits of paper and plastic floated in huge mud holes in the middle of the street. Small children with swollen bellies played among the vendors. Megan wanted to remember everything she saw, because it was all part of the country she already loved.

A mother handed Megan a baby boy who looked about nine months old. The boy had glassy eyes and the lethargic look of someone with malaria. Megan held the child while his mother repeated in a whisper, "Money for medicine, please. Money, please."

Megan motioned for the mother to follow her to the clinic. With only a limited amount of money she had brought with her into the country, she knew she couldn't give it all away, and she reasoned that it was best for the mother to find medical help for her child. With the mother and child in tow, she hurried on her way to find the clinic.

Once she was inside the building, Megan's eyes adjusted to the darkness of the waiting room. The walls were lined with mothers holding sick babies. Megan directed her new friend to a woman sitting at the desk. Once the mother was registered, she took a seat in the long line. As

Megan looked at the mothers in the room, she saw looks of hopelessness on their faces.

The director, Ethel, had come from Holland three years before, just after the civil war in Guinea-Bissau, to start the clinic. Now the facilities included a day-care center, a school, and a feeding program for street children. The school was where Megan would work.

"I began to see children on the streets," Ethel explained, "and I asked them why they didn't go home. I found out that mothers send their small children to the market to beg, steal, or perhaps sell a couple of packages of tissues. At any rate, the child is to come home with a certain amount of money. If for some reason the child cannot meet his mother's demands, he knows that a beating awaits him when she finds out. So he stays in the city and sleeps on the streets. At least that way he knows he will avoid the beating."

Megan walked through the schoolrooms and envisioned the classes she would soon teach. There were no textbooks, notebooks, or pencils. She had known she would be teaching in an under-supplied school system designed on a colonial model, but she was not prepared for the lack of teaching aids in the classrooms.

The director explained the mentality of the country. "You have to understand that the attitude here is accepting whatever fate has to offer. The people pretty much roll with the punches. They have a saying here: 'A log, as long as it stays in the water, will never become a crocodile.' They just accept things and let them go. Neither the children nor the adults try to become 'crocodiles.' They are mostly 'logs' and let life happen. That's why we have to tell them about Jesus Christ and a life that is better than this one."

Megan left the center and walked back to her flat. She had come here to make a difference, and she determined that whatever she did, she would teach "crocodiles" and not "logs."

Guinea-Bissau is a tiny country located just north of Guinea and is considered one of the 20 poorest countries in the world, with 50 percent of the population living below the poverty line. Most of the country's nearly 1.3 million residents depend on subsistence agriculture and the export of cashew nuts to make a living.

Under Portugal's control the people received very little education. Now, 25 years later, because of internal conflict and lack of infrastructure, the educational system is still not in place.

Guinea-Bissau is now open to the gospel and is allowing missions agencies to enter the country not only to do humanitarian work but also to evangelize.

Prayer Points

- Pray that the church will respond to the needs of this destitute country with a biblical worldview and medical, educational, business, and financial resources for the sake of future generations.
- Pray that God will give the church cutting-edge ideas to reach this generation with the gospel.
- Pray that food will be provided to the children who are dying of malnutrition.
- Pray that the church will have compassion on these precious people.
- Pray that believers will respond to their responsibility to preach the gospel in this nation. Since the coup of 1998, the government has lessened its restrictions on establishing churches.
- Pray that young people will be properly educated so that they will know how to build a better country.
- Pray that the existing church in Guinea-Bissau will repent for the sins of their forefathers and pray and fast for their nation.
- Pray that the church will sense the urgency of reaching the young people, since the life expectancy is barely more than 50 years.

Quick Reference

Ethnic Breakdown: Balanta 30%, Fula 20%, Manjaca 14%, Mandinga 13%, Papel 7%, European and Mulatto 1%, other 15%

Type of Government: Multiparty republic

Economy: Agriculture 78%, Industry, Services, and Commerce 14%, Government 8%

Per capita income: U.S.$250

National debt: U.S.$921 million

Economic conditions: Extremely poor

Education

Quality of education: There is a severe shortage of schools and teachers.

Gender discrimination against girls: Girls have limited access to education, especially in rural areas.

Religion

Religious concerns: Not enough Christians are reaching this country that is now open to the gospel.

Status of the church: Small church but growing steadily. The Christians need discipleship, leadership, and evangelism training.

Are Christians being persecuted? No

Societal Viewpoint Toward Children

Are they viewed as precious? Yes

Are there street children? Because of the economy, children work as street vendors selling small items.

Is there a large population of orphans? No

Are there child soldiers? No

Is child labor a problem? Children are routinely used in the labor force.

India

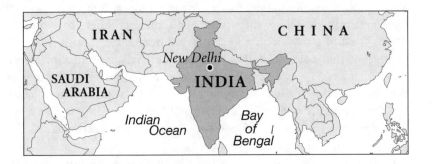

Major Languages: Hindi, Bengali, Marathi
Total Population: 1,014,004,000
Population 0–34: 697,354,000
Life Expectancy: 63 years
Religion: Hindu/other 79.83%, Muslim 12.50%, Christian 2.40%, Sikh 1.92%, traditional ethnic 1.40%, Buddhist 0.80%, Jain 0.35%, nonreligious 0.55%, Baha'i 0.23%, Parsee 0.02%
Literacy Rate: male 66%, female 38%

*D*elite concentrated intensely as she squatted on the floor of her family's tiny one-room home, surrounded by stitched soccer half balls. To keep her eyes free for her intricate work, she had pulled her short, dark brown hair back into a tight pigtail. Over and over, she meticulously pushed two needles through prepunched holes along the edge of a black vinyl pentagon, crossed the two threads, and pierced the next hole, never stopping.

Delite's movements were quick, and she knew precisely how to vary the order of the black and white pieces. She'd had plenty of time to learn, since she had been doing this for the past six months. Her only breaks were eating, sleeping, and attending school for a few hours each afternoon. She was only eight years old.

Her family earned about 500 rupees, or U.S.$20, each month stitching the soccer balls part-time. This covered their monthly rent and half of their electricity bill.

They lived in urban Bhargo Camp, in Punjab's Jalandhar district, where thousands of parents and children work from morning until night producing all kinds of sports equipment—volleyballs, soccer balls, nets, and cricket gear.

C hildren in India work because families need more income than parents alone can make to provide for the household's basic necessities. Parents often cannot afford to feed their children, and sometimes they have incurred debts, so they must send their children to work. Over 300,000 children work in the carpet industry alone. Many work under conditions that amount to bonded labor. Officials are reluctant to prosecute offenders, because families need the money and the problem is so rampant. In all of India there are an estimated 11.3 million child laborers.

Child prostitution is also a major problem. According to one international labor organization, 15 percent of the country's estimated 2.3 million prostitutes are children.

Human Rights Watch cites the practice of dedicating or marrying prepubescent girls to a Hindu deity to serve as a "servant of god," a continual problem in several northern states. These young girls do not marry but are taken from their families to live in the temple and serve as prostitutes for the Hindu priests.

Inadequate health care in India is a serious problem. Many villages are without any kind of dispensary. A person needing medical assistance must pay cash for services and purchase all medicines that are to be administered. Disease among children is serious and is most often the result of lack of potable water. Diarrheal diseases are the primary cause of death in early childhood.

Statistics indicate that the same pattern of AIDS that hit Africa in the 1980s is poised to enter India on a full-blown scale in the near future. At the end of 1997, 48,000 children were infected with HIV, and an estimated 110,000 children had lost their mothers or both parents to AIDS.

Throughout the country, mothers prefer to have a boy instead of a girl, which has resulted in a growing difference in the ratio of males to females. Often a pregnant woman will have an abortion if she finds out that the child she is carrying is a female. (Female children will require the parents to provide a dowry at the time of marriage, which makes a girl less desirable.) Human-rights groups estimate that at least 10,000 cases of female infanticide occur yearly. The government has passed laws prohibiting the use of amniocentesis and sonogram tests for the purpose of sex determination, but there has been little follow-up by the authorities in prosecuting those doctors who continue to perform these tests. The practice is still popular with women.

India, with a population of over one billion, needs our prayers. The children of the country are its hope and future. Pray that the government will recognize the treasure they have in the minds of their children.

Prayer Points

- Pray for God to send anointed believers with cutting-edge ideas who will work among children, teens, and young adults.
- Pray for Christians to establish homes that will nurture, educate, and care for abandoned children and teenagers who are sexually and emotionally abused, then banished from the family because of the shame.
- Pray for children who are robbed of their childhood because they must work to help the family survive. Pray for God to prosper families so that their children can attend school and positively impact their nation.
- Pray for the children who live on the streets under horrific, inhumane conditions. Pray that churches and ministries will reach out to them and present the gospel to them.
- Pray that the Christian community will lead the way in ministering to AIDS victims.
- Pray for parents to receive the understanding that children—both boys and girls—are gifts from God.
- Pray that poor families will keep their children and not abort, abandon, or murder them. Pray that these poor families will receive training and well-paying jobs.
- Pray for "girl widows." If an older husband dies and his widow is still a teenager, she cannot remarry. Often such girls provide cheap labor for their in-laws for the rest of their lives.
- Pray that the middle- and upper-class young people who are attracted to the music and lifestyles portrayed on TV shows and movies from the West will not be ensnared by the ungodly part of Western culture.

Quick Reference

Ethnic Breakdown: Indo-Aryan 72%, Dravidian 25%, Mongolian and other 3%
Type of Government: Federal republic
Economy: Services 45%, Industry 30%, Agriculture 25%
Per capita income: U.S.$340
National debt: U.S.$98 billion
Economic conditions: Extremely poor

Education
Quality of education: Government does not provide compulsory free education. Only 59 percent of children 5 to 14 attend school. There is a severe shortage of schools and teachers.

Gender discrimination against girls: Not much importance is placed on education for girls.

Religion

Religious concerns: Evangelism is restricted.

Status of the church: The church is steadily growing but needs discipleship, leadership, and evangelism training in a hostile environment.

Are Christians being persecuted? Yes

Societal Viewpoint Toward Children

Are they viewed as precious? No

Are there street children? Yes. Because of the economy, children work as street vendors, selling small items. Many children live on the streets.

Is there a large orphan population? Yes

Are there child soldiers? No specific data available.

Is child labor a problem? Children routinely work in the labor force because their parents cannot afford to feed them. They may work as bonded laborers.

Indonesia

Major Languages: Indonesian, Malay, Chinese
Total Population: 224,784,000
Population 0–34: 181,148,000
Life Expectancy: 68 years
Religion: Muslim 80.30%, Christian 16.00%, Hindu 1.90%,
   traditional ethnic 1.00%, Chinese 0.50%, Buddhist 0.30%
Literacy Rate: male 90%, female 78%

*T*welve-year-old Anna and her six-year-old brother are homeless children who fend for themselves on the streets of the capital city of Jakarta. In 1998 Anna's mother lost her job as a hotel maid. At first she tried to work odd jobs to get food for her six children, but the money was never enough. Anna remembers going to bed hungry because there was only a handful of rice to feed the whole family. Then came the day when there was nothing to eat. Her mother gathered the children and told them they were being evicted from their small flat and she had no way to take care of them. The three oldest children were each assigned a younger child to provide for in the best way possible.

At first Anna thought she could earn a living for herself and her brother by walking up to people on the streets and making funny faces. She would dance, and if people stopped long enough, she would tell a joke. If she made someone laugh, she could then ask for money. It wasn't long before her antics caught the attention of a local pimp, who offered them protection from the other children living on the streets, food, and a place to sleep. Anna consented. Now she and her brother are among the 20,000 street children of Jakarta who are at risk for sexually transmitted diseases and every work of iniquity.

One horrific consequence of the recent Indonesian economic landslide is an increase in the number of children who cannot be cared for by their families. Many families are forced to make difficult decisions regarding their children. This downward spiral of Indonesia's economy combined with an unstable political situation has thrust multitudes of children into the streets to live and work. The present generation of children could very well become a lost generation because of the devastation they have experienced. This period in Indonesia's history is unlike any other time—unstable economy, civil unrest, and hatred in the name of religion. The plight of the children threatens to create a culture that, if not immediately attended to, will have repercussions throughout the world in years to come.

Since 1998 over 5,000 Muslims and Christians have been killed in widespread civil unrest, with well over 5,000 more Christians forced to convert to Islam. The situation intensifies as *jihad* soldiers, reportedly trained by the Taliban, continue to attack Christians. Presently over 63,000 Christians are trapped in the Tentena area, waiting for the arrival of jihad soldiers who have vowed to slaughter them. Although Christians make up less than 10 percent of Indonesia's 224 million people, they are the group most targeted for extinction by radical militant Muslims.

It is extremely difficult for any child living on the streets to avoid falling into the world of prostitution. Researchers at Atma Jaya University in Jakarta found that all children working on the streets are abused or sodomized within their first three months, if not by adults, then by other street children. The smaller children and girls, under the impression that in exchange for sexual favors they will be protected, allow themselves to be traded between the older boys.

Because of the recent economic downturn, 46 percent of school-age children have dropped out of school in the past three years. These children often make their way to the streets to earn a living for themselves or to supplement their family's income. The street children are more prone to become involved in drugs and prostitution. It is not uncommon for a family to sell a daughter into prostitution to help relieve the economic pressure of another mouth to feed.

The health-care system has been hit hard by Indonesia's economic downturn. According to recent U.N. data, as many as 37 percent of toddlers may be suffering from some form of malnutrition, up from 9.8 percent in 1995. Specifically, researchers have begun to document an increase in children suffering from deficiencies of vitamin A, iron, and protein. One nongovernmental organization estimated that the deaths of up to 180,000 children were related to malnutrition.

Whether the Indonesian government realizes it or not, it will take a supernatural act of God to rescue this nation for the sake of generations to come.

Prayer Points

~· Pray for the 8 million preschool children who are undernourished. Inadequate diets threaten to cause mental retardation.

~· Pray for the 6.4 million children aged 7 to 15 who are not able to attend school.

~· Pray for the 20 million children who are not being educated.

~· Pray for the children who work long hours in horrible conditions for industrial factories and do not receive the same wages as adults who work the same hours.

~· Pray that the children who survive by collecting and reselling garbage will be trained in jobs that will support them.

~· Pray for the children who are dying of curable complications from respiratory tract infections, diarrhea, and other illnesses. An estimated 7 percent of Indonesia's children die before age one. One child dies every two minutes.

~· Pray that children will be able to live in an atmosphere where they can learn and play.

~· Pray for the children whose parents have been murdered. Pray that they will know God, who is the Father of the fatherless, and that they will be able to forgive the perpetrators.

~· Pray for the children who live in the areas of civil unrest like East Timor, that they will be safe and there will be peace in the land.

~· Pray for innovative Christian programming to reach the youth.

~· Pray for humane laws to be passed to protect the children.

~· Pray for the tens of thousands of street children.

~· Pray for children, teens, and young adults to be seen as precious in Indonesia.

Quick Reference

Ethnic Breakdown: Javanese 45.0%, Sundanese 14.0%, Madurese 7.5%, Coastal Malays 7.5%, other 26.0%

Type of Government: Independent republic

Economy: Services 44%, Industry 35%, Agriculture 21%

Per capita income: U.S.$980

National debt: U.S.$140 billion

Economic conditions: Extremely poor, recovering from economic depression

Education

Quality of education: There is a shortage of schools, teachers, and supplies.

Gender discrimination against girls: Not much importance is placed on education for girls.

Religion

Religious concerns: Evangelism is restricted.

Status of the church: Many incidents of anti-Christian violence. The church needs discipleship, leadership, and evangelism training in a hostile environment. Churches need to work together to reach all of Indonesia with the gospel.

Are Christians being persecuted? Yes. Hundreds have been martyred. Even so, the church has grown tremendously.

Societal Viewpoint Toward Children

Are they viewed as precious? No

Are there street children? Yes. Children are forced to the streets to eke out a living. Because of the downturn in the economy, their families do not have enough money to care for them.

Is there a large population of orphans? Yes

Are there child soldiers? Yes, serving as jihad soldiers.

Is child labor a problem? Largely because of the economic crisis, thousands of children are working as prostitutes and bonded laborers.

Iran

Major Languages: Persian, Turkic, Kurdish
Total Population: 65,620,000
Population 0–34: 48,018,000
Life Expectancy: 70 years
Religion: Muslim 99.02%, Baha'i 0.52%, Christian 0.33%, other 0.10%, Jewish 0.03%
Literacy Rate: male 82%, female 69%

*B*ecause of a continuing economic crisis, children beg on the streets of Iran in increasing numbers. One visitor described her experience. "Every day as I return home from the market, I feel a gentle tug on my *monto* [dress] as a child bids for my attention. He asks for money to buy food for his family or, on more prosperous days, offers to resell to me at an inflated price candy he has purchased. I buy the candy, knowing I am helping a family survive. Then when I go to sleep at night I can say that I have fed a child, and a perhaps a family, for that day because I bought a candy bar I didn't want."

Another child, Zahra, is required by her parents to make her living by begging on the streets in the capital city of Tehran. She is too young to work, and begging is her only hope of getting the money required by her parents. If she is caught stealing, she could have her arm amputated in an electric guillotine. As a result she would never be able to work, and her only means of earning a living would be to beg for the rest of her life.

The visible evidence of the economic condition of Iran is the children on the streets looking for money for their family's next meal. Iran needs our prayers.

*P*rior to 1976 Iran was ruled by the *shah,* who held a pro-Western stance. Political discontent led to a revolution. On January 16, 1976, Ayatollah Ruhollah Khomeini came to power and on April 1 established the new Islamic Republic of Iran. During the transition time Iraqi leader Saddam Hussein took advantage of the civil unrest to attempt to reclaim the Shatt al Arab, a waterway that forms the boundary between the two countries, as well as seize an oil-rich region in western Iran. The United Nations brokered a cease-fire in July 1988 but not before Iran's economy was in ruins. Almost every Iranian family experienced the loss of a loved one, and in some families two generations of men were killed. Iran has not recovered from the militant governmental takeover by the ayatollah and the war with Iraq.

Because of the implementation of strict Islamic law, many doctors, dentists, and other professionals left the country in search of a better life. The results for those left behind were disastrous. Today there are shortages of vaccines, and many once rare childhood diseases threaten a large section of the population. Once sufficient in food production, Iran now has major shortages, as farmers lack good seed, farming implements, and spare parts. Water is scarce because the irrigation systems are in serious disrepair. Western embargos on exports to Iran have caused major shortages for factories and severely hampered the country's heavy industry.

The people of Iran find pleasure in simple things, like visiting with family and friends. The youth search for fun at parties where drugs may be readily available. Heroin in its unprocessed form may be found at gatherings. Although the penalty for selling drugs is severe, such as being hung by the neck from a crane in the middle of the busy city, dealers still take the risk by bringing in opium from other countries, such as Afghanistan and Pakistan.

In addition to their lack of value in the workplace and the small importance placed on their education, girls in Iran suffered when Khomeini lowered the marriage age for females from 18 to 13. Girls as young as nine, even seven in some cases, could be married if a physician signed a certificate attesting to their sexual maturity.

There are Christians in Iran, but persecution is severe. Often those who are converted seek refuge in other countries. In October 1996 International Christian Concern reported yet another murder of an Iranian Christian pastor. His body was found hanging from a tree in a secluded forest. The Rev. Mohammed Ravanbaksh was killed shortly after he had reportedly been detained and questioned by the Iranian police. He was the fourth Christian leader to have been murdered in less than three years.

Visas into Iran are next to impossible to obtain for one to see firsthand the condition of the country. Only God can change a country and bring down walls that appear impossible to penetrate. God sets up governments, and God causes them to fall. Doors need to open for the sake of the millions there who have no hope or joy and have not had the good news preached to them.

Prayer Points

⌐· Pray for the Lord to open doors for Christian workers to enter the country through relief efforts, businesses, and other creative ways.

⌐· Pray for supernatural protection for the national Christians as they find opportunities to share their faith.

⌐· Pray for Iranians living abroad to know Jesus Christ as Lord and Savior and return to their homeland to evangelize.

⌐· Pray for reversal of laws that allow girls to marry as young as seven years of age.

⌐· Pray for abolishment of the *siqeh* marriage, which allows a man to marry a woman for as little as 30 minutes.

⌐· Pray for the children, who can be executed for crimes when they are as young as 9 years for girls and 16 years for boys.

⌐· Pray for children, teens, and young adults to be treated as special gifts from the Lord.

⌐· Pray for the minds of this generation not to become warped as a result of living under such horrific tyranny.

⌐· Pray for the youth of Iran to know God and be used by Him to take the gospel of Christ to their nation.

⌐· Pray for the families of the 20,000 girls and women who were executed in the early years of Khomeini's rule who are still suffering grief and shame over these executions.

Quick Reference

Ethnic Breakdown: Persian 51%, Azeri 24%, Gilaki and Mazandarani 8%, Kurd 7%, Arab 3%, Lur 2%, Baloch 2%, Turkmen 2%, other 1%

Type of Government: Theocratic republic

Economy: Services 45%, Industry 34%, Agriculture 21%

Per capita income: U.S.$4,700

National debt: U.S.$21.9 billion

Economic conditions: Poor

Education

Quality of education: Primary school for ages 6–12 is compulsory. Little is known about the quality of education, but instruction includes mandatory Koranic curriculum.

Gender discrimination against girls: Not much importance is placed on education for girls.

Religion

Religious concerns: Spirituality is heavily influenced by Shiite Muslims. Evangelism is prohibited. National Christians must worship underground.

Status of the church: No national church exists.

Are Christians being persecuted? Yes

Societal Viewpoint Toward Children

Are they viewed as precious? Yes

Are there street children? There is a growing problem with street children.

Is there a large population of orphans? No specific data available.

Are there child soldiers? No specific data available.

Is child labor a problem? Children are used in the labor force.

Iraq

Major Languages: Arabic, Kurdish, Persian
Total Population: 22,676,000
Population 0–34: 18,069,000
Life Expectancy: 67 years
Religion: Muslim 96.85%, Christian 1.55%, other 1.10%, nonreligious 0.50%
Literacy Rate: male 71%, female 45%

*I*n April 1997 George Capaccio and two colleagues broke U.N. trade sanctions on Iraq to stage a mercy mission and take medical supplies and children's toys into the country. The group of three from Chicago were moved by the fact that up to 750,000 children are estimated to have died as a result of the strict U.N. sanctions imposed by the U.N. Security Council in 1990 after Iraq invaded Kuwait. One of the group remarked, "When one scratches beneath the surface, Iraq is literally dying under the weight of the embargo. Malnutrition is endemic, reaching 50 percent to 60 percent of the population outside of Baghdad. More than half the country drinks water infected with typhoid, cholera, and E-coli bacteria."

Jan Goodwin, a news reporter, wrote in her book *Price of Honour* about her visit to Iraq and her observations of the devastating economic conditions. "The scene that saddened me most was a young woman sitting on the ground in a black *abaya* and *hijab* trying to sell a chicken that she had raised for D. 30 [less than one American dollar], even though she and her six children had not eaten meat for two years. Fatima, age 30, lost her husband in 1986 in the Iran-Iraq War. Her war pension was barely enough to feed her family with bread. She had brought two chickens to the market that day, but in the rush of the crowd, a passerby had accidentally stepped on the head of one and killed it. Since it had not been Islamically slaughtered, Muslims considered it *haram* (forbidden) and refused to buy it. I purchased the dead chicken and told her to feed it to her children, but I wasn't sure, as hungry as she and her family were, that they would violate the Muslim code."

*F*our days after Iraq invaded Kuwait in 1990, the U.N. imposed trade sanctions, which are the underlying cause of the devastating economic situation in Iraq. The result has been rampant inflation. Children five years old and under are dying at more than twice the rate they were a decade ago because of lack of adequate food and medical attention. Mothers left widows as a result of the war between Iran and Iraq now struggle to support children on a government pension that will not even buy a candy bar at today's prices. Even though the United Nations has allowed Iraq to trade oil for food and medicine, the program has not been as successful as was originally intended. The Iraqi government reportedly stockpiles medicines and food sent to them, refusing to distribute it.

Children are expected to spy on their parents in much the same way as Russian children did under Stalin and report their activities. The parents are then tortured. Human-rights organizations have cited many violations. There are reports of Iraqis using an electric drill on prisoners' eyes, ears, and knees or using an ax to cut off women's breasts. Besides committing horrific tortures, Iraqis have killed an estimated 200,000 Kurds, and tens of thousands of other Iraqis have been executed under the Hussein regime. The vast majority of them are tortured before being killed.

Northern Iraq is home to nearly one million Christians. The Iraqi believers provide the pool from which President Hussein procures his domestic help. Hussein is said to trust them more than the competing Islamic factions in Iraq.

The children of Iraq have known nothing but war and hardship for over a decade. Not only have they lost fathers and grandfathers, but they are expected to train to defend their country against any enemy. For six years the government has held three-week training courses in weapons use, hand-to-hand fighting, rappelling from helicopters, and infantry tactics for children from 10 to 15 years of age. Families who do not send their children to train as "Saddam Cubs" are threatened with confiscation of their food-ration cards and withholding of school examination results.

The people endure Saddam Hussein's harshness partly because it is the national mentality that their destiny is tied to the person who rules the country, a concept that is also prevalent in other Islamic countries. While the ruler sets up his kingdom, the children suffer. Iraq needs our prayers and our God-given authority to rescue this generation from fear and tyranny.

Prayer Points

⌐· Pray that the government will not restrict relief efforts coming into the country.

⌐· Pray for Iraqi Christians to find ways to share Christ's love with friends and neighbors.

⌐· Pray for the removal of U.N. sanctions and the underlying causes that are compromising the lives of children through the Iraqi government's withholding of food, medical supplies, vitamins, and baby formulas.

⌐· Pray for God to appear to Iraq's leaders through dreams and visions.

⌐· Pray for the young people growing up in this generation that the tyranny they have lived with won't turn them into tormentors.

⌐· Pray that the young people who have fled with their families to neighboring countries for refuge will find Christ.

⌐· Ask God to reveal Himself to children, teens, and young adults through dreams and visions.

⌐· Pray for the children ages 10 to 15 who are forced to train under tough physical and psychological strain for up to 14 hours a day as "Saddam Cubs."

⌐· Pray that President Saddam Hussein will be concerned for the welfare of his people, especially for the generation that will one day be making decisions for Iraq.

Quick Reference

Ethnic Breakdown: Arab 80%, Kurdish 15%, Turkoman, Assyrian, and other 5%

Type of Government: One-party socialist military state

Economy: Services 81%, Industry 13%, Agriculture 6%

Per capita income: U.S.$2,000

National debt: U.S.$130 billion

Economic conditions: Poor. Children are suffering from the embargo.

Education

Quality of education: Education is mandatory through elementary school. Instruction includes mandatory Koranic curriculum.

Gender discrimination against girls: Not much importance is placed on education for girls.

Religion

Religious concerns: Evangelism is prohibited. Conversion to Christianity is punishable by death.

Status of the church: National Christians must worship underground.

Are Christians being persecuted? Yes

Societal Viewpoint Toward Children

Are they viewed as precious? No, although the birth of a boy is celebrated more than the birth of a girl.

Are there street children? No specific data available.

Is there a large population of orphans? Yes

Are there child soldiers? Yes. Children are forced into military service.

Is child labor a problem? The employment of children below 14 years of age is prohibited except in small-scale family enterprises.

Israel

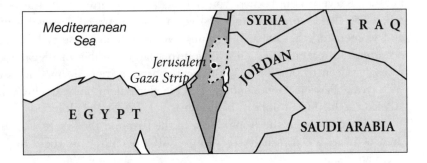

Major Languages: Hebrew, Arabic, English
Total Population: 6,974,000
Population 0–34: 3,489,000
Life Expectancy: 79 years
Religion: Jewish 80.65%, Muslim 14.60%, other 2.50%, Christian 2.25%
Literacy Rate: male 97%, female 93%

Many of the young people of Israel are crying out for meaning in their lives. Everywhere they are surrounded by war and violence as hatred between the Jewish and Muslim communities runs high. With precious few places to turn for a reprieve from the tensions, the television program Y2 Heart has been an oasis for the youth of Israel. Y2 Heart Rock ministry airs a daily music program formatted to youthful taste. Featuring popular contemporary Christian music groups, the TV show attracts those who are searching for meaning and an answer to the violence that surrounds them.

Richard Frieden, director of the program, writes, "Please pray for the young people in Israel who are watching our *Y2* show. The days are so challenging here with the increasing strife, and the souls of youth are under such enormous attack.... We are so overwhelmed by the sense of God's mercies...to reach His children. I am very encouraged today! May it encourage your hearts to know that your prayers are heard!"

There are few outreaches to the young people who are searching for truth. One mother spoke of her daughter's search for meaning in life—a search that took the daughter to India and ended with her embracing Hinduism. Saddened at the girl's rejection of the family's Jewish beliefs, the mother admitted she knew many Jewish young people who had taken the same path.

One major concern is the rise in the abortion rates among young girls in Israel. Some blame the Israeli draft policy for the increase. At the age of 18 every able-bodied youth in Israel is drafted into the army, where men and women train and live in close quarters. Throwing men and women together at such a young, vulnerable age results in a high occurrence of pregnancies. In addition to a large number of illegal abortions, between 15,000 and 17,000 legal abortions are performed in Israel each year. Patrick Goodenough, a CNS Jerusalem bureau chief, has labeled the killing of unborn babies in Israel the "Silent Holocaust."

Without hope in the Jesus Christ of the past and the future, the children of Israel are presently searching. Will the church be there to give them answers?

Since its inception in 1948, Israel has been in a constant state of war with most of its Arab neighbors. In the 1967 War, Israel added to its territory the Golan Heights, the West Bank, the Gaza Strip, and East Jerusalem. The international community does not recognize Israel's sovereignty over any part of these occupied territories.

Children are viewed as precious in Israeli society and are given an education up through grade 10 or until they reach the age of 15, whichever comes first. The Arab segment of the country fares worse when it comes to education. It most often experiences the brunt of teacher shortages, school-building disrepair, and a scarcity of textbooks. This may account for the fact that only 54 percent of the Arab children finish high school, as compared to 89 percent of the Jewish children. The Arab children may be the most at-risk children in Israeli society.

Child abuse, unreported in the past, has now become the topic of government awareness programs. There are five shelters for children at risk in the country. While this problem may not be on the rise, it is coming to the surface as a situation that needs to be addressed.

In the past, drug abuse among the youth was not a problem. Now, however, the use of drugs is becoming more accepted, and users are beginning at an increasingly younger age. This upward trend in drug abuse may also account for the growing number of youths who are running away from home and living on the streets. While the numbers are not significantly high, they are worth noting, as they may be the start of a trend.

Israel needs children's programs that promote good moral values. Some ministries like Y2 Heart Rock are working to fill the demand for such youth programs.

Pray for the youth of Israel.

Prayer Points

⌣· Pray for the peace of Jerusalem (Psalm 122:6) and that Jewish children will one day know Yeshua.

⌣· Pray for an end to the ongoing violence and hatred so that this generation of young people will learn to love and live at peace with all nationalities living in Israel.

⌣· Pray for God to raise up peacemakers in this generation to help reconcile the children of Isaac and Ishmael.

⌣· Pray that child abuse and prostitution will be exposed and eradicated.

⌣· Pray for this generation to come to know Jesus Christ as their personal Savior and lead others to Christ.

⌣· Pray for wise leaders who will seek God for guidance, realizing that the decisions they make today will impact generations to come.

⌣· Pray for television programming that will convey the gospel with an anointing that will draw young people to the Lord.

⌣· Pray for Christian workers to freely share the love of Christ with Jews, Arabs, and Gentiles living in the land.

⌣· Pray that Jewish and Arab leaders will find a resolution to their problems for the sake of future generations.

⌣· Pray for an end to the extremely high number of abortions being performed in the country.

Quick Reference

Ethnic Breakdown: Jewish 80.1% (Europe/America-born 32.1%, Israel-born 20.8%, Africa-born 14.6%, Asia-born 12.6%), non-Jewish 19.9 % (majority Arab)

Type of Government: Parliamentary democracy

Economy: Services 81%, Industry 17%, Agriculture 2%

Per capita income: U.S.$15,920

National debt: U.S.$18.7 billion

Economic conditions: Endangered by the effects of the Palestinian/Israeli conflict and a drastic drop in foreign visitors.

Education

Quality of education: School system is well organized.

Gender discrimination against girls: Girls are being educated.

Religion

Religious concerns: Evangelism is restricted.

Status of the church: The church is growing but needs cutting-edge programs to reach out to the Jews, Arabs, and others.

Are Christians being persecuted? No

Societal Viewpoint Toward Children

Are they viewed as precious? Yes

Are there street children? Street children are a slight problem.

Is there a large population of orphans? No specific data available.

Are there child soldiers? No

Is child labor a problem? There are no reports of child labor.

Japan

Major Languages: Japanese, English, Korean
Total Population: 126,550,000
Population 0–34: 53,543,000
Life Expectancy: 81 years
Religion: Shinto and Buddhist 69.61%, new religions 24.43%,
    nonreligious/other 4.27%, Christian 1.56%, Muslim 0.12%, Baha'i 0.01%
Literacy Rate: male 99%, female 99%

"Chizura, eat your dinner!" her mother yelled.

The small child pushed the remaining rice around in the bottom of her bowl and made circular designs with the ends of her chopsticks.

Frustrated because their toddler took so long to finish her meal, Chizura's mother and stepfather began to take turns beating the child. At first they gave "spankings," but after each spanking, Chizura still refused to eat, so her parents grew angrier and began applying heavier blows.

This was not the first time Chizura had tested her parents' patience by wasting time at meals. Finally Chizura's mother grabbed a mop handle and beat the child's back. Chizura's stepfather lit a cigarette and held the hot end against her tender flesh. It was not long before her small body grew limp and was unable to respond to their blows. That night Chizura died from the injuries to her body.

Chizura is only one of the 6,932 cases of child abuse reported between 1990 and 1999 in Japan. Dr. Jun Saimara, head of social work research at the Japan Child and Family Research Institute, fears there are many more such cases, because only the more serious instances are reported to the police. Japanese parents are, for the most part, caring and helpful toward their children. But Dr. Saimara cites smaller households, increasing isolation from neighbors and society, and lack of family structure as the reasons for the upsurge in child abuse.

According to a report from Keith Carey, U.S. Center for World Missions, abortions in Japan are also on the rise, with an estimated 10,000 babies aborted daily. Often an abortion is seen as an act of honor when a mother knows that her child, by being aborted, will be spared from a life of poverty or disgrace.

In academic competition Japanese children perform very well, partly because their parents have high expectations and often exert a great deal of pressure on them. Cases of suicide have been reported as a result of such pressure. Students must pass strenuous exams to enter college, and the family can be disgraced if they fail. Another result of academic pressure is known as *hikikomri,* where a person retreats to a life of seclusion, often not coming out of his or her room or house for years on end. While most children strive to please their parents, some realize the futility of their efforts, knowing they will never be able to measure up to parental expectations.

The older generation is concerned for the young people, whom they see turning away from the values and work ethic of their ancestors. The current cultural trend is to embrace a more pleasure-oriented lifestyle than did prior generations.

A practice that has recently risen to the surface is that of *ijime,* or intimidation. At junior high and elementary levels a child may receive much verbal abuse. Some Japanese authorities believe the increase in bullying may be a result of violent Nintendo games, videos, and TV programs.

Many of the ills of Japanese society are common to developed nations. Materialism has become a way of life, crowding out an awareness of the need for a personal Savior. Nonetheless, the youth of Japan have shown great interest in soul gospel music and Christian rock music, often taking overseas tours to visit churches that are famous for their lively Christian worship. One rock musician has founded over 15 gospel singing groups across the country.

Yoido Full Gospel Assembly has planted a national church in Japan. The church has over 3,000 members and is still growing.

Japanese girls often request a Christian wedding because of the beautiful, elaborate ceremonies. While young couples may not understand the full significance of what a Christian minister says, such weddings are a wonderful way to reach out to them.

Prayer Points

╰· Pray for Christian singing groups to be used powerfully by God to impact the young people for Christ.

⌣· Pray for the Japanese youth to come to know that only God—not materialism, drugs, or sex—can fill the vacuum in their hearts.

⌣· Pray that parents will feel God's love for their children. Social pressures have caused an alarming increase in abuse, neglect, and suicide among children.

⌣· Pray that the Japanese would realize that abortion is murder and not honorable in God's eyes.

⌣· Pray that the national church will be proactive in reaching children, teens, and young adults who are contemplating suicide. Pray that young people will find the comfort of the Prince of Peace and that suicides will cease.

⌣· Pray that God will send more laborers into Japan to spread the gospel and that the existing churches will grow and become grounded in their knowledge of God's greatness and holiness.

⌣· Pray for the government to take a harsh stand against child prostitution and trafficking of young women, that there will be a deterrent to these practices. Pray that the women and children involved will come to know the Lord and that He will heal them.

⌣· Pray that the Japanese will become educated on AIDS statistics and realize that AIDS is a very valid concern, especially among those who are promiscuous.

⌣· Pray that the government will shut down the large number of pornographic websites that contain lewd images of children. In 1998 INTERPOL (International Criminal Police Organization) estimated that 80 percent of websites with pornographic images of children originate in Japan.

Quick Reference

Ethnic Breakdown: Japanese 99.4%, other 0.6%
Type of Government: Constitutional monarchy
Economy: Services 63%, Industry 35%, Agriculture 2%
Per capita income: U.S.$39,640
National debt: None
Economic conditions: Suffering the effects of economic recession

Education
Quality of education: Pressure is placed on children to do well in school, and this may result in undue stress. School system is well organized.
Gender discrimination against girls: Girls are being educated.

Religion
Religious concerns: Demonic forces associated with idolatry in temples and ancestral worship in homes have never been decisively challenged.

Status of the church: The church needs discipleship training. Some churches are
   attempting to work in unity to reach Japan and to send missionaries to other
   10/40 nations. The church is wealthy.

Are Christians being persecuted? Yes

Societal Viewpoint Toward Children

Are they viewed as precious? Yes, but child abuse is on the rise and child
   pornography is a serious problem.

Are there street children? No

Is there a large population of orphans? No

Are there child soldiers? No

Is child labor a problem? There is a growing concern about teenage prostitution.

Jordan

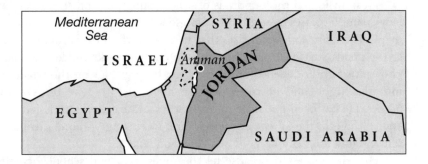

Major Languages: Arabic, English
Total Population: 4,999,000
Population 0–34: 3,853,000
Life Expectancy: 72 years
Religion: Muslim 96.19%, Christian 2.75%, nonreligious/other 1.00%,
    Baha'i 0.03%, other 0.03%
Literacy Rate: male 91%, female 80%

*E*very day eight-year-old Hussein leaves his house to go to school. In his backpack, along with books and his lunch, his mother places 20 packages of gum and 21 candy bars.

She always gives him the same instructions. "I'm sending you one candy bar that you may eat yourself. You must sell the rest. Be a good boy and don't walk out in the street in front of a car. When you try to sell to someone in a car, knock gently on the window so as not to make anyone in the car mad at you." She pats her son on the back and stands at the front door to watch him walk to school.

Hussein looks back to see if his mother is still standing in the doorway of their home. For almost a year he has been taking extra items in his backpack to sell on the streets. He remembers years before, when he would help his father in the souvenir shop they owned in Amman. They had a thriving business selling to tourists from all over the world who were visiting the ancient city of Petra located in Jordan. Two years ago the fighting started in the West Bank, and the tourists stopped coming.

At first a few people continued to visit, but then almost no one came. Soon Hussein's father had to close the doors of his shop and sell his merchandise on the streets for next to nothing. He found work in a local factory, which then closed, too. He began to drink because there was no money. Hussein's sisters and mother suffered the most. Many nights

Hussein watched as his father drank and his mother cried because there was no food to eat and no money to pay the rent.

Hussein joined the hundreds of other young boys on the streets who hawk simple wares like candy bars, small packets of tissue, and city maps. There are so few tourists that he frequently returns home with all of the goods still in his backpack. Each day he works harder because he knows his family depends on him. Often he stays out on the streets late into the night, and at times strange men offer to take him to their homes. He has been obedient to his mother and has never gone with anyone, although the offers of money are increasingly more difficult to refuse. How long can he hold out? He wonders....

Hussein is blessed because he continues to attend school for half of each day. He wants to attend high school next year, but he knows this will be difficult. Many of his friends have had to quit school altogether to work longer hours.

J ordan is looking for ways to stimulate the economy. The recent downturn in the tourism industry has left the country economically strapped. In an effort to help, Saudi Arabia recently agreed to grant Jordanians work visas. Visas had previously been denied because of Jordan's alliance with Iraq in the Gulf War.

The country is in desperate need of aid to help sustain the fragile economy until it can restore tourism or shift its income base to another industry. The government asked the Ministry of Social Development to address the increasing problem of child vendors, and in some cases children have been physically removed from the streets. The effects have been short-lived as, out of necessity, the children return to peddle their wares.

The new king, Abdullah bin Hussein, is trying to create an atmosphere of peace between Jews, Muslims, and Christians. As a new ruler, he has the opportunity to change his country economically and spiritually. He needs much prayer, for the task ahead of him is great.

Prayer Points

～· Pray for families of pastors and ministry leaders to be able to successfully handle the stresses and demands of the ministry.
～· Pray that the young people seeking answers in life will find that Jesus Christ is the answer.
～· Pray that the young people who are coming to Christ will be properly discipled.

- Pray for more ministries to reach out to children, teens, and young adults in an effective way. Pray that God will give Christian leaders creative ideas that will impact the youth.
- Pray that the Iraqis, Sudanese, and Filipinos who work in Jordan will be reached with the gospel.
- Pray that God will deliver the hundreds of thousands of Iraqi refugees in Jordan from their harsh conditions and that they will receive a good education.
- Pray for the economy to be greatly improved for the sake of future generations.
- Pray for the church to have cutting-edge strategies to reach this generation with the gospel.

Quick Reference

Ethnic Breakdown: Jordanian 32.4%, Palestinian Arab 32.1%, Iraqi Arab 14.0%, Bedouin Arab 12.8%, Syrian Arab 5%, other 3.7%

Type of Government: Constitutional monarchy

Economy: Services 72%, Industry 25%, Agriculture 3%

Per capita income: U.S.$1,510

National debt: U.S.$8.4 billion

Economic conditions: Poor

Education

Quality of education: The government is committed to education, but its efforts are constrained by limited financial resources. Currently Koranic curriculum is taught, but a law has been passed to allow biblical instruction in Christian schools.

Gender discrimination against girls: Girls are being educated, although less importance is placed on education for girls than that for boys.

Religion

Religious concerns: Evangelism is restricted. Conversion from Islam is prohibited.

Status of the church: There are 11 evangelical churches. Most converts come from the nominal Christian population.

Are Christians being persecuted? No

Societal Viewpoint Toward Children

Are they viewed as precious? Yes

Are there street children? Yes

Is there a large population of orphans? No

Are there child soldiers? No

Is child labor a problem? Because of the poor economy, children work as street vendors selling small items.

Kazakhstan

Major Languages: Kazakh, Russian
Total Population: 16,733,000
Population 0–34: 10,196,000
Life Expectancy: 64 years
Religion: Muslim 60.50%, Christian 24.66%, nonreligious/other 14.27%,
    Buddhist 0.50%, Jewish 0.04%, Shamanist 0.03%
Literacy Rate: male 100%, female 99%

*K*arin approached her father carefully. She desperately wanted to attend the English camp being held at a youth center in the country not far from the city of Almaty.

"Father," she almost whispered, "some people from America will be conducting a camp this summer. It's an English-speaking camp." She waited for him to respond.

"I suppose you want to go?" he replied.

"Yes, I would like very much to attend."

"I don't mind. As a matter of fact, I would like for you to learn English." He turned away, leaving Karin to contemplate how easy it had been to ask.

The English camp was wonderful, and Karin learned a lot. The camp speaker gave the children the opportunity to invite Jesus Christ into their hearts, and Karin prayed the prayer of salvation. She knew things were different after that prayer, and she wondered what would happen once she told her parents. Her father and mother had known nothing but atheism and Communism all their lives, and now their daughter was a Christian. What would they do? Every night as she read the Bible the camp teacher had given her, something touched her heart. Surely God would help her as she talked to her mother and father about her conversion.

At first their reaction, especially her father's, was one of anger. Her father refused to allow her to attend church, and she stayed home out of obedience. Then he softened and finally agreed to let her go to part of the Sunday service. It was important to him that she return home by noon on Sunday for the midday meal with her family, and she obeyed. Each day she drew her strength from the Word of God and reminded herself that, while the meetings were important, it was the Bible that would truly change her life.

Karin still lives at home, and at age 20 she can participate in all the church activities she desires. She faithfully prayed and witnessed to her family in true lifestyle evangelism. Not easy for a teenager! Where her talk of God once drew angry arguments, there is now a softening in her strongly atheistic family. This past Christmas she was asked to pray before the traditional holiday meal. Everyone at the church believes that one day Karin's whole family will come to know Jesus Christ.

The government of Kazakhstan has made it clear that the country belongs to the Kazakhs. Even though the president has encouraged Russians to stay, they feel unwelcome and are returning to Russia in large numbers. This exodus has caused not only technological setbacks but also setbacks in the health-care system. Many women and children have no clinics, especially in the rural areas.

Sadly, the abortion rate in Kazakhstan, especially in the former capital city, Almaty, is commensurate with that of the former Soviet Union. Women use abortion as a means of birth control and may have as many as 5 to 10 abortions in a lifetime.

The people of Kazakhstan embrace Islam as their principal religion, yet only about 40 percent of them are practicing Muslims. They have adopted a form of religion that includes shamanistic and Zoroastrian elements along with Islam. Seventy years of Communist rule left a spiritual void that needs to be filled. If Christians do not give the people answers to their questions and present the gospel to them, the people will once again fully embrace Islam. At this point the government is committed to remaining a secular state.

The young people are hungry to know about God. They like music from the West, TV, and the Internet. One prayer journeyer tells about two young girls being converted through listening to a recording of DC Talk. These two girls are now being educated in the West.

Summer camps are one of the most successful outreaches in all of the former Soviet republics and have proven to be a wonderful evangelistic tool. Pray for more churches in the West to perceive the need to help youngsters learn about Jesus Christ through such camps. Pray that they will be financed and staffed with godly men and women who love children.

Prayer Points

- Pray for Kazakh leaders to reject ethnic religious extremism and oppression.
- Pray for the centuries of spiritual bondage to be broken. Kazakhs are nominal Muslims, but fear of spirits is often stronger than their religious beliefs. Meanwhile, Saudi, Turkish, and Iranian Muslim missionaries are pouring into the country.
- Pray for many more Christian missionaries to work among the Kazakhs.
- Pray for spiritual health and maturity in the newly established churches consisting of national believers. Pray that believers will be properly discipled.
- Pray for Christians working among Kazakh college students, those translating the Kazakh Bible, the urban and rural church-planting teams, and those working with the Jesus film and radio broadcasts.
- Pray for international students to be reached with the gospel.

Quick Reference

Ethnic Breakdown: Kazakh 53.4%, Russian 28.2%, Ukrainian 3.0%, German 2.5%, Uzbek 2.3%, other 10.6%
Type of Government: Republic
Economy: Services 60%, Industry 30%, Agriculture 10%
Per capita income: U.S.$1,330
National debt: U.S.$7.9 billion
Economic conditions: Poor

Education
Quality of education: A severe shortage of schools and teachers is currently developing.
Gender discrimination against girls: Girls are being educated.

Religion
Religious concerns: Evangelism is restricted.
Status of the church: The constitution provides for freedom of religion, and the various denominations worship largely without government interference. The national church is growing and needs discipleship and leadership training.
Are Christians being persecuted? Yes. Converts to Christianity may be harassed by family, friends, and government authorities. Muslims who convert to Christianity may be killed.

Societal Viewpoint Toward Children

Are they viewed as precious? Yes

Are there street children? No specific data available.

Is there a large population of orphans? No specific data available.

Are there child soldiers? No specific data available.

Is child labor a problem? The constitution does not specifically prohibit forced and bonded labor of children, although there are no reports of abuses in this area.

Kuwait

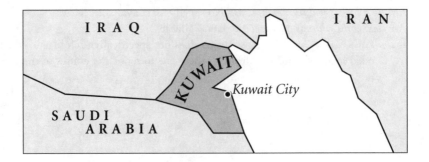

Major Languages: Arabic, English, Persian (Farsi)
Total Population: 1,974,000
Population 0–34: 1,320,000
Life Expectancy: 76 years
Religion: Muslim 87.43%, Christian 8.17%, Hindu 2.50%,
    nonreligious/other 1.10%, Baha'i 0.50%, Buddhist 0.30%
Literacy Rate: male 95%, female 83%

Sabah remembers the day when, as a young student, she marched to the polling stations in a demonstration for women's suffrage. She carried a banner that said, "The Voice of the Women Is in the Nation's Interest." That was in 1996, and women still do not have the right to vote in Kuwait.

During the Iraqi invasion in October 1990, the emir and the crown prince stated that once the war was over, women would receive better treatment, but they failed to follow through on any of their promises. In the war, women fought with the male soldiers against the Iraqis. Many risked their lives by wearing *abayas* to hide resistance documents and arms from the Iraqis, carrying them safely to the soldiers on the front lines. Yet there seemed to be no appreciation for all they did—they still had no voice in Kuwait.

Sabah was grieved when she was denied a scholarship to study at a university in London because she was a woman. It didn't matter that she was the top student in her class. She adjusted and still loved her country, but she wished Kuwait would change, and it wasn't happening quickly enough. Even her father, a liberal Shiite Muslim, often encouraged her to work to see women receive better treatment in Kuwait, yet he still held strong reservations about women being able to vote.

One of Sabah's greatest fears was that the growing fundamentalist Islamic movement would take over before her country changed for the betterment of women and children. There would be no hope for the plight of women under Islamic rule. The fundamentalists would enforce *sharia* (Islamic law), which would mean stricter dress codes for women, and the country would be indoctrinated with strongly anti-Western sentiment. Already violence had broken out when professors or newspaper articles suggested that women should not be required to wear veils that restricted their view while working in dangerous jobs at the university.

Some of Sabah's friends embraced the strictness of the Islamic law. It was an answer for those who wanted to fill the void in their lives. Even though they had nice cars, designer clothes, and money to spend as they pleased, they were looking for guidance and solutions in shaping their lives, and the platform of Islam, "Islam Is the Solution," seemed to provide the answer.

Shortly after the Iraqi invasion, Sabah's father determined that Kuwait was no place for a woman, and Sabah went to London to stay with family members while the war took place. The horror stories of rapes, beatings, and abuses by the Iraqis were plentiful, and Sabah was glad she left. When exposed to the West, she learned to like the people and saw new ways she could help her own country. She learned about means to solve the government's dilemma. The problem was that her own people would not listen to her. No matter how much she knew or understood about politics, no one in Kuwait would listen.

Sabah belongs to one of the many wealthy families in Kuwait, and though it is true that she suffers from her lack of a political voice, many in the country are poor and suffer much more. Almost 300,000 Bedouins or nomads were declared non-Kuwaitis in the early 1990s. The nomads had been required by the government to register in the 1950s, but many were illiterate and did not know that the registration process took three visits or more to the government office. They thought, "We were born in Kuwait, and our parents were born in Kuwait, so we are Kuwaitis." In the mid-90s those who had not registered were declared non-Kuwaitis, ousted from their jobs, and asked to leave their homeland. With no money, education, or means to leave, they now occupy the slums and scrounge for their very existence.

Rich oil reserves have given the children of Kuwait advantages in education, health care, and material goods. The consequence of such affluence without the knowledge of Jesus is a materialistic generation. Kuwait needs intercessors who will pray for the children to know Jesus Christ. The fields are open for those who will go into the country to work, use their "tent making" to stand in the gap, and believe God for the people of Kuwait.

Prayer Points

⌐· Pray for continued commitment to the welfare of children in Kuwait.

⌐· Pray for Christian families living in Kuwait to share their faith with their neighbors and demonstrate the love of Christ in a tangible way.

⌐· Pray for entire families, from the youngest to the oldest, to accept Jesus Christ as Savior.

⌐· Pray for this generation to be properly educated and trained to effectively run the country.

⌐· Pray for more workers who are trained in vanguard ministry to reach young people with the gospel and that they in turn will spread the gospel among their Muslim neighbors.

⌐· Pray for God to draw the children and young people of Kuwait to Him.

⌐· Pray for the physical and emotional healing of those who were injured and traumatized during the Iraqi invasion.

⌐· Pray that Kuwaiti-born nomads will be recognized as Kuwaitis and receive the benefits of citizenship.

Quick Reference

Ethnic Breakdown: Kuwaiti 45%, Other Arab 35%, South Asian 9%, Iranian 4%, other 7%

Type of Government: Nominal constitutional monarchy

Economy: Industry 55%, Services 45%

Per capita income: U.S.$17,390

National debt: U.S.$6.9 billion

Economic conditions: Thriving economy

Education

Quality of education: School system is well organized. Instruction includes mandatory Koranic instruction.

Educational discrimination against girls: Girls are encouraged as much as boys to get an education.

Religion

Religious concerns: Evangelism is strictly prohibited.

Status of the church: No national church exists, only expatriate churches.

Are Christians being persecuted? Yes. Christians have been detained, questioned, and charged by government authorities.

Societal Viewpoint Toward Children

Are they viewed as precious? Yes

Are there street children? No specific data available.

Is there a large population of orphans? No

Are there child soldiers? No specific data available.

Is child labor a problem? No specific data available.

Kyrgyzstan

Major Languages: Kirghiz (Kyrgyz), Russian, Uzbek
Total Population: 4,685,000
Population 0–34: 3,273,000
Life Expectancy: 63 years
Religion: Muslim 78.08%, nonreligious 13.60%, Christian 7.83%,
 Buddhist 0.35%, Jewish 0.12%, Baha'i 0.02%
Literacy Rate: male 99%, female 95%

Carol traveled from Chicago to visit her aunt who lived on the out-skirts of Bishkek, the capital of Kyrgyzstan. Amazed at how thin her aunt and her cousins were, Carol said nothing. Her aunt always pre-pared special meals for guests, but this time each meal consisted of the same thing—a variation of cabbage and potatoes. On the third day Carol's aunt apologized. "We have little to eat, but what we have you are welcome to share with us."

It was not just the meals that showed how bad things were in Kyrgyzstan. As Carol walked around her aunt's yard, she missed the beautiful flower garden she had known as a child. There had always been an abundance of roses, daisies, and peonies, but now every inch of the yard was bare dirt with new shoots of various kinds of vegetables. Her aunt referred to the yard as her "kitchen garden." Each tiny plant that sprouted was meticulously cared for every day, like a precious treasure, even though the spring temperatures hovered around freezing.

Another surprise greeted Carol as she followed her teenage cousins to the market one day. Families lined the streets selling soap, razor blades, used books, and anything they could spare from their homes. While Carol admired the people for their ingenuity, the underlying reality was that the economy of Kyrgyzstan was shaky at best.

The country that once had been known for its excellent educational system and high literacy rate was now not even educating all the children, many of whom were working on the streets. Carol saw firsthand what a country looks like at the intersection of Communism's downfall and a free market economy's emergence.

Economists believe that Kyrgyzstan stands a better chance of overcoming its financial woes than any of the other former states of the Soviet Union. It still has a long way to go, however, to be able to provide even the bare educational, medical, and social services for its citizens that were in place under the old system. The average Kyrgyz family spent 69.9 percent of its income on food in 1993, compared to 34.1 percent in 1990.

Nestled in the mountain ranges between China, Kazakhstan, and Uzbekistan, tiny Kyrgyzstan is considered the most democratic society of all the states of the former Soviet Union. While the Kyrgyz are trying to move to a free market society, the path has been difficult and plagued with setbacks. The country has little to develop. The crime rate and the number of organized gangs have increased considerably over the past few years. Children suffer the most from the economic struggles, and the government has expressed concern over the numbers of children who are presently living on the streets.

Chronic water pollution, a result of outdated systems and previous disregard for environmental concerns, wreaks havoc among the people. It brings many diseases such as diarrhea and typhus, taking a toll on the children and the elderly.

Though often inadequate, the health-care system under the Soviets provided free coverage for everyone, but now citizens often receive poor care because the medical personnel are not well trained. Pharmaceuticals, medical supplies, and equipment are insufficient, and facilities are generally inadequate and unsanitary. Doctors and hospitals may require upfront payment, often in U.S. dollars, and many of the residents are unable to pay. Kyrgyzstan produces no vaccines of its own and almost no medicines or pharmaceuticals.

The trafficking of women and young girls from Kyrgyzstan to Turkey, the United Arab Emirates, and other countries for work in the sex industry is a huge problem. Kyrgyz girls are commonly promised legitimate work abroad and find themselves indebted to their traffickers for travel expenses. They are then pressured to work in the sex industry to repay the debt.

Prayer Points

- Pray for God to deliver this newly independent republic from poverty.
- Pray for nationals to be trained to successfully run their country.

~· Pray for corruption within the government to end. The visa and registration departments commonly receive bribes from traffickers to forge documents.

~· Pray for the young women and girls who are often abused that the Lord's protection would cover them. Pray that women will have a voice in the government.

~· Pray for the protection of young women who leave home for jobs but are sold into prostitution.

~· Pray for God to meet the basic needs of the poverty-stricken children for shelter, food, clothing, and vaccinations.

~· Pray for unity among believers, leadership and discipleship training for Christians, balance in teaching, and wisdom in outreach.

Quick Reference

Ethnic Breakdown: Kirghiz 52.4%, Russian 18%, Uzbek 12.9%, Ukrainian 2.5%, German 2.4%, other 11.8%

Type of Government: Republic

Economy: Agriculture 45%, Services 35%, Industry 20%

Per capita income: U.S.$700

National debt: U.S.$1.1 billion

Economic conditions: Poor

Education

Quality of education: The educational system is deteriorating from an acute lack of governmental support and material resources.

Gender discrimination against girls: None

Religion

Religious concerns: Evangelism is restricted.

Status of the church: The majority of Christians are Russian Orthodox. There are two Kyrgyz churches in Bishkek, with about 2,000 believers in the country.

Are Christians being persecuted? No, although periodic tension exists between conservative Muslims and foreign missionaries in rural areas.

Societal Viewpoint Toward Children

Are they viewed as precious? Generally, but social pressures are affecting families, resulting in abandonment of children caused by parents' lack of resources to care for them.

Are there street children? Yes

Is there a large population of orphans? No specific data available.

Are there child soldiers? No specific data available.

Is child labor a problem? Families frequently call on their children to work and help support the family. Many children work as beggars and street vendors. There are reports of girls trafficked for the purpose of forced prostitution.

Laos

Major Languages: Lao, French, English
Total Population: 5,497,000
Population 0–34: 4,227,000
Life Expectancy: 51 years
Religion: Buddhist 61.05%, traditional ethnic 31.20%, nonreligious/other
 4.20%, Christian 1.85%, Muslim 1.10%, Chinese 0.50%, Baha'i 0.10%
Literacy Rate: male 74%, female 48%

The Minister of the Department of Religious Affairs addressed the group that had assembled to hear his speech. "You must renounce your faith in this man Jesus Christ. The government will not forgive anyone who believes in this cult."

Ti Soi had walked a long way to find out where her husband was and perhaps talk with the minister. After the minister's open demonstration against Christians, she realized there was no hope of getting her husband released from prison. She wanted desperately to raise her hand and say, "Mr. Minister, our government says there is religious freedom in this country, and yet you hold my husband because he is a believer. What about him? And what about me? I have no way to make a living without my husband. I have four children who will need food in the morning. Can you let him go?"

Ti Soi dared not say anything. If she did, she knew it would only make things more difficult for herself and her husband. Instead she listened.

The minister spoke in a deliberate manner, as though he were addressing a crowd of 10,000. "We, as the government, must do away with Christians. They are the number one enemy of the state, devised in the West and implemented in our country as an imperialist foreign religion that is backed by the political interests of Western devils. If you or anyone you know belongs to this sect, you have until the year 2001 to renounce this belief or to leave your mother country of Laos." He cleared his throat.

"We in Laos have religious freedom for Buddhists and for the Phi, but no others." He raised his voice even louder. "Those religions are not foreign to us, but Christianity is."

Ti Soi turned and walked away. Thoughts of her children ran through her mind. The children were so tiny and innocent. How would she face them? What would she say when the last bit of rice was gone tonight and the morning came when they would need food? Was it good to be a Christian when her children were the ones who suffered?

She had visited her husband once since he was taken away. On her visit she found the prison conditions crowded, and she learned that her husband had been tortured. He was fed gruel and water only once a day. Yet she could see a glow on his face and something strangely happy about him. Dedicated to his belief in Christ, he had decided not to renounce his Christian faith, but what about his children? Would they understand persecution? Hunger? Rejection?

At home Ti Soi sat down at the table and put her head in her hands. She wanted to cry, but she had to be brave. She fought thoughts of starvation and persecution. Tomorrow she was going to have to go to the government office and sign papers renouncing faith in Jesus Christ. This trial was too hard. Instead of crying, she prayed for food, comfort, and wisdom.

Ti Soi felt quieted, but she knew she was on the verge of giving up her faith. That night as she lay on her mat she thought of a better land where they could worship as they pleased. Finally she drifted off to sleep.

Ti Soi was awakened the next morning by a timid knock on the door. Tim Sigh, another believer, was at the door. "Here is rice and some pork. Eat well today, my sister." He was gone. God had supplied the need for the day, and that was sufficient for her. She and her family would be sustained for the moment. Tomorrow would take care of itself.

*L*aos is troubled with internal problems, to a large extent as a result of the ongoing civil war. The country also suffers from environmental problems, chronic marginal food production, and lack of access to health care and education for the children. The economy is underdeveloped, which negatively affects transportation and communication. Laos depends on large amounts of international aid (mainly from Japan) to meet its food needs.

The government has not allowed Christianity to grow among the people and for the past two years has instituted what it calls "The Program" to close down all house churches while retaining official churches to give foreigners the impression of religious freedom in the country. So far Laos has not been able to attract as many foreign investors as other central Asian countries have. All of these problems directly or indirectly affect children and young people. Laos needs our prayers.

Prayer Points

- ᴄ· Pray for children who are sold by their parents into slave labor and sex rings run by corrupt government officials. Many are taken to Thailand. Pray that God will protect these precious ones and they will hear and believe the gospel.
- ᴄ· Pray for the exposure and prosecution of those involved with child prostitution and child pornography.
- ᴄ· Pray for the safety of Christians and their families, labeled as the number one enemy by the Laos government. Pray that they will have the courage to spread the gospel in this hostile environment.
- ᴄ· Pray for Christians who are being forced to sign statements renouncing their faith in Jesus Christ to be courageous and faithful to Christ.
- ᴄ· Pray for safe water, adequate sanitation, and proper immunization for young people.
- ᴄ· Pray for an improved educational system that is equally fair to boys and girls.

Quick Reference

Ethnic Breakdown: Lao 50%, Phoutheung (Kha) 15%, Tribal Thai 20%, Meo, Hmong, Yao, and other 15%

Type of Government: Lao People's Democratic Republic (Communist)

Economy: Agriculture 56%, Services 25%, Industry 19%

Per capita income: U.S.$350

National debt: U.S.$2.32 billion

Economic conditions: Extremely poor

Education

Quality of education: Enrollment rates are low. Not much value is placed on education in this society.

Gender discrimination against girls: Domestic chores may take precedence over education.

Religion

Religious concerns: Evangelism is prohibited.

Status of the church: There are only a few Christians in the country and no national church. Christians must worship underground in individual homes.

Are Christians being persecuted? Yes

Societal Viewpoint Toward Children

Are they viewed as precious? Yes. It is a disgrace not to have children.

Are there street children? Yes

Is there a large population of orphans? No specific data available.

Are there child soldiers? No specific data available.

Is child labor a problem? Children are commonly employed by their families. Some
   children are sold into slave labor and sex rings.

Lebanon

Major Languages: Arabic, French, English
Total Population: 3,578,000
Population 0–34: 2,505,000
Life Expectancy: 71 years
Religion: Muslim 59.76%, Christian 31.93%, Druze 7.00%,
    nonreligious/other 1.30%, Jewish 0.01%
Literacy Rate: male 91%, female 82%

*M*other late again, Ani?" Joseph asked.
        "Yes, sir." Ani hung her head and kicked a pebble with her toe.
    Joseph closed the door to the school and turned the lock. As the school janitor, he was always the last one to leave the building. "I hate to leave you by yourself. You want me to wait with you?"
    "No, Mr. Masouf, I'll be all right. Mother will be here soon. She's probably at the church doing something."
    "Knowing your mother, she's tending to someone's needs," he replied.
    "You're right." Ani agreed with Mr. Masouf, but she was still disappointed. This was the third time this week her mother had been involved with someone else's "need" while she waited, twice at school and once at her piano lesson.
    Ani's mother, Zivort, had worked hard all her life in the Catholic Orthodox Church. She spent many hours taking care of others. For Zivort, the whole country needed help. Since the civil war, the needs in Lebanon were everywhere and so was Zivort. Their house was always filled with people who'd had their homes bombed or couldn't go home for the night because there was fighting in their neighborhoods. "Ani, can this family sleep in your room tonight? It's just for one night, dear," and Ani would sleep in the kitchen next to the pantry, on the hard floor.

She hated it every time someone strange showed up at the door. Ultimately it meant she was either going to be out of her bedroom or have less food to eat.

"War doesn't have any favorites. It hits everyone," her mother often said. "We are Christians, so we must help the people in our country and show them the love of God. How will they know Jesus Christ if we don't show them?"

Resentment rose up in Ani. She purposed that when she got older, she would never, never take a stranger into her home. She was going to have a small place so that no one else would come to stay with her. Whether she was a Christian or not, she wasn't going to help anyone—not ever.

"Ani, I'm so sorry I'm late." Zivort held out her arms to hug her daughter, but Ani turned away and walked past her mother. She would later regret her resentment, but during her youth she hated every outside intrusion on their family's life.

When Ani was an adult, she had an encounter with God and met Jesus Christ as her personal Savior. Then she understood her mother's love for others. Today Ani and her husband pastor a church of over 5,000 people in another country. They have outreaches to street children, refugees, and an orphanage. Ani credits her mother with showing her how to minister to people and how to make her relationship with the Lord vibrant and effective in the community.

The 16-year civil war (1975–1991) wreaked havoc in Lebanon. It paralyzed the country, cutting the national output in half and almost destroying the economic infrastructure. Lebanon is still in a state of recovery, with many buildings destroyed and its people suffering. Because of the effects of the war, one in five Lebanese under the age of 20 is illiterate. Boys are favored to receive an education, and girls are encouraged to stay home and help the family with chores. Primary school is free but not compulsory, and if a girl child continues her education, she will most likely have to attend a private school.

Many children, war orphans, or economic casualties roam the streets and survive by begging or working at menial jobs, often in abusive situations. An estimated 16 percent of the street children are Palestinian. Drug addiction and crime are increasing. The health-care system, once one of the best in the Middle East, has not been able to recuperate from the overload placed on it by the war. The government has been unable to establish child-welfare programs to combat the problems children face.

The children of Lebanon need our prayers.

Prayer Points

◞· Pray for continued progress in Lebanon's rebuilding of the war-torn physical and financial infrastructure.

◞· Pray for the opening of more Christian schools.

◞· Pray for God to heal the Lebanese people of bitterness, hatred, and disunity that resulted from the long war.

◞· Pray for the development of programs and institutions devoted to improving conditions for children.

◞· Pray for intolerance toward violence against young women.

◞· Pray for God to prompt more and more ministries, especially those seeking to reach children, teens, and young adults, to return to Lebanon.

◞· Pray that those traumatized by the war will hunger for the peace that only Jesus Christ can bring them.

◞· Pray for TV programming like SAT-7 and their partners and for finances to continue to bring life-changing programs to children, teens, and young adults.

Quick Reference

Ethnic Breakdown: Arab 95%, Armenian 4%, other 1%
Type of Government: Republic
Economy: Services 61%, Industry 27%, Agriculture 12%
Per capita income: U.S.$2,660
National debt: U.S.$8.8 billion
Economic conditions: Poor. The civil war seriously damaged Lebanon's economic infrastructure and cut national output by half.

Education
Quality of education: Only primary education is provided free of charge by the government, and even then it is not compulsory.
Gender discrimination against girls: Domestic chores take precedence over education in lower-income families.

Religion
Religious concerns: Allows evangelism.
Status of the church: The church needs to be more proactive in evangelism.
Are Christians being persecuted? No.

Societal Viewpoint Toward Children
Are they viewed as precious? They are not well protected.
Are there street children? Yes
Is there a large population of orphans? No specific data available.
Are there child soldiers? No specific data available.
Is child labor a problem? Children are used in the labor force.

Libya

Major Languages: Arabic, Italian, English
Total Population: 5,115,000
Population 0–34: 3,889,000
Life Expectancy: 65 years
Religion: Muslim 96.50%, Christian 3.00%, Buddhist 0.30%,
  nonreligious 0.20%
Literacy Rate: male 88%, female 63%

*I*n 1960, when Colonel Qaddafi, Libya's new dictator, expelled all foreign missionaries, Mubarak watched his best friend, James, board a plane for the United States. Every year Mubarak thought about his childhood friend and how they had celebrated holidays together—Christmas for James and Ramadan for Mubarak. Closer than brothers, they had talked about Jesus and Muhammad, and Mubarak had prayed to ask Jesus Christ into his heart. Now, as he looked back, he was sure it was just a child's fancy. *Surely it had no meaning*, he thought, but still he had the nagging feeling that perhaps there was some significance to a child's simple prayer.

When they were about 12 years old, Mubarak and James played together in Mubarak's backyard and would sit on a rock to look up at the stars. Now, whenever Mubarak looked up into the heavens, he thought of his friend James and the comfort he had felt when he asked Jesus into his heart. He had received a letter from James about a year after he left. It was a friendly note about school, church, and his new soccer team, but Mubarak's father was irate. He feared the authorities would come to their home and ask questions about the foreigner's letter. Mubarak hid the letter under a stone in his backyard and read it every day, but he never responded to it.

For 25 years the two countries were unable to trade with each other. Although America needed Libya's precious oil and Libya needed medical supplies and computer technology, neither country attempted to reestablish political relations.

As time passed, Mubarak forgot to look at the letter from his friend. His family moved away from the house with the stone and its hidden secret. The stars never left him, however, and they constantly reminded him that God had a special place in his heart for him.

Mubarak became a man with grown children of his own. He served his country as a soldier and went to college to become a geological engineer. He had a good wife, and all his children lived nearby, but something about his friend James and the stars hovered over him as a constant reminder that he belonged to a God greater than he could imagine.

One day as he sat in his office and stared at his computer, he asked himself, *What if I look on the Internet and try to find my friend James?* He worked on his computer continually and often used the Internet but had not ventured beyond work-related projects. He had never before tried to locate anyone on the international directory, and he reasoned, *Why not?* Impulsively, he quickly typed in the address of the Internet directory and found 14 names that matched his friend's—James Bellmont Rhodes. Only one of the names had an address in Illinois, James's home state. Quickly he jotted down the address and telephone number. Mubarak picked up his company phone and dialed the international number. James answered with a sleepy voice. The two men caught up on the past 40 years of their lives. They exchanged the dates they had married, the names of their children, and their vocations. James was now a minister.

The two men agreed to correspond by e-mail. Over the course of the next three months, they conversed over the Internet. James was particularly careful not to mention prayer, the name of Jesus, or missionaries to Mubarak. Eventually they were able to meet in Chicago, where Mubarak was attending a conference. There Mubarak found answers to his questions about Jesus.

The children of Libya fare better than those in many other Muslim nations. Education is mandatory until age 15, and the country encourages girls to go to school. Traditionally, girls may be kept home to help with chores or removed from school at puberty to minimize contact with the opposite sex. Medical care is adequate and available for most of the population, especially in urban areas.

Libya has great wealth because of its oil reserves, but it remains closed to the West and to the gospel. There are very few ways children can hear the good news. Pray for the doors to be opened so that this present generation of children will be able to hear about Jesus Christ.

Prayer Points

⌐· Pray for an end to the drug-abuse problem among the students and young people of Libya.
⌐· Pray for the barbaric practice of FGM to be abolished.
⌐· Pray for Jesus Christ to reveal Himself to Libya's youth in dreams and visions.
⌐· Pray that children, teens, and young adults will have an insatiable desire to have a personal encounter with Jesus Christ.
⌐· Pray for divine strategies in reaching the nation with the gospel.
⌐· Pray for the young women of Libya to reach out for Jesus Christ as the remedy for their powerlessness and oppression.
⌐· Pray that Colonel Mu'ammar Qaddafi will have wisdom to govern righteously for the sake of the children, teens, and young adults.
⌐· Pray for the recent converts.

Quick Reference

Ethnic Breakdown: Berber and Arab 97%, Greek, Maltese, Italian, Egyptian, Pakistani, Turkish, Indian, and Tunisian 3%
Type of Government: A military dictatorship described by the government as *Jamahiriya* (governed by the masses)
Economy: Industry 31%, Services 27%, Government 24%, Agriculture 18%
Per capita income: U.S.$6,510
National debt: U.S.$4 billion
Economic conditions: Stable

Education
Quality of education: Instruction includes mandatory Koranic curriculum.
Gender discrimination against girls: Not as much emphasis is placed on education for girls as for boys, though girls are encouraged to attend school.

Religion
Religious concerns: Evangelism is prohibited.
Status of the church: No national church exists.
Are Christians being persecuted? Yes

Societal Viewpoint Toward Children
Are they viewed as precious? Yes
Are there street children? No specific data available.
Is there a large population of orphans? No
Are there child soldiers? No specific data available.
Is child labor a problem? There are no reports of bonded child labor.

Malaysia

Major Languages: Bahasa Melayu, English, Chinese
Total Population: 21,793,000
Population 0–34: 15,005,000
Life Expectancy: 71 years
Religion: Muslim 58.00%, Buddhist/Chinese 21.59%, Christian 9.21%, Hindu 5.00%, nonreligious/other 4.50%, traditional ethnic 1.20%, Baha'i 0.40%, Sikh 0.10%
Literacy Rate: male 89%, female 79%

*T*he children sang with all the enthusiasm of a national choir. They belted out songs of praise and raised their hands in worship to the Lord—an unusual sight for this Muslim nation. Who were these children, and why were they singing with such exuberance? They were students at an "underground school" located on the outskirts of Penang, Malaysia.

One Friday, Anny, the school principal, played the guitar while the children sang for a special guest, Florence, a missionary from Uganda who spoke about her work among AIDS orphans. At the end of Florence's talk, a child began to pray for the orphaned children who lived in Africa. Several children walked to a posted world map, placed their hands on the continent of Africa, and prayed fervently.

Anny finished the praise and worship session with the song "Jesus, I Adore You." She then dismissed the children to their classrooms.

Walking across the courtyard with her guest, Anny explained her vision for training the children. "I want them to know Christian principles. They need to learn young."

Florence expressed her concern for the school. "What if the government finds out you're sponsoring a Christian school? You know that's forbidden. What will you do?"

"The worst the authorities would do is shut us down. They would most likely not prosecute me, but it's worth the risk to see the children grow spiritually and gain a heart for those in the world who are less fortunate than they are," she said.

"Your country is blessed, and it's good that you teach the children to spread the gospel," Florence replied.

"I have a children's intercessory prayer group that meets in my home once a month. We meet tonight. Would you like to come?"

Florence responded quickly. "I'd love to. I've never seen children pray as intercessors."

Anny went on to explain that for two years she had kept a diary of the prayers the children had prayed and the answers they had received. Many of the children had had dreams and visions. One child with an intense burden for the children of Sudan had seen a vision of Jesus visiting a refugee camp in Kenya, where he touched a child and called him to preach the gospel to his people.

Two weeks after the child's vision Anny picked up a newspaper and found a story about Emmanuel, one of the lost boys of Sudan, whom the Lord had called to preach while he was at a refugee camp in Kenya. Coincidence? Anny didn't think so.

Anny described many more answers to prayer that the children had received. She was very glad that the children were learning not only about Jesus but also how to pray for the nations.

*C*hristianity is the fastest-growing religion in Malaysia. Because it is against the law to proselytize Muslims and ethnic Malays, the church has grown mainly among the Chinese. The government acts as a watchdog over any religious activity. Even the content of the sermons delivered in the mosques comes under its scrutiny.

Malaysia is a relatively prosperous country, rich in rubber and tin. The government and the industrial sectors have worked hard to make the country economically stable so as to compete in the world's market. Even the 1999 recession did not keep Malaysia from continued economic growth.

Children are viewed as precious, and the family circle is tight because many generations live under one roof. Educational achievement is highly prized among students of all ages. Nevertheless, with all its prosperity and educational goals, Malaysia has a notable child prostitution problem, especially in the larger cities.

The young people love to visit each other and enjoy videos. They have a strong liking for rock music and many of the teen fads that are popular in the West. Christian contemporary music bands have been able to provide a witness to them.

Prayer Points

- Pray that the church will seek God for his strategic plan to reach Malaysia with the gospel.
- Pray that the church will have a strong prayer burden for children, teens, and young adults.
- Pray that Christian parents will not be caught up in their careers, leaving children in the care of unsaved caregivers.
- Pray against ungodly influence on the young people through TV, secular rock music, computer games, and the Internet.
- Pray that this generation of children, teens, and young adults will know and follow Jesus Christ and be properly discipled.
- Pray for the young people who are rebelling against parental, school, and other authorities.
- Pray that incest and sexual exploitation of children will be eradicated, that God will protect these precious ones from such hideous acts, and that the government will continue to sternly prosecute such cases.
- Pray that the new churches will be strong in evangelism, discipleship, and church planting. Pray that Christianity will continue to be the fastest-growing religion in the country.

Quick Reference

Ethnic Breakdown: Malay and other indigenous 58%, Chinese 26%, Indian 7%, other 9%
Type of Government: Constitutional monarchy
Economy: Industry 46%, Services 42%, Agriculture 12%
Per capita income: U.S.$3,890
National debt: U.S.$43.6 billion
Economic conditions: Stable after recovering from 1999 recession.

Education
Quality of education: School system is well organized. Twenty percent of the national budget is spent on education.
Gender discrimination against girls: Girls are being educated.

Religion
Religious concerns: Evangelism is restricted.
Status of the church: Christianity is the fastest-growing religion in the country. Believers need training in discipleship, leadership, and evangelism.
Are Christians being persecuted? Restricted but not persecuted

Societal Viewpoint Toward Children

Are they viewed as precious? Yes, but the government recognizes that sexual exploitation of children and incest are problems.

Are there street children? Child beggars are tolerated.

Is there a large population of orphans? There are some orphans.

Are there child soldiers? No

Is child labor a problem? Child labor occurs in certain sectors of the country. Forced and bonded labor by children is prohibited and generally rare, although occasional trafficking of girls for the purpose of forced prostitution is a problem.

Maldives

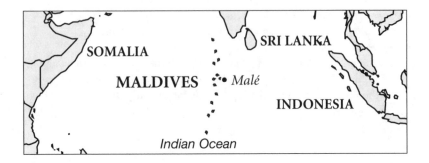

Major Languages: Maldivian Divehi, English
Total Population: 301,000
Population 0–34: 236,810
Life Expectancy: 62 years
Religion: Muslim 99.41%, Buddhist 0.45%, Christian 0.10%,
   nonreligious/other 0.03%, Hindu 0.01%
Literacy Rate: male 93%, female 93%

*A*minath Moonisa, a 17-year-old Maldivian, was arrested in 1998, not because she had committed a crime but because she had received Jesus Christ as her personal Savior and no longer wanted to be called a Muslim. In Aminath's country few converts, although they are believers, call themselves Christians. Converts do not want to be persecuted for changing their religion. Aminath, though, decided to take a stand and publicly declare her faith. She is one of more than 50 people who have been arrested for becoming Christians. Conversion to any religion other than Islam is against the law.

Aminath was taken into custody and subjected to interrogation, imprisonment, and possible death. During her arrest the government seized her passport, her Christian books, and her personal correspondence, photos, and other personal possessions. At the same time, a Voice of the Martyrs source reported that at least 19 Christian expatriates were coerced into signing statements and were "expelled for life" from the Maldives.

Few people are willing to endure the consequences of making their conversion public. It was a heroic act for Aminath to publicly proclaim her conversion. She is to be commended and should be held up in prayer because her boldness will give other new converts the courage to take a stand for Christ. As Christians come forward, pressure will be exerted to

144

allow citizens the freedom to embrace religion as a personal choice, not because of a mandate from the government.

*T*he government of the Republic of Maldives prides itself as being "100 percent Muslim," and even the Maldivian constitution states that it is against the law for a citizen to embrace any faith other than Islam.

Change is taking place because the Maldives are not as isolated as they once were. More people are coming to the country, and along with the people come the ideas of different cultures. Because of this, society is polarizing between a younger generation that has been influenced by Western culture and older residents, who are more fundamental in their beliefs, including their practice of religion.

In the past, attempts have been made to scramble radio and TV stations that were able to send signals into the Maldives. The government wants the country to be left as it is and fears what is new and different. However, the islands are fast becoming one of the most popular tourist attractions as visitors come to the beautiful crystal clear waters for some of the most spectacular scuba diving in the world. Change is inevitable. Pray that as Christians come to enjoy the ocean, they will bring Christian literature and Bibles with them to be left behind for the young people of the Maldives who are searching for God to fill a void in their lives.

Foreigners may worship as they choose if they do so privately. Conversion of a Maldivian is in violation of *sharia* (Islamic law) and may result in the loss of a convert's citizenship.

Maldivians have incorporated their traditional superstitions into Islam. In spite of the heat, they build houses with no windows or they close the windows tightly to keep out the evil spirits. They also leave a kerosene lamp burning to appease the spirits.

Maldivian fathers have a reputation for being distant from their families. They often share meals with their children but do not communicate with them. The children, besides not knowing the closeness of an earthly father, have very little chance to learn about their heavenly Father.

The government pays for the health care of its citizens and has done an excellent job of increasing the life expectancy of the people. Tuberculosis and malaria have been drastically reduced, and village chiefs have been encouraged to administer medications and vaccines.

Prayer Points

- Pray that suspicion of Christianity and centuries of prejudice will be removed and the gospel will be freely preached.

◡· Pray that students traveling abroad will hear the gospel, receive Christ, and reach their families with the good news.

◡· Pray that this generation and their families will receive Jesus Christ as their personal Savior and will be taught that believers have authority over evil spirits.

◡· Pray that the Bible and Christian materials will be translated into their language.

◡· Pray for drastic changes to take place in the hearts of the leaders so that they will accept the gospel for their own sake and for future generations.

◡· Pray for God to prepare the way for Bibles, Christian literature, and Christian broadcasts, especially programming that will reach children, teens, and young adults, to come into this country legally.

◡· Pray that Maldivians working in the tourism industry will hear the gospel, accept Christ, and evangelize others.

◡· Pray that parents will show their children love and affection and that this generation will know God as their Father.

◡· Pray that the divorce rate will be reduced in the Maldives. Since there is no negative stigma attached to divorce, it is very common for Maldivians to marry early and often.

◡· Pray that young people will be attracted to Christian music with lyrics that contain a gospel message.

Quick Reference

Ethnic Breakdown: Maldivian 98.4%, Sinhalese 0.6% %, Gujarati 0.2%, Malayali 0.1%, Tamil 0.1%, other 0.6%

Type of Government: Republic

Economy: Services 62%, Agriculture 20%, Industry 18%

Per capita income: U.S.$990

National debt: U.S.$188 million

Economic conditions: Stable

Education

Quality of education: The school system is well organized. Instruction includes mandatory Koranic curriculum.

Gender discrimination against girls: Women have traditionally been disadvantaged, particularly in terms of education and the application of Islamic law. Parents may not allow girls to leave their home island for an island having a secondary school.

Religion

Religious concerns: The government prohibits evangelism, making it difficult to present the gospel.

Status of the church: A missionary work has been established and local churches are beginning to grow. The Bible has not been translated into their language.

Are Christians being persecuted? Yes

Societal Viewpoint Toward Children

Are they viewed as precious? Generally, but families have a reputation for being distant and rarely express any affection.

Are there street children? No

Is there a large population of orphans? No specific data available.

Are there child soldiers? No

Is child labor a problem? Children work in family fishing, agricultural, and commercial activities.

Mali

Major Languages: French, Bambara
Total Population: 10,686,000
Population 0–34: 8,471,000
Life Expectancy: 47 years
Religion: Muslim 87.00%, traditional ethnic 10.98%, Christian 1.92%,
  nonreligious 0.10%
Literacy Rate: male 39%, female 23%

Getting water from the local pump is more than a daily chore for a young Malian woman. This activity is her social contact with the world and means life for her family, who wait for her to return to their hut from her morning trek to the pump. Ten liters of water weigh 22 pounds, a fifth of a woman's body weight. Often, a woman will carry at least 20 liters in an aluminum pot large enough to hold a computer monitor.

To move the water from the cement floor surrounding the outdoor hand pump to the top of her head, the woman will solicit the help of one of the other women at the pump. The two of them take hold of the pot's edges and lift the pot straight up between them. When the pot is level with her head, the woman ducks underneath it and places it on the wad of rolled-up cloth she always wears when fetching water. The cloth is the cushion between the woman's skull and the pot of water. The friend lets go, and the woman spends a few seconds finding her balance. Then, with one hand steadying the load, she turns and starts toward home, which might be a 20-minute walk through mud huts and donkey manure.

Since the droughts of the 1970s and '80s, water is even more precious to the families of Mali. The pump may be the only source of clean drinking water for the village of 2,000 to 3,000 people. Everyone knows that pump water is clean and that drinking well water will make a family sick. Many Malian children die every year from impure drinking water that causes diarrhea.

The pump is where the young woman will visit with other women and hear village gossip. The woman's trip to the pump may be her only excuse for going outside of her family's Muslim home unescorted.

The people of Mali need the Living Water of the Word of God. Most Malians are moderate in their religious beliefs and tolerant of the Christian message. The government of Mali welcomes Christian workers and is seeking to contain those who oppose Christian ministries. In the past Saudi Arabian and Libyan oil dollars have funded and strengthened the Islamic movement, encouraging the people to despise Christians. While Mali is open to the gospel, laborers are few.

The children of Mali have very few opportunities for a better life than that of their parents. With a current life expectancy of 47 years, the lives of the children are shortened because of disease, poverty, and exploitative labor.

Most Malians are poor and cannot afford to send their children to school. Parents must provide school uniforms along with textbooks. Often education is cut short because it becomes necessary for the child to work in the fields and help with chores at home. A male child stands a better chance of going to school longer because it is believed that a man needs an education more than a woman. Only 23 percent of the women in Mali can read and write.

The people have a desire for large families, which causes the birthrate to be high and places a great demand on the land, of which only a scant 2 percent can be cultivated. The Malian child, seen as a celestial, social, and material being, is handled with great care. Many communities consider a child to be part of the cosmos before he is born—a gift from God, an ancestor, an evil spirit, a social product, and a community possession.

Prayer Points

- Pray that God will bless this nation so that the children will not have to be a large part of the workforce.
- Pray that the government will be successful in halting the trafficking of children and return them to Mali. There are reports that children are being sold to work on plantations in Cote d'Ivoire.
- Pray that there will be great improvements in health care for children, teens, and young adults.
- Pray that the young professional and skilled workers will be able to

use their abilities to build a strong nation and not have to go abroad to find jobs.

╰· Pray that entire villages, some of which are totally illiterate, will learn to read and write.

╰· Pray that the church will make reaching millions with the gospel a priority, especially because of the short life expectancy of the Malians.

╰· Pray that since evangelism is allowed, the church will respond to the open door God has given us. Praise God that Malians are free to change their religion without repercussion.

╰· Pray that God will send rain upon the land and restore His blessing upon Mali. At present only 2 percent of the land can be cultivated. Mali agriculture was once very prosperous.

╰· Pray that excellent health care and education will be available for pregnant mothers, which will reduce the high mortality rate.

Quick Reference

Ethnic Breakdown: Mande 50% (Bambara, Malinke, Soninke), Peul 17%, Voltaic 12%, Songhai 6%, Tuareg and Moor 10%, other 5%

Type of Government: Republic

Economy: Agriculture 46%, Services 33%, Industry 21%

Per capita income: U.S.$250

National debt: U.S.$3.1 billion

Economic conditions: Mali is one of the world's 10 poorest nations.

Education

Quality of education: There is a severe shortage of schools and teachers. Chores take precedence over education.

Gender discrimination against girls: Not much importance is placed on education for girls.

Religion

Religious concerns: Christians need to partner with the local church to reach the Malians with relief and the gospel.

Status of the church: People are free to change their religion. Foreign missionary groups operate in the country and can freely evangelize.

Are Christians being persecuted? No

Societal Viewpoint Toward Children

Are they viewed as precious? Yes

Are there street children? Yes. Many of them are boys between the ages of 6 and 15 years, including many from Senegal and Guinea as well as Malians.

Is there a large population of orphans? No specific data available.

Are there child soldiers? No specific data available.

Is child labor a problem? Yes. An estimated 54.5 percent of children between the ages of 10 and 14 work.

Mauritania

Major Languages: Hassaniyah Arabic, French
Total Population: 2,668,000
Population 0–34: 2,107,000
Life Expectancy: 51 years
Religion: Muslim 99.84%, Christian 0.16%
Literacy Rate: male 50%, female 26%

*A*t first I didn't know what was happening. I kept thinking that maybe I was losing my mind." Eighteen-year-old Amal cried as she spoke. "Every night I would dream about this man and He would ask me if I knew who He was. In my heart I knew, but I couldn't say His name—Jesus Christ.

"He would ask me if I believed in Him, and I would have this overwhelming desire to fall at His feet in worship. I would wake up and look around the room. I could feel His presence, but He wouldn't be there. The dream happened so many times that I finally went to my father and told him.

"My father is the *imam* for our village and practices witchcraft. Many people come to him for healing and advice about the future. His advice is often very good. I have always respected him and thought he was the best father a girl could have. We've had a unique relationship in that we've been very close. This is not the case with most girls and their fathers in a Muslim society such as ours in Mauritania.

"Ever since I was a child, my father has told me that when I reached the age of 18, I would inherit the family's powers. He groomed me to know how to handle the powers I would receive.

"When I told my father about the dreams, he was very calm and told me just to come to him whenever they happened and he would help. On several occasions I went to him in the middle of the night, but finally he realized that a power greater than the one he served was coming to me. Eventually he stopped trying to help by his incantations and 'cleansing' of my room.

"At that point he thought the solution was for me to get married. He felt that if I had a family of my own, the dreams would stop. My deep desire to know Jesus Christ would be replaced by my devotion to my husband and the business of attending to his needs. At the age of 16, I was married, but the dreams only intensified.

"Immediately after the birth of my first child, a little girl, Jesus visited me. His presence was so strong that when I awoke I called out, 'Jesus, come into my life and make me like You.' I didn't know what that meant, since I had no idea who Jesus really was, but there was such a peace that came over me. I kept it to myself for many days as I sat in His presence and told Him how much I loved Him.

"As my 18th birthday approached, I realized that the ceremony would take place. I went to my father and told him I had accepted Jesus Christ and did not want the family's powers.

"My husband and my father agreed to take my child and lock me away. A few days later they drove me to a nearby town and left me with no money or anyone to help. I found a small church in the town and asked to speak to the priest, who was a wonderful man. He told me about Jesus Christ and introduced me to a group of people who met secretly to worship Jesus. I now have a Bible of my own and have been able to help a lot of other women who are seeking to know God for themselves. Someday I may see my child and my husband, but if I never do, I have found a treasure greater than anything I could have ever imagined."

Very few would be willing to pay the price Amal has had to pay for putting her faith in Jesus Christ. In Mauritania a person who converts to Christianity is in danger of losing not only her family but also her life.

Mauritania is a desert country with 57 percent of its people living below the poverty line. Although the government is trying to develop jobs for its young people and women, progress has been slow.

Only 10 percent of school-age children attend primary school. Girls are often kept from school because they are needed at home to help the family with chores and to tend to younger siblings. They may be taken from school when they reach puberty to minimize their contact with boys.

Despite the laws and penalties against conversion, there are a growing number of national believers, who desperately need supportive prayer.

Prayer Points

~· Pray for an increase in the literacy rate.

~· Pray for creative ways to present the gospel in a society where the majority of the people can't read.

~· Pray that God will expedite translation of the Bible into the Hassaniyah dialect.

~· Praise God that the Jesus film is available in Hassaniyah. Pray that children, teens, and young adults will want to repeatedly watch this version of the film and that God will use it to confirm in their hearts that Jesus Christ is the Son of God and their Savior.

~· Pray that Jesus Christ will appear to this generation supernaturally through dreams and visions.

~· Pray that God will powerfully use this generation, once it is saved, to witness about Jesus Christ.

~· Pray for the "Muslim-background believers" (MBBs) who have converted to Christianity to be discipled so that they will fulfill God's purpose for their lives. Pray that they will be protected.

~· Pray that God will give the expatriate Christian community strategies to present the gospel in a hostile environment.

~· Pray that the practice of gavage (the force-feeding of young girls to make them more attractive) will cease.

Quick Reference

Ethnic Breakdown: Maure (Moors) 82%, Black Africans 18%
Type of Government: Republic
Economy: Services 43%, Agriculture 33%, Industry 24%
Per capita income: U.S.$460
National debt: U.S.$2.5 billion
Economic conditions: Extremely poor; 57 percent of the population lives below the poverty line.

Education
Quality of education: Only 10 percent of the children attend primary school, and the percentage that attends high school is even smaller. Instruction includes mandatory Koranic curriculum.
Gender discrimination against girls: Yes

Religion
Religious concerns: Evangelism is prohibited.
Status of the church: The national church is underground.
Are Christians persecuted? Yes. Law forbids Mauritanians from even hearing the gospel. Conversion to Christianity is illegal and punishable by death.

Societal Viewpoint Toward Children

Are they viewed as precious? No

Are there street children? Yes. The abundance of children located in urban areas and the lack of adequate schools have created a situation where more children are on the streets.

Is there a large population of orphans? No specific data available.

Are there child soldiers? No specific data available.

Is child labor a problem? Children are routinely used in the labor force.

Mongolia

Major Languages: Mongol, Kazakh
Total Population: 2,616,000
Population 0–34: 1,905,000
Life Expectancy: 67 years
Religion: nonreligious/other 41.59%, shamanist 31.20%, Buddhist 22.50%, Muslim 4.00%, Christian 0.71%
Literacy Rate: male 88%, female 77%

*M*ore than one morning Jeff awakened to find that the fire had gone out in the small wood stove that sat in the middle of his *ger* (tent). Although he loved winter and had been raised in a small town in New England, where snow was a way of life, this was winter in Mongolia, where temperatures often dipped below -50 degrees Fahrenheit.

Jeff loved the people, the winters, and his ger, but this was his choice, and he could go back to his warm home in the States at any time. The Mongolians who lived here endured year after year of harsh winters that could easily make people look 10 years older than they were.

Jeff taught English as a second language at the local high school and helped work on a greenhouse project after hours. He attended the small local church of 21 believers, all of them young adults about his age. The small gathering began to meet after a Christian rock band traveled to Mongolia to give a concert. The young people had been hungry to hear about the gospel, but the same was not true of the older generation. While they welcomed Jeff and the help he gave the village, the older people made it clear they were not interested in knowing about this "new religion." Because Jeff had seen much greater openness among the youth, he had hope for the next generation of Mongolians, who desperately needed Bibles. As an outsider, Jeff was limited in what he could do. Since he knew that he could not bring Bibles into the village, he prayed for others to do so. The elders respected him for following his own beliefs, but they strictly forbade him to witness. He tried to walk a middle road so that his time in Mongolia would not be shortened and he would be able to accomplish as much as possible during his two-year commitment.

He wrote in his journal, "I woke up this morning to a chilling wind howling about my ger. I used the remainder of my wood to start a fire in my stove. In the quiet darkness of the morning, huddled next to my stove and sipping hot coffee, I ask myself, 'Is it worth it? Am I really making a difference in the lives of the people? Is it really worth being this cold?' Then I remember my fire that I built with my own hands, and how that small fire has kindled enough heat to keep me alive, and I know I am building a small fire here among the people that will warm their souls and give them a hope for eternity."

*M*ongolians are very proud of their history and traditions. They trace their heritage to the great warrior Ghengis Khan, who formed the Mongol nation in 1206. During the 16th century, the Manchus gained power and Tibetan Buddhism became the primary religion. The Communists took over the country in the 1920s, and the country remained under Soviet rule until the early 1990s. The past 70 years of atheistic domination has left a spiritual vacuum in the country. At least one generation of Mongolians has been raised and educated to have no religious beliefs. The country shows some promise of opening up to Christianity, but the people are also remembering the old days before Communism and are turning to Buddhism in large numbers. In 1991 there was only one monastery and 100 Buddhist monks, known as *lamas*. Today there are over 134 monasteries with more than 2,000 lamas. The law does not permit the building of Christian churches. Consequently there are no church buildings in the country. Native Americans have been able to reach the Mongolians with the gospel better than any other group of Christian workers.

The young people are more open than the older generations to new ideas. While rock music is very appealing, it is by no means Christian rock they have the opportunity to hear. Any type of music from the West is very much in demand. Please pray for the youth of Mongolia that the longing in their hearts for truth will be satisfied with the knowledge of Jesus Christ.

Prayer Points

- Pray that the young people who thirst for answers that Buddhism cannot provide will be introduced to Jesus Christ in a culturally sensitive manner. Ask God to replace their hunger for material riches with a hunger for Him.

⌣· Pray that young believers will become mature in their faith and be able to discern truth from error.

⌣· Pray for the economy of this nation and for the salvation of its leaders.

⌣· Pray that Christian aid programs will be carefully implemented for the maximum benefit of the children who are malnourished.

⌣· Pray for legislation that will protect women and children from abuse. Ask God to heal and protect these victims of abuse from suffering further pain.

Quick Reference

Ethnic Breakdown: Mongol 90%, Kazakh 4%, other 6%
Type of Government: Multiparty republic
Economy: Services 43%, Agriculture 33%, Industry 24%
Per capita income: U.S.$310
National debt: U.S.$715 billion
Economic conditions: Extremely poor

Education
Quality of education: There is a severe shortage of schools and teachers. The government has been unable to keep pace with the educational needs.
Gender discrimination against girls: No

Religion
Religious concerns: Evangelism is restricted. The government has imposed limits on proselytizing, and bureaucratic harassment of groups that seek to register hinders free practice of religion.
Status of the church: There are very few Christians in the country. The need for discipleship and leadership training is great.
Are Christians being persecuted? Yes. Conversion to Christianity is discouraged, and converts may be detained and/or harassed.

Societal Viewpoint Toward Children
Are they viewed as precious? Yes
Are there street children? There are between 400 and 2,000 street children.
Is there a large population of orphans? There are some orphans. The government does not have the resources to improve the welfare of children. Nongovernmental organizations continue to assist orphaned and deserted children.
Are there child soldiers? No specific data available.
Is child labor a problem? There are some instances of forced labor. Children may be kept out of school to work. There is evidence that Mongolian children work in the sex trade in Asia and Eastern Europe.

Morocco

Major Languages: Arabic, Berber dialects, French
Total Population: 30,122,000
Population 0–34: 21,675,000
Life Expectancy: 67 years
Religion: Muslim 99.85%, Christian 0.10%, Jewish 0.05%
Literacy Rate: male 57%, female 31%

*C*hildren lie randomly on piles of fishing nets and cartons in the wholesale market. A few sleep in the doorways of nearby shops. Dirty and cold, they don't seem to mind that the morning air brings a heavy settling of moisture. A closer look reveals that the children are all boys. Although it is difficult to determine their age, they appear to be between 2 and 18 years of age.

Aman walks among the children and takes note of each one. Some he recognizes but not all. New faces show up every day along the wharf, and he tries to make room for them in his refuge. As a psychologist, he has been assigned to try to get the children off the street—a responsibility he was given after the Moroccan government, in a joint effort with the United Nations, published a report in 1995 about the increasing problem of street children and child prostitution in Casablanca.

The children are a part of Morocco's growing sex trade. Those lying about the streets represent only a small fraction of the number who actually work in the brothels. Girls usually live in rooming houses, six or more to a small room, where they await "clients." Aman works with these children day in and day out to get them out of harm's way. He talks candidly about the difficulty of winning the children's trust. "About 1,000 children live on the streets of Casablanca. They will lie and run away because they believe we will put them in jail, but that is not our purpose. We offer a sports program, educational workshops, and meals.

We make only two conditions for the children—no glue sniffing and no quarreling." Aman's program makes some effort to reunite the children with their families, and he tries to get them to go to school.

"We don't meet with a lot of success, but we try to reach the boys before they find favor with foreigners who, once they spot them, clean them up, dress them neatly, and usually keep them for the rest of their stay. Gulf Arabs and Westerners will pay between $115 and $172 to be with the children."

The street children, unaware of the dangers of STDs and AIDS, believe that antibiotics can cure AIDS. Some 48 percent of the street boys Aman knows have been sexually abused, often by the older boys on the street, tramps, or men working as "guards" for cars left in the streets and parking garages. In return for sexual favors, guards often allow boys to sleep on the streets without being harassed or detained.

Aman is not a Christian but a Muslim. His work with the children is done as a Muslim and as a psychologist and offers no way for the children to change their lives from the inside out. The number of street children may be growing in Morocco, but workers who are there to reach out to those children are very few.

M oroccan law allows for the prosecution of adults having sex with children, but shame and fear of not being believed deter most youngsters from reporting that they have been raped or otherwise abused. It is often a small step for a child, after being abused, to turn to prostitution to earn a living and pay for the prevalent habit of glue sniffing. The children will do almost anything for glue, which costs around 20 dirhams (U.S.$2.30).

Morocco provides free elementary and high school education. Attendance is especially low in rural areas, which lack teachers and schools. Education for girls is not a priority. In addition, many boys stay at home to help their families farm the land.

In recent years Christian TV stations, such as SAT-7, have broadcast programs in Arabic into Morocco. These children's programs are very successful.

Prayer Points

- ⌣· Pray for God's protection over the many street children who are being physically and sexually abused.
- ⌣· Pray for Christian workers to minister to these children with programs that will impact their lives to know Christ and become a vital part of society.

- ⌣· Pray for an end to the sex trade and child prostitution in Morocco.
- ⌣· Pray for the healing of the more than 40 percent of the population under age 15 who are sick with malaria, typhoid, trachoma, tuberculosis, and gastrointestinal infections.
- ⌣· Pray for the plight of children with disabilities in Morocco, for Christian ministers to work with them and tell them of the love of Jesus.
- ⌣· Pray for Moroccan leaders to have hearts softened to the needs of the children.
- ⌣· Pray for Christian organizations that work specifically with children to have divine wisdom on how to reach them through television and radio programming.
- ⌣· Pray for stability in the political, economic, and educational struggles in the country.
- ⌣· Pray that Morocco would withdraw from the country of Western Sahara (which they hold illegally) and that the Sahrawi families living in refugee camps in Algeria would return to their homeland.
- ⌣· Pray for the government to allow the people of Western Sahara the right to vote for self-determination.

Quick Reference

Ethnic Breakdown: Arab and Berber 99.1%, Jewish 0.2%, other 0.7%
Type of Government: Constitutional monarchy
Economy: Agriculture 50%, Services 35%, Industry 15%
Per capita income: U.S.$1,110
National debt: U.S.$19.1 billion
Economic conditions: Poor

Education
Quality of education: There is a severe lack of schools and teachers. Children may be kept out of school for farming. Instruction includes mandatory Koranic curriculum.
Gender discrimination against girls: Many parents place less value on education for girls than for boys. Domestic chores take precedence over education.

Religion
Religious concerns: Evangelism is prohibited.
Status of the church: Nationals must worship underground.
Are Christians being persecuted? Yes. Those whose proselytizing activities become public face expulsion.

Societal Viewpoint Toward Children
Are they viewed as precious? No

Are there street children? A growing number of children are living on the streets in urban areas because of lax education laws, migration to the cities, and the lack of available jobs for parents.

Is there a large population of orphans? No specific data available.

Are there child soldiers? No specific data available.

Is child labor a problem? Children are routinely used in the labor force as house servants, in farming, and in handicrafts. Forced prostitution is prevalent, particularly in towns with military installations and large numbers of tourists.

Myanmar

Major Languages: Burmese, Shan, Karen
Total Population: 41,735,000
Population 0–34: 28,748,000
Life Expectancy: 63 years
Religion: Buddhist 82.90%, Christian 8.70%, Muslim 3.80%, Chinese 3.00%, traditional ethnic 0.80%, Hindu 0.50%, nonreligious/other 0.30%
Literacy Rate: male 80%, female 78%

Nazu and Sue Lee, both teenagers, help their respective parents in a small confectionary business that gives their families income to eke out a living on a daily basis. One December day the two girls walked into town to buy brown sugar. They took the path they had walked all their lives, but this time was different. Just before they reached the last bridge going into town, they met four soldiers dressed in civilian clothes. Nazu recognized one of the men as an army sergeant stationed near their village.

The soldier stepped in front of the girls and demanded, "Where are you going?"

Frightened, neither girl could answer. Both of them stood on the bridge, frozen.

The men laughed as the sergeant taunted the girls. "Well, if you don't know where you're going, then you can come with us."

The soldiers dragged them into the nearby forest and took turns raping them. Afterward the sergeant warned them not to tell anyone; otherwise they would kill them and their families.

As soon as they were released, Nazu and Sue Lee hurried back to their village to tell their parents and the village leaders. The parents arranged a meeting with the battalion commander to discuss the rape. The commander ordered his soldiers to line up and asked the two girls to point out the men who had raped them.

Not finding the four soldiers in the lineup, Nazu asked, "Are there any soldiers who are not here?"

"We do have other soldiers," the commander said, "but at the moment they are on duty in another part of the province." The angry commander lashed out at the girls. "You mean to tell me that you caused all this confusion and work and you can't even find your offenders? I believe you gave yourselves freely to the men you accuse, and now you try to blame it on them. I will not stand for this!" With that he slapped the girls and their parents and fined them, ordering them to pay the fines within three days or go to prison. The girls returned to their village, embarrassed and ashamed for what had taken place.

Is there justice? What happens when people have no rights and all the privileges of legal retribution belong to the elite? Is there anyone to stand in the gap and help those who have no one to speak up on their behalf? Let's pray Proverbs 31:8–9 for these precious children.

*M*yanmar is under the rule of one of the most barbaric military regimes ever to have existed. In an effort to stay in power, the regime continues to repress the country's ethnic minorities and prodemocracy groups. Human-rights abuses abound and include torture, imprisonment, arbitrary executions (particularly in the areas of ethnic tension), forced relocation, extortion, looting, destruction of villages and fields, and forced labor. The dictatorship spends over 50 percent of its national budget on the military.

The U.N. Human Rights Commission's reporter, Rajsoomer Lallah, in his report on Myanmar, stated that the worst violence committed by the military was against the ethnic minorities, which make up over 40 percent of Myanmar's population. In the states of Karen, Karenni, and Shan, up to one million people have been forced to leave their homes with only what they can carry. They live in relocation sites, where their freedom is severely limited. Over two million people have been internally displaced inside Myanmar, with over 400,000 in Karen and Karenni alone. They are hiding in the jungles, existing in a fragile and uncertain life, with temporary shelter, very little food, and virtually no medical care. Malaria, typhoid, dysentery, and malnutrition are widespread, particularly among the children. The situation is desperate.

A mother of three who fled her village and spent the next four years hiding in the jungle said, "My greatest fear was not the enemy but keeping my children healthy. I was terrified they would get malaria or dysentery. Finding food was very hard. We were often on the run. I fled carrying one child in my arms and one on my back."

God has a way out for these desperate people in this war-torn land. Christians are called to pray for the children and the youth in Myanmar and to believe for their deliverance.

Prayer Points

⌣· Pray for the resources needed to feed the 50 percent of Myanmar's children who are suffering from malnutrition.

⌣· Pray for a just and democratic government to replace the current military regime and rebuild the country with political and religious freedoms.

⌣· Pray for protection of the children against forced military service, rape, and prostitution, most often at the hands of those in the government.

⌣· Pray for a reformed health-care system that will provide service to all the people, not just to the elite.

⌣· Pray for an end to child prostitution.

⌣· Pray for an end to military conscription of children. Girl soldiers need protection, as they may be forced to be sex slaves for officers.

⌣· Pray for protection and courage for Christians to continue to evangelize and to disciple believers.

Quick Reference

Ethnic Breakdown: Burmese 55.8%, Burmese Shan 6.5%, Arakanese 4.2%, Sgaw Karen 3.5%, White Karen 3.3%, other 26.7%

Type of Government: Military regime

Economy: Agriculture 59%, Services 30%, Industry 11%

Per capita income: U.S.$1,790

National debt: U.S.$5.9 billion

Economic conditions: Poor

Education

Quality of education: Education beyond elementary school is available only in the larger towns and cities. Despite a compulsory education law, almost 50 percent of children never enroll in school, and only 40 percent of them complete the five-year primary school course.

Gender discrimination against girls: Domestic chores may take precedence over education. Girls may marry young.

Religion

Religious concerns: Evangelism is prohibited.

Status of the church: The growing group of believers in the country need discipleship and leadership training.

Are Christians being persecuted? Yes

Societal Viewpoint Toward Children

Are they viewed as precious? No

Are there street children? Yes

Is there a large population of orphans? Yes

Are there child soldiers? Yes. Myanmar has one of the highest numbers of child soldiers of any country in the world. Young girls recruited as child soldiers may
end up as sex slaves for their officers.

Is child labor a problem? Yes. Tens of thousands of other children are forced to
work for the military as porters, servants, and even minesweepers. Child
prostitution and the trafficking of girls for the purpose of forced prostitution
are problems.

Nepal

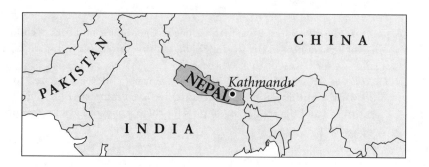

Major Languages: Nepali, Tibetan, Hindi
Total Population: 24,702,000
Population 0–34: 18,593,000
Life Expectancy: 58 years
Religion: Hindu 74.82%, Buddhist 16.00%, Muslim 5.00%, Christian 1.89%,
   other religions 1.70%, nonreligious/other 0.50%, Sikh 0.06%, Baha'i 0.03%
Literacy Rate: male 63%, female 28%

A medical team traveled to Nepal to set up an outreach in a city near Kathmandu. A Hindu priest brought his five-year-old daughter, who had been paralyzed on her right side for over three months, to the clinic. After the doctor examined her, he said to her father, "There is nothing we can do for your daughter, but we serve a God who does miracles. He healed people in the past when they believed in him and prayed. Will you allow us to pray for your daughter and ask Jesus to heal her?"

Reluctantly the father agreed and stood nearby as the team gathered around the child, laid hands on her, and prayed in unison for the healing power of Jesus Christ to make her whole. After praying, the team members stood back and watched to see what would happen. The little girl sat up, and the doctor lifted her off the examination table and gently placed her tiny feet on the floor. Immediately the girl began to walk across the room.

The father covered his mouth and began to cry. "I should know this Jesus who healed my daughter."

The doctor then led the Hindu priest in a prayer of repentance and acceptance of Jesus Christ, and the team rejoiced about the healing of the child and the gift of salvation that was given to her father.

*I*lliteracy is a major problem in Nepal. Only 63 percent of the men and 28 percent of the women are able to read. Schools are few, and poorer families often do not see the value of sending their children to receive an education.

A girl may be considered a burden to her family. She is literally a guest in her father's home until she marries, and then she becomes a guest in her husband's home. This attitude, along with the fact that young girls often marry older men, gives rise to the continuing domestic violence within the country. Violence within the home is considered a private matter and will not be interfered with by local authorities.

Nepal has one of the highest percentages of child prostitution in the world. It is not uncommon for an impoverished family to sell a daughter into prostitution so that the other family members may enjoy a few more months of food or a new television set. Once she is sold, the girl could end up in a brothel in India, only to be released when her owners find she is infected with an STD or AIDS. There is no returning home for these young women because of the stigma attached to their profession. It has been estimated that over 200,000 women have already been sold into slavery in India, and at least half of them have contracted AIDS.

Very little medical treatment is available for those with AIDS or other diseases. Goiter, a disease associated with iodine deficiency, is endemic in certain villages in the hills and mountains. In most villages more than half of the population has goiter, and the incidence of deafness and mental retardation is high. Leprosy and malnutrition are serious problems, especially in the rural areas.

According to a recent UNICEF report, child brides are common, with 40 percent of all marriages consummated when girls are under the age of 14. If a girl from a poor home is not forced into an early marriage, she may be sold to a businessman who purchases children for bonded labor. Her family will give her as collateral for a loan, and when the lender calculates interest on the loan, the girl never makes enough to repay the debt. An estimated 40,000 children work as bondservants in Nepal.

Even with all of Nepal's societal issues, the gospel is spreading throughout the land faster than was dreamed possible. Recent estimates put the number of Christians around 400,000, and press reports indicate that 170 Christian churches operate in Kathmandu alone. The door has cracked open for Nepal.

Prayer Points

- Pray for economic stability in Nepal so that the standard of life for children will be improved.

꙳· Pray for Nepal, the only officially Hindu kingdom, to see the kingdom of Jesus Christ through its youth.
꙳· Pray for an end to the chronic problem of malnutrition. An estimated 50 percent of children die before age five.
꙳· Pray for God to use Christian organizations to teach the Nepali people to improve food production, literacy, and medical standards.
꙳· Pray for God to help each girl understand that He values and loves her.
꙳· Pray for an end to child prostitution in Nepal.
꙳· Pray for the protection of girls as young as six who are being raped and forced into incestuous sexual acts. Pray for God to heal their emotions and that they will know the pure love of Jesus Christ.
꙳· Pray for the protection of young believers in Nepal from cults that are targeting them.
꙳· Pray for church plants geared toward the Nepali youth culture.

Quick Reference

Ethnic Breakdown: Nepalese 55.7%, Maitili 10.8%, Bhojpuri Bihari 7.8%, Newar 2.9%, Awahi 2.6%, other 20.2%
Type of Government: Constitutional monarchy with bicameral parliament
Economy: Agriculture 41%, Services 37%, Industry 22%
Per capita income: U.S.$200
National debt: U.S.$2.4 billion
Economic conditions: Extremely poor

Education
Quality of education: Although education is not compulsory, the government provides free primary education for all children between the ages of 6 and 12, but many families cannot afford school supplies or clothing.
Gender discrimination against girls: Not much importance is placed on education for girls.

Religion
Religious concerns: Evangelism is restricted.
Status of the church: Christian churches are few but growing.
Are Christians being persecuted? No

Societal Viewpoint Toward Children
Are they viewed as precious? No
Are there street children? No specific data available.
Is there a large population of orphans? No specific data available.
Are there child soldiers? No specific data available.
Is child labor a problem? An estimated 40,000 children work as bonded laborers. Forced prostitution and trafficking of young girls remain serious problems.

Niger

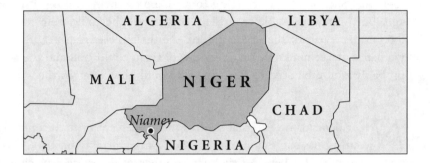

Major Languages: French, Hausa, Djerma
Total Population: 10,076,000
Population 0–34: 8,061,000
Life Expectancy: 41 years
Religion: Muslim 97.59%, traditional ethnic 2.00%, Christian 0.40%,
  Baha'i 0.01%
Literacy Rate: male 21%, female 7%

*R*ays of hot sun streaked through the tall oak tree, providing small patches of shade for the bleak playground. Children played games of tag while a group of boys kicked a ball fashioned from old rags. A woman stood at the door of a building made of sticks and bamboo and rang a bell, and the children scurried into their classroom.

The dark classroom was packed with about 30 children who looked like third graders. There were no textbooks, no visual aids, no paper, and not one student had the usual crudely made black slate so common in rural African schools. The teacher walked around the room with a doubled-up piece of wire, which she frequently pointed at a talking student. This was a nongovernmental school in Niger.

Fatima, a 10-year-old girl, knows this is her last chance to learn. Her family is Muslim, and she will be taken out of school once she becomes old enough to marry, possibly within the next two years. Even knowing this, she feels blessed because she can read and write when only 7 percent of the girls in Niger are literate. She will most likely marry an older man, have children, tend the household, and work in the fields.

The future looks dismal for Fatima, but there is some hope for her because she is being given an opportunity that millions of other children in the country do not have—she is going to school.

One day a woman came to her village and asked people if they would like to know about Jesus Christ. She handed out pamphlets, and Fatima took one. She found it interesting to read about a man who lived so long ago, but no one was able to explain to her how he could help her find food or get a pair of shoes. Many took the little pieces of paper from the woman, but Fatima knew that very few of them could read and the paper probably would be used to start fires or would blow away in the wind.

Niger depends on external sources for 50 percent of its income. The country has some uranium and other minerals, but in the 1980s a severe famine and collapse of the uranium market devastated the country. The economy has never recovered, and the economic future appears bleak. Most of the people are subsistence farmers, small traders, or herders. About 40 percent of Niger's 10 million people now face famine because of poor harvests.

Niger is open to the gospel, yet church growth has been slow. This could be due to lack of fellowship between churches, failure to coordinate projects, and lack of mature leaders. The country is 98 percent Muslim, with Islamic beliefs sometimes mixed with animistic rituals.

Niger's health-care system is severely inadequate. About half of the population has no access to doctors or hospitals. Each year many people die from parasites and malaria. Iodine deficiency and the subsequent occurrence of goiter create a high risk factor. The situation is so severe that a child 10 years old has already lived a fourth of his or her life.

The children of Niger face a dismal future with no hope to better themselves. They need schools and simple dispensaries, and their parents need jobs. We must pray for their government to clearly understand that children are the future of the country and must be educated.

Prayer Points

⌐· Pray for God to protect young girls, who may potentially enter into marriage between the ages of 12 and 14. Pray for God to assure them of His love.

⌐· Pray for additional Christian schools in Niger so that children can be educated and hear the good news.

⌐· Pray that students attending Islamic University near Naimey will be reached with the gospel.

⌐· Pray for God to raise up churches that will develop strategic partnerships to reach children, teens, and young adults.

⌣· Pray for the church to put aside personal differences and work together in unity to reach their country.

⌣· Pray for legislation that will make all forms of FGM illegal.

⌣· Pray for God to use Christian organizations to improve availability of medical services.

⌣· Pray for God to protect physically abused women and convict their husbands of the physical and psychological harm they are causing their wives.

Quick Reference

Ethnic Breakdown: Hausa 56%, Djerma 22%, Fula 8.5%, Tuareg 8%, Beri (Kanouri) 4.3%, Arab, Toubou, and Gourmantche 1.2%

Type of Government: Republic

Economy: Services 42%, Agriculture 40%, Industry 18%

Per capita income: U.S.$220

National debt: U.S.$1.3 billion

Economic conditions: Extremely poor

Education

Quality of education: There is a severe shortage of schools and teachers. Instruction includes mandatory Koranic curriculum.

Gender discrimination against girls: Yes. Only about 40 percent of those who finish primary schools are girls.

Religion

Religious concerns: Evangelism is restricted.

Status of the church: The church needs discipleship and leadership training.

Are Christians being persecuted? No, but there is some intolerance and harassment.

Societal Viewpoint Toward Children

Are they viewed as precious? Yes, but boys are valued more than girls.

Are there street children? Yes

Is there a large population of orphans? No specific data available.

Are there child soldiers? No specific data available.

Is child labor a problem? Rural children regularly work with their families from a very early age.

Nigeria

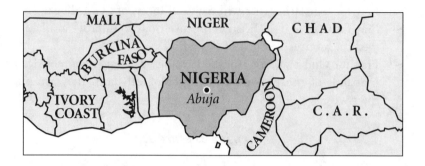

Major Languages: English, Hausa, Yoruba
Total Population: 123,338,000
Population 0–34: 95,748,000
Life Expectancy: 52 years
Religion: Christian 52.61%, Muslim 41.00%, traditional ethnic 5.99%, nonreligious/other 0.40%
Literacy Rate: male 67%, female 47%

C rystal entered the compound and asked where the baby was. A child about 10 years old directed her to one of the huts. As she entered the dark room, Crystal saw a lifeless form lying on the floor. The small body looked like a worn-out rag doll. An older woman knelt beside the child. She waved her hand to chase away the flies, which were quickly replaced by another horde that descended on the child's face. The baby's short, shallow breathing told Crystal that soon the infant would be another AIDS statistic.

"How old is he?" Crystal asked. During her year in Nigeria as a nurse, she had been by the side of many who, like the child who lay before her now, came to an untimely death.

The old woman shrugged her shoulders and muttered that he was a year old, maybe older.

"He looks like he could be four months old at the very most," Crystal commented. "How many people in your family have died of AIDS?" she asked.

"Both of his parents are dead. His mother was my daughter, and when she got sick, she came back here to die. He was born while she was dying. It's a shame that so many are dead. So many." She shook her head in disbelief.

The child's big eyes opened and fixed on Crystal. Too weak to move, he seemed not to mind the flies or the putrid smell that came from the pot boiling on a small charcoal burner positioned in the corner of the hut. Brown liquid bubbled and sent up a cloud of steam that made its way to the thatched roof and collected in drops of moisture that fell on him. The extreme heat, the smell, and the humidity made the small living area almost unbearable.

"What is that?" Crystal asked, pointing to the pan.

The woman nodded toward the boiling pot. "Keeps away evil spirits. They come with the disease my daughter brought to us. We must chase them away."

Crystal sat on the floor and picked up the child's limp body. Since he had only a few moments left to live, she wanted him to have one person in this world hold him close and tell him that God loved him. That was the least she could do.

The grandmother sat on her haunches and stared out the door at the bright sunlight. "Many, many die." She shook her head. "They die so sick, unable to eat, and with a bad cough. It's a bad, evil spirit. The medicine doctor cannot help. He tells me to boil the roots, but they do not help. You cannot help. All of our young people die. We have no parents for so many children. I am an old woman, yet I must keep many children because they have no parents. It is a sad day in our country."

"You are right, Mama," Crystal said affectionately to the old woman. She held the child close and rocked back and forth, offering what little comfort she could in his final moments. "But there are things we can do. We can tell the people of this country there is hope. We can tell them about Jesus Christ, and we can tell them how to prevent the disease. These people don't have to die."

Carefully she laid the baby back on the mat. No longer was life left in his small frail body. Without showing any emotion, the grandmother took a cloth and began to wrap him for burial.

*T*he mortality rate for children in Nigeria is high, with almost one in every five children dying before the age of five. AIDS is one of the culprits. As of 2000, more than 20 million people have died of AIDS worldwide since the epidemic began. AIDS is considered to be the leading cause of death in Africa. In 1999 it was estimated that 5.4 percent of Nigerians (2.6 million people) were infected with AIDS. The child Crystal held is only one of the 1.4 million Nigerian children who have lost one or both of their parents to AIDS.

Primary education is compulsory but not enforced, and many times children leave school to work. There is a lack of infrastructure to provide adequate schools. Girls are often encouraged to stay home and help with chores.

One ray of hope is that the newly elected president is a Christian. Pray that he will be able to unify Nigeria and build a stable government (the country has had six coups in the past 20 years).

Prayer Points

⌐· Pray for the children, teens, and young adults who are infected with the AIDS virus. As you read this, hundreds are dying of AIDS.

⌐· Pray that God will spare the lives of AIDS victims so that they will have an opportunity to hear and respond to the gospel.

⌐· Pray that the government will launch an extensive campaign to educate its people on prevention measures against AIDS.

⌐· Pray that President Olusegun Obasanjo, who professes to be a Christian, will be used by God to impact this nation.

⌐· Pray for political stability for the sake of children, teens, and young adults.

⌐· Pray for creative outreaches to impact the lives of the young people with the gospel.

⌐· Pray that God will raise up young Christian leaders who will not seek power for themselves but will be used by Him to impact their nation in extraordinary ways.

⌐· Pray that God will give this generation creative ideas in business, education, and health care so that they will be freed from abject poverty.

⌐· Pray that God will show the leaders that the minds of their young people are national treasures so that they will make education a high priority.

Quick Reference

Ethnic Breakdown: Hausa and Fulani 29%, Yoruba 21%, Ibo 18%, Ijaw 10%, Kanuri 4%, Ibibio 3.5%, Tiv 2.5%, other 12%

Type of Government: Elected civilian government

Economy: Agriculture 54%, Services 40%, Industry 6%

Per capita income: U.S.$260

National debt: U.S.$29 billion

Economic conditions: Extremely poor

Education

Quality of education: There is a shortage of teachers. Enrollment has declined because of continuing deterioration of public schools and increased economic pressures on families.

Gender discrimination against girls: A girl may be kept home to help with chores and tend younger siblings. She may also marry young.

Religion

Religious concerns: Evangelism is restricted.

Status of the church: The Nigerian church has experienced rapid growth, which has greatly accelerated over the past 15 years. Nigeria has become one of the major missionary-sending countries of the developing world.

Are Christians being persecuted? Yes

Societal Viewpoint Toward Children

Are they viewed as precious? Yes

Are there street children? The number of street children in Lagos in 1994 was 15,000.

Is there a large population of orphans? Yes

Are there child soldiers? Yes

Is child labor a problem? Children are routinely used in the labor force to supplement family incomes. Children are reportedly sold into forced labor or into prostitution.

North Korea

Major Languages: Korean, Chinese, Russian
Total Population: 21,688,000
Population 0–34: 13,026,000
Life Expectancy: 71 years
Religion: nonreligious 64.31%, traditional ethnic 16.00%, Chondogyo 13.50%, Buddhist, 4.50%, Christian 1.69%
Literacy Rate: male 96%, female 94%

In 1948, when Korea was divided into two countries, Communist authorities set about to rid North Korea of the practice of religion. Young Mee was a first grader when the war ended and was surprised when a new teacher took over her class.

The new teacher seemed kind and challenged the class of 30 children to play a new game. "Today, boys and girls, we are going to play a game, and the winner will receive a wonderful prize." Everyone sat mesmerized as the teacher described what they were to do to win the "prize." It was simple. That day they were to go home and look for a book that their parents might have. The search was to be a secret, and not even their parents were to know about the game.

Having never received a prize before, Young Mee could hardly wait until her parents read a bedtime story to her from the black book so that she could find out where it was hidden. That night after her parents had gone to bed, she slipped into the kitchen and found the book behind a loose brick near the oven. Carefully she took the book from its hiding place and put it with her schoolbooks. The next day she eagerly presented the book to her teacher. Young Mee, along with 14 others who had played the game successfully, received royal treatment at school. For their prize each one received a special red scarf. Young Mee's parents had not allowed her to join the club that had given out the red scarves, so she knew her parents would be especially proud that she had received the prize without becoming a member. She hurried home from school to an empty house. Her parents, who had always been there, did not come home that night; nor were they there the next morning when she awakened. Before she had a chance to ready herself for school, some men came, packed her belongings, and took her to a communal home for children.

Forty years later Young Mee attended a house church and found the secret of the black book. She accepted Jesus Christ into her heart. Imagine her surprise as she discovered that her parents were in heaven waiting for her—she would see them again.

Young Mee's story is not unique. Communist authorities have used many children like her to spy on their parents and grandparents.

*C*hildren in North Korea are starving. The number of those dying is hard to confirm. American and South Korean officials have estimated that 2 million to 3 million people have starved to death, while North Korea estimates that only 220,000 have died from starvation. Since North Korea is isolated from the rest of the world, it is difficult for relief agencies, which are often denied access into the country, to make accurate assessments.

Reports of cannibalism, emaciated babies, and people foraging for grass and bark continue to reach the outside world. People have eaten dogs, cats, and even rats in their attempts to survive. The country's deepening economic slide has been fueled by acute energy shortages, poorly maintained and aging industrial facilities, and a lack of new investments. The agricultural outlook, though slightly improved over previous years, remains weak. The combined effects of serious fertilizer shortages, successive natural disasters, and physical limitations—such as a lack of arable land and a short growing season—have reduced staple grain output to more than one million tons less than what the country needs to meet even minimum international requirements. The small amounts of international food aid have been critical in supplementing the population's basic food needs. The impact of other forms of humanitarian assistance, such as medical supplies and agricultural help, has been largely limited to local areas. Even with aid, malnutrition rates are among the world's highest as a direct result of starvation and famine-related diseases.

Over the past five years North Korea has suffered a series of droughts, floods, tidal waves, and other natural disasters. Many of its citizens flee to China in search of food and some security. If captured, they are sent back to North Korea, where they are killed. The Chinese government will prosecute any Chinese caught harboring a North Korean.

Prayer Points

⌣· Pray for all the children tricked by the government into turning their Christian parents over to the authorities to be reached with the gospel.
⌣· Pray for God's protection for the Christians of North Korea.
⌣· Pray that all will hear and receive the gospel.
⌣· Pray for strategies to reach children, teens, and young adults with the gospel.
⌣· Pray that God will send food to feed the starving children.
⌣· Pray that the dictatorial stranglehold the Communist party has on North Korea will be broken.
⌣· Pray that God will use the current famine to persuade the government to allow Christian relief workers to enter the country.
⌣· Pray for God to raise up Joshuas and Calebs to impact this country.
⌣· Pray for the Communist leader of North Korea, Kim Chong-Il, that his deception and hardness of heart will be removed and that he will make decisions in the best interest of the people.

Quick Reference

Ethnic Breakdown: Korean 99%, Han Chinese 0.07%, other 0.93%
Type of Government: Democratic People's Republic of Korea
Economy: Mining and Manufacturing 60%, Agriculture 25%, Services and other 15%
Per capita income: U.S.$949
National debt: U.S.$12 billion
Economic conditions: Extremely poor

Education
Quality of education: Well-organized school system.
Gender discrimination against girls: No

Religion
Religious concerns: Evangelism is prohibited. The official religion is the cult of Kim Il-Sung, the father of the present leader.
Status of the church: Numerous underground house churches. The church needs discipleship and training.
Are Christians being persecuted? Yes, Christians suffer and are killed, but their number is growing despite the persecution.

Societal Viewpoint Toward Children
Are they viewed as precious? Yes.
Are there street children? No specific data available.
Is there a large population of orphans? No specific data available.
Are there child soldiers? Initial draft registration is at age 14, and preinduction physicals take place at age 16.
Is child labor a problem? No specific data available.

Oman

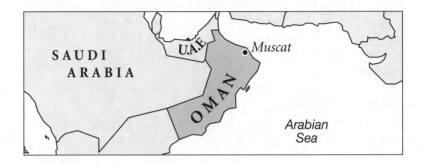

Major Languages: Arabic, English, Baluchi
Total Population: 2,533,000
Population 0–34: 1,826,000
Life Expectancy: 72 years
Religion: Muslim 92.66%, Hindu 3.00%, Christian 2.54%, Buddhist 1.20%, nonreligious/other 0.40%, Baha'i 0.20%
Literacy Rate: male 79%, female 57%

*I*t was an exciting day, like none other she had experienced. Nadia gave specific instructions to each of the servants, then opened the box that held the beautiful cake she had purchased at the European bakery for her daughter's birthday. Carefully she placed 18 candles on top of the elaborately decorated cake. Nadia had every reason to be proud of her daughter. Kabbi had just received top academic honors in high school and next fall would start her university studies. It was a bittersweet time as this would most likely be their last summer together as a family. The following summers would be filled with travel.

"Where is she?" Kabbi's father, Omar, asked. Nadia knew Kabbi was his favorite of their three daughters. He had even purchased a new car for her birthday, but Kabbi didn't know.

"I think she's in the front room talking with her friend Rima," Nadia answered. "Rima just returned from Paris today."

Omar's face looked troubled. "Nadia, you know I don't like her associating with Rima. She's too Western—too loose. She has such an eye for boys."

"Kabbi is a smart girl. She will keep our ways. Don't worry so much. Besides, Kabbi and Rima have been friends since they were children." She waved her hand at her husband and turned back to the cake.

Kabbi was delighted with her father's present. "Oh, Father, the car is awesome!" she exclaimed. "Let me take it for a ride," she pleaded.

Later Nadia would remember the night of her daughter's 18th birthday with sadness and tears. Kabbi and Rima sneaked out of the house that night after everyone was in bed and drove into town. Rima had convinced Kabbi that they would not get caught. There was a knock on the door in the early hours. The police had caught Rima and Kabbi with two boys, kissing. Both families were upset, but Kabbi's father had been beside himself.

Nadia listened as Kabbi pleaded with her father. "Father, I'm so sorry. Please forgive me," she cried over and over.

Omar would have none of her begging. He was a man of little patience, and Nadia knew he had reached his limit. Kabbi had dishonored him, and she would have to pay. Nadia never thought she would live to see the day when Omar would hate this child as much as he had loved her.

Nadia tried to comfort her daughter, but she herself was distraught, not knowing what Omar would do. Kabbi had sobbed, "Father loves me. He won't harm me, will he, Mother?"

In the end her death was simple. Omar had Kabbi drowned in the swimming pool. He stood over her lifeless body and made his final pronouncement. "For dishonoring me and your family, I sentence you to death." He walked away and never mentioned Kabbi's name again.

H onor killings, like that of Kabbi, are an accepted practice in Oman. Any actions that indicate that a girl has compromised her father's values receive severe reprimands from him or her family.

Prior to 1970 no schools existed for girls. The most recent figures available from the Ministry of Education report an enrollment rate nearing 90 percent for all girls eligible for elementary school. Women are now allowed to enter college and obtain degrees in areas closed to them in the past. Although the educational scene looks promising, even a well-educated girl is expected to follow strict Muslim rules of behavior when it comes to submission to her father or husband.

The government of Oman anticipates that its rich oil reserves will be depleted around 2014 and is looking to develop a thriving tourist trade to replace the export of oil. This redirection of the country's economic priorities could provide an open door for the gospel to enter the country. It is estimated that the Christian population consists almost entirely of foreign workers, with perhaps no more than 20 indigenous believers.

Prayer Points

‿• Pray for an end to the practice of honor killings.

- Pray that the Lord will give Christians powerful strategies to reach children, teens, and young adults.
- Pray for Christian radio and TV programming to impact youth with the gospel.
- Pray that the Lord will remove the spirit of witchcraft that hovers over the entire area.
- Pray that sexual immorality will be removed, including at the highest level of authority.
- Pray that strict enforcement by the newly formed Ministry of Religious Affairs prohibiting evangelism will be loosened. Such prohibition could seriously hinder the freedom and movement of Christian churches in Oman.
- Praise God for the newly formed House of Prayer that has been established in the country.
- Pray that God will bless the gathering of church congregations for prayer, praise, and worship and that He will be glorified in these meetings.

Quick Reference

Ethnic Breakdown: Omani Arab 48.1%, Southern Baluch 15.0 %, Bengali 4.4%, Gulf Arab 3.2%, Persian 2.8%, other 26.5%
Type of Government: Monarchy
Economy: Services 57%, Industry 40%, Agriculture 3%
Per capita income: U.S.$4,820
National debt: U.S.$4.8 billion
Economic conditions: Thriving economy

Education
Quality of education: School system is well organized.
Gender discrimination against girls: Yes

Religion
Religious concerns: Evangelism is prohibited.
Status of the church: The estimated 20 indigenous Omani believers must worship underground. There is a need for discipleship and leadership training.
Are Christians being persecuted? No, because there is little or no witness.

Societal Viewpoint Toward Children
Are they viewed as precious? Yes.
Are there street children? No specific data available.
Is there a large population of orphans? No
Are there child soldiers? No
Is child labor a problem? There are no reports of child labor.

Pakistan

Major Languages: Punjabi, Sindhi, Urdu
Total Population: 141,554,000
Population 0–34: 106,254,000
Life Expectancy: 63 years
Religion: Muslim 96.08%, Christian 2.31%, Hindu 1.50%, Baha'i 0.06%,
    other 0.03%, traditional ethnic 0.02%
Literacy Rate: male 50%, female 24%

One 16-year-old wife found herself in a traditional marriage, only to learn that her in-laws were not satisfied with her modest dowry. They insisted she go back to her family and demand a TV and a VCR. Because she knew that her family had no funds for this outrageous request, she sold her wedding jewelry and purchased the items, but soon there were other requests she could not meet. Since divorce is not an option in Pakistan, her in-laws attempted to kill her. One night her mother-in-law poured gasoline over her, and she awoke just in time to see her husband strike the match. She was badly burned over her entire body. They took her to a hospital, where she later died—but not before she had told her story. This young girl had no place to turn, no one to take her in, no one to console her throughout her terrible ordeal. Even the neighbors who heard her screams dismissed them as the cries from another commonplace beating. The police dismissed the case, and the girl's in-laws were free to find another bride for their out-of-work son.

Dowry burnings are virtually ignored by the country's legal and religious authorities. Newlywed young women whose dowries are considered insufficient, despite prenuptial agreements, are burned to death by their husbands or in-laws when their families are unable to contribute more. During a 10-month period in 1991, 2,000 women under the age of 25 died in such cases. Other killings may have gone unreported. The relative of one badly burned woman told hospital authorities, "We didn't report it to the police because we didn't want to create a scandal. Anyway, if she survives, she will have to go back to her husband. It will be bad enough for her as it is."

Reports of persecution and human-rights violations against Christians, women, and children leak out of Pakistan at an alarming rate considering the majority are censored or unreported because the acts are regarded as private in nature. Christians and other minority religious groups have no legal redress in the Pakistani courts, and their testimony counts for only half that of a Muslim. They are not allowed to file charges, even in cases of theft, rape, or murder.

On October 12, 2000, a military coup led by General Pervez Musharraf caused grave concern among human-rights groups. Musharraf signed a constitutional amendment establishing Islam as the sole, supreme religion of the country, subjugating all other religions to the laws of Islam according to the Koran. Many leaders see this act as a death warrant for the religious minorities of Pakistan and believe that Pakistan could very well witness the same unrest and violence as Indonesia, where Islamic forces are demanding a stricter enforcement of the Koran.

The economy of Pakistan is plagued with problems—prostitution, child labor, and lack of opportunities for the youth of the country. The number of heroin addicts in the larger cities is growing, creating an entire subculture of children without the basic necessities who may be used for begging and child labor. It is reported that because so many children work, the carpet and brick industries would collapse if those under the age of six were taken home.

Women are under the strict supervision of their nearest male relative, and when a young woman marries, her first cousins are given priority as marriage partner candidates. If the woman has no marriageable relative, her family, to keep the dowry money, may hold a wedding for her without a groom.

Who will go? Who will pray for these children and women? What price will the children and young people of Pakistan have to pay before Christians rise to the level of intercession that says, "Enough is enough!" God wants us to take our place in prayer. An army of laborers is needed to help the marginalized in Pakistan, a nation at the crossroads.

Prayer Points

- Pray for children who suffer from severe abuse. Pray that they will be able to forgive their offenders. Pray for the offenders that they will stop abusing children.

⌣• Pray for children who begin working as young as age four in the carpet and brick industries that they might be able to enjoy their childhood. Children who work in these dangerous jobs often have developmental problems because of malformed and crippled hands.

⌣• Pray for the hundreds of children, mostly girls, who are rejected by their parents and left on the doorsteps of relief agencies.

⌣• Pray for those who are persecuted and are victims of outrageous human-rights violations, especially the children and young women.

⌣• Pray that parents who abandon their babies in garbage dumps will realize the sin they are committing against their children and God. Pray that those who destroy their children through horrific, ungodly abuse will repent and receive God's mercy.

⌣• Pray that businesses that hire young children will be publicly exposed.

⌣• Pray for an end to dowry burnings and murders. A dowry burning usually ends in the death of the young woman. Pray that the perpetrators will be prosecuted and convicted of this hideous crime and punished.

Quick Reference

Ethnic Breakdown: Punjabi 61%, Sindhi 12%, Urdu 9%, Baloch 3%, Northern Tribes 2%, Tribal People of Sindh 1%, Patan 10%, Hunza 0.5%, Dravidian 0.74%, Tibetan 0.34%, Turkic 0.1%, other 0.32%

Type of Government: Military

Economy: Agriculture 44%, Services 30%, Industry 26%

Per capita income: U.S.$441

National debt: U.S.$32 billion

Economic conditions: Extremely poor

Education

Quality of education: For the general population, education has little or no value. Instruction includes mandatory Koranic curriculum.

Gender discrimination against girls: Not much importance is placed on education for girls. Girls may be removed from school at puberty to minimize contact with males.

Religion

Religious concerns: Evangelism is prohibited.

Status of the church: There are a small number of committed believers. The conversion of a Muslim to Christianity is punishable by death. Christians need leadership and discipleship training.

Are Christians being persecuted? Yes

Societal Viewpoint Toward Children

Are they viewed as precious? No

Are there street children? Because of the growing drug problem, the number of street children has increased.

Is there a large population of orphans? This is a growing problem as AIDS becomes more prevalent.

Are there child soldiers? No specific data available.

Is child labor a problem? The labor force is dependent on children.

Qatar

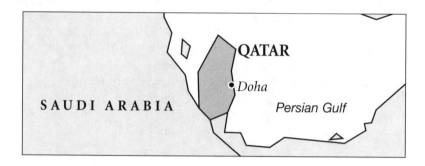

Major Languages: Arabic, English
Total Population: 744,000
Population 0–34: 419,076
Life Expectancy: 73 years
Religion: Muslim 79.43%, Christian 10.47%, Hindu 7.20%, Buddhist 1.80%,
    nonreligious/other 0.90%, Baha'i 0.20%
Literacy Rate: male 84%, female 81%

"Mother, look what I found!" Six-year-old Omar proudly produced a small picture of the Ayatollah Khomeini. Ghazi took the picture and studied it carefully.

"What is it?" the boy asked.

"It's a picture of a famous holy man in Islam, my child." Ghazi tucked the picture into the pocket of her skirt and looked around the beach to see if anyone had seen her son's discovery. All around her, children ran in and out of the water, catching the waves that washed over their small feet. A few men lay sunbathing. One man yelled to his children to be careful not to venture out too far into the ocean. Women dressed in *abayas* sat on blankets spreading out food for the day's picnic. No one, as far as Ghazi could tell, had seen Omar pick up the picture.

"Where did it come from?" Omar asked.

"Oh, probably a worker from Iran brought it to Qatar," his mother explained, "perhaps to use as a bookmark for a book he was reading at the beach. This man in the picture is famous in Iran but not here."

"Why did you take the picture from me? Can I see it again?" Omar bombarded her with questions.

"You may not see it again. You cannot look on such a picture. Now go back into the water and enjoy the rest of your vacation with your friends."

"But, Mother, I found it. I want to have my treasure back. Besides, you said he was a holy man. Don't we believe in holy men?"

Ghazi patted her son on the shoulder. "Yes, we do, but we are forbidden to have a shrine or a picture that honors a holy man. You must understand that we are not like other Muslims. We believe that Allah will punish those who honor a specific man. There is no god but Allah, and we must reverence him."

"Then we must destroy the picture, even though the man is holy?"

"That is true. You see, we belong to the Wahhabi Muslims, who have a different interpretation of Islam than in Iran, where the man in the picture came from. Our people have even destroyed famous mosques and shrines in our own country that have been dedicated to holy men. There is no one holy but the one god, and that is Allah. Remember that no man stands above god."

Omar squinted his eyes from the sun and looked up at his mother. "Then I want to worship only one god, like you and Father do."

"Allah will be pleased with you, my son." Ghazi squeezed Omar's hand and watched him as he ran to join his friends chasing waves. *Such innocence*, she thought as she watched him laugh and try to skip over a sand castle his friend had just built. She took the picture from her pocket, tore it into small pieces, and tossed them into the water. One by one the fragments floated out to sea.

*T*he Wahhabi Muslims worship and revere only Allah. They are expected to keep themselves free from anything that might detract from Allah's central and supreme place in the universe. Nothing is to be compared to him, and no earthly authority is to stand in his place.

The Wahhabi have tried to destroy all mosques and shrines dedicated to sheiks and holy men. Some of the most sacred sites of Shiite Islam, such as Karbala and Nejaf (in southern Iraq), were razed during times of war. The zeal the Wahhabi have to worship one god is what many Christians believe will ultimately bring them to know the God of our Lord Jesus Christ.

Qatar is one of the most prosperous countries in the Middle East, with a per capita income of U.S.$11,600 and a social welfare system that provides educational and medical programs that outdistance any other Muslim country. Qatari enjoy free education, free housing, free health care, and free electricity. Oil was discovered in Qatar in 1932, which many people believe was Allah's reward to them for the harsh life they endured in the desert.

At this time the Qataris are vehemently opposed to Christianity, but they do tolerate it somewhat in the foreigners who come to work in oil-related jobs. The workers may worship as they please, and the government is making plans to allow Christians to build a church in the country.

Prayer Points

- Pray for the church to have powerfully anointed ministries that will reach children, teens, and young adults with the gospel.
- Pray for SAT-7 to develop cutting-edge Christian TV programming that will be watched by children, teens, and young adults and will give a clear presentation of the gospel.
- Pray for an end to "crimes of honor" in which a male relative assaults or kills a female because of alleged sexual misconduct.
- Pray for Christian music to impact teens and young adults.
- Pray for young people to begin seeking their purpose in life and that the search will lead them to Jesus Christ.
- Pray that the desire of the Qataris for purity (reflected in the Wahhabi sect's beliefs and practices) will lead them to search for the truth in Christ Jesus.
- Pray for Christians to find creative ways to share their faith with Qataris in a culturally sensitive manner.
- Pray for the Lord to raise up young leaders who have a heart for Him to witness to their family and friends.

Quick Reference

Ethnic Breakdown: Arab 40%, Pakistani 18%, Indian 18%, Iranian 10%, other 14%
Type of Government: Traditional monarchy
Economy: Services 50%, Industry 49%, Agriculture 1%
Per capita income: U.S.$11,600
National debt: U.S.$10 billion
Economic conditions: Thriving economy

Education
Quality of education: School system is well organized. Instruction includes mandatory Koranic curriculum.
Gender discrimination against girls: Girls are being educated but are excluded from certain curriculums (religion, commerce, technical studies) and steered toward teaching careers.

Religion
Religious concerns: The government prohibits evangelism. Conversion can be punishable by death in the public square.

Status of the church: No national church exits. Expatriate Christians need discipleship, leadership, and evangelism training to be more effective.
Are Christians being persecuted? No

Societal Viewpoint Toward Children
Are they viewed as precious? Yes
Are there street children? No
Is there a large population of orphans? No
Are there child soldiers? No
Is child labor a problem? There are no reports of child labor problems.

Saudi Arabia

Major Languages: Arabic, Persian, Hindi
Total Population: 22,024,000
Population 0–34: 15,720,000
Life Expectancy: 68 years
Religion: Muslim 92.83%, Christian 4.54%, nonreligious/other 1.40%,
    Hindu 0.60%, Buddhist/Chinese 0.42%, Sikh 0.19%, Baha'i 0.02%
Literacy Rate: male 71%, female 50%

*F*ateema was arrested three years ago for letting her ankles show in public. At the police station she was booked and charged with indecent exposure. "All I did was put some shopping bags in the trunk of my car. When I bent over, my ankles showed under my *abaya*," Fateema explained. "For this I was arrested?"

For her punishment she was assigned to the custody of her nearest male relative, an uncle she was not eligible to marry. She could not go out in public without him, and at 19 she was virtually a prisoner for the rest of her single years. "It was very difficult for me to get to my classes at the university. I did manage to get a degree in mathematics but stopped there. I would have liked to continue my education, but the arrangements were much too difficult. Now I am married, so I go out with my husband. Those years were very difficult, but I had to accept what was handed me."

Fateema is not alone in her experience of harsh sentences placed on women whose freedom to move about is limited. Strict Muslim law, which may or may not follow the Koran, is enforced in every aspect of life in Saudi Arabia. The sheik can issue *fatwas*, which are his interpretation of the law, anytime he wishes. Once a fatwa is stated, it becomes Islamic law for everyone under his jurisdiction.

In November 1990, after it was declared illegal for a woman to drive a car, making Saudi Arabia the only Islamic country to do so, 47 women in the city of Riyadh assembled in a grocery store parking lot, dismissed their chauffeurs, and drove a 15-car convoy through the city's downtown area. The women were mainly students at King Saud University in the capital city. The police promptly arrested them and accused them of renouncing Islam, an offense punishable by death in Saudi Arabia.

Twenty-five months after the incident, the women as graduates were still banned from working. One young woman had just accepted a teaching position, but two days after the driving incident was told to go home from her job and has not worked since.

Young women have very little freedom in Saudi Arabia and no voice or vote in the laws that govern their lives. Honor killings of young girls who are caught in compromising situations with a man are acceptable. One of the most publicized executions in recent years was the beheading of Princess Misha'il bint Fahd bin Mohammad. A marriage had been arranged for the princess to an older man. When she became attracted to a man her own age and tried to leave the country to have freedom to marry him, she was caught. Her grandfather insisted she be executed. The story reached the British press, and because Western newspapers carried the story exposing the inequality of justice in Saudi Arabia, all the British expatriates working in the country were sent home.

Hangings, beheadings, and other executions may be done in public squares during rush hour as an example to all those who are tempted to break the law. Saudi Arabia has been cited on many counts of human-rights violations. All Saudi citizens are considered Muslims and are restricted from practicing any other religion. Conversion by a Muslim to another religion is considered apostasy and under *sharia* (Islamic law) is punishable by death. The only non-Muslim worship is by expatriates living in the country, mainly workers in the oil industry and oil-related fields.

Saudi Arabia has the largest reserves of oil in the world (26 percent of the total) and is the largest exporter of petroleum. Because of the petrol dollars, the country has good health-care and educational systems. Girls may be educated if it is a family priority. If the family sees no value in providing an education for a girl, who will become the property of her husband's family once she is married, she will stay home and help with family chores.

Since Saudi Arabia is closed to Christians, children have no access to the gospel. One ray of hope is in Internet access and TV programs that cross all political barriers.

Prayer Points

⌣· Pray that this generation of young people will not be overtaken by materialism. Pray that they will desire to have a relationship with Jesus Christ and know His purpose for their lives.

⌣· Pray that young people studying abroad will be reached with the gospel. Pray that they will return home and have an impact on their families for Christ.

⌣· Pray that believers will seek the Lord for His strategic plan to reach the children, teens, and young adults among the untargeted people groups—the Fayfa, Indonesian, Kabardian, Mahra, Persian, and Turk.

⌣· Pray that this generation of young people will question the cruel treatment of Saudi citizens and the arbitrary fatwas that are issued by the government.

⌣· Pray that young men and women will work to change the unreasonable rules and regulations put on women.

⌣· Pray that teens and young adults will listen to Christian radio and watch Christian television programs over satellite. Pray that the programming will challenge their way of thinking.

⌣· Pray that the Saudi government will stop financing the worldwide spread of Islam. Pray that leaders will have Damascus Road experiences like Paul's!

⌣· Pray that human-rights groups in the West will be able to expose human-rights atrocities as barbaric practices.

Quick Reference

Ethnic Breakdown: Saudi Arab 74.2%, Bedouin Arab 3.9%, Gulf Arab 3.0%, Punjabi 2.4%, Urdu 2.2%, other 14.3%

Type of Government: Monarchy

Economy: Industry 47%, Services 47%, Agriculture 6%

Per capita income: U.S.$7,040

National debt: U.S.$28 billion

Economic conditions: Thriving economy

Education

Quality of education: Education is not compulsory; however, the school system is well organized. Instruction includes mandatory Koranic curriculum.

Gender discrimination against girls: Since the 1980s girls have received education equal to that received by boys.

Religion

Religious concerns: Open evangelism and public worship by non-Muslims are prohibited.

Status of the church: No national church exists. There is an expatriate church that needs cutting-edge strategies to evangelize in a hostile Muslim environment.
Are Christians being persecuted? Yes

Societal Viewpoint Toward Children
Are they viewed as precious? Yes
Are there street children? No
Is there a large population of orphans? No
Are there child soldiers? No
Is child labor a problem? Foreign criminal rings reportedly bought and imported children with disabilities to the country for the purpose of forced begging.

Senegal

Major Languages: French, Wolof, Pulaar
Total Population: 9,987,000
Population 0–34: 4,695,000
Life Expectancy: 62 years
Religion: Muslim 92.07%, Christian 4.76%, traditional ethnic 2.97%, Baha'i 0.20%
Literacy Rate: male 43%, female 23%

*I*n March 2001 Udo, one of the directors of a large school in Dakar, became fearful as he watched the number of children attending the after-school Christian teaching program grow from 100 to more than 300 in a very short time. Uneasy about the phenomenal growth and possible reactions from the mostly Muslim parents, he quickly sent home "permission slips" to inform parents of the program and make sure they had consented to their children's attendance. Because Senegal is 94 percent Muslim, it may be considered shameful for Muslim parents to have their children attend a Christian event.

Udo said, "Many times we don't really know what the parents are thinking. We have been here for some time, and though we believe the parents support us and like what we do, no one has ever commented or thanked us for helping with their children. I was sure the parents would not sign the slips and the program would be closed. However, to our complete surprise, virtually every parent signed the paper to give permission for their children to attend the Christian instruction sessions."

Still not satisfied with the results, and in an effort to make the parents fully understand that the instruction sessions were Christian, Udo levied additional requirements for the parents. They had to write out their full names and addresses along with a written statement giving permission for their children to attend the program.

Udo laughed as he related the outcome of his second request. "This was too much for the parents. Half of them, the brave ones, gave their full names and addresses. The other half came with their children during one of our instructional sessions and pleaded with us that their children be allowed to attend. One parent emphasized that he had no problems with his child attending the ministry but that he had problems with giving his full name and address.

"I had to make a difficult decision, so those children whose parents had not given me their names and addresses went home. I was sad to see them go, but we had to make sure the parents understood we were teaching the children about Jesus Christ. Otherwise we would have repercussions from the local *imams* later.

"While it was sad for those children who had to go home, we were able to continue and grow with those who were willing to commit to our teachings."

*U*do is one of many headmasters who are providing instruction for the children in Senegal. He sees doors open to those who will work with the children, which is not true in most Muslim countries. Over the years Christian schools have shown a measure of success in Senegal and have therefore received the greatest share of the government funding for education. It is interesting to note that most of the children attending these Christian schools are from Muslim backgrounds.

While the work through schools is promising, the overall picture is bleak. The country faces internal urban problems of chronic unemployment, juvenile delinquency, and drug addiction. Senegal is considered one of the poorer countries in West Africa. Abuse against women is of serious concern for human-rights groups. Much of the abuse may be the result of tradition and the status of women in the society. Men are given priority for food and medicine, with women and children given lesser consideration.

Prayer Points

- Pray for Muslim children to be allowed to attend Christian schools for their education. Pray that once they hear about Jesus Christ, they will witness to their parents.
- Pray for God to cast out the fear of taboos and customs that restrict the types of nutritional food women and children are allowed to eat. Forty percent of the children die before reaching five years of age.
- Pray for police intervention in incidents of wife beating. Spousal abuse is very common, but police do not usually intervene in domestic disputes.

⌐· Praise God that FGM has been banned in this country. Pray that the Toucouleur and Peulh ethnic groups will adhere to this legislation and stop the practice completely.
⌐· Pray for a strong, unified, fruit-bearing church to be salt and light to this dark nation. Currently, most of the Christians are scattered, poorly taught, and living a lifestyle that does not honor God.
⌐· Pray for cutting-edge strategies to reach children, teens, and young adults with the gospel.

Quick Reference

Ethnic Breakdown: Wolof 43.3%, Pular 23.8%, Serer 14.7%, Jola 3.7%, Mandinka 3%, Soninke 1.1%, European and Lebanese 1%, other 9.4%
Type of Government: Republic under multiparty democratic rule
Economy: Services 61%, Industry 20%, Agriculture 19%
Per capita income: U.S.$600
National debt: U.S.$3.4 billion
Economic conditions: Extremely poor

Education
Quality of education: There is a severe shortage of schools and teachers.
Gender discrimination against girls: Not much importance is placed on education for girls.

Religion
Religious concerns: Evangelism is restricted. The government monitors foreign missionary groups and religious and nonreligious nongovernmental organizations.
Status of the church: Severe lack of discipleship.
Are Christians being persecuted? No. However, groups have been expelled when their activities were judged to be political in nature and a threat to public order.

Societal Viewpoint Toward Children
Are they viewed as precious? Yes
Are there street children? Organized street begging by children who are Koranic students results in a significant interruption of their education.
Is there a large population of orphans? No specific data available.
Are there child soldiers? Reportedly, children have been fighting with the Casamance Separatist Movement, but no precise figures are available. Other sources say no children have ever fought during this 20-year-old conflict.
Is child labor a problem? Children may be kept out of school to work on family farms.

Somalia

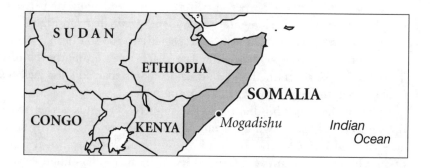

Major Languages: Somali, Arabic, Italian
Total Population: 7,253,000
Population 0–34: 5,694,000
Life Expectancy: 57 years
Religion: Muslim 99.95%, Christian 0.05%
Literacy Rate: male 36%, female 14%

As a child Farkan watched his father avoid the pain of poverty and hopelessness by chewing *khat,* a powerful plant that acts as an amphetamine. Every day Farkan's father got out of bed, worked a couple of hours, and then headed to the market to buy enough of the bitter leaf to get him through the rest of the day. The daily purchase of khat and chewing tobacco left the family little money for food. Farkan remembers going to bed many nights in their crowded hut listening to the sounds of his younger sisters crying from hunger. Two of his sisters eventually died from malnutrition.

Growing up, Farkan promised himself that he would never chew khat. He would work hard and make a decent living for his family. Maybe he would even go to school—that is, if the government could get a school established in the city. He had never seen a school because they didn't exist anymore in his area of Somalia. All his great plans amounted to nothing when at the age of 10 he began to run with the wrong crowd. One theft led to another until he landed in jail with a 20-year sentence. Now there is little hope—crime is a way of life for him.

Men like Farkan may never know how to change their lives because Christians are almost nonexistent in Somalia. The years of civil war

197

and lack of any central government have left Somalia in a state of chaos without schools, hospitals, social programs, or government infrastructure.

Somalia has only a 25 percent literacy rate, and only 10 percent of the children who enter elementary school will graduate from high school. Schools are so scarce that some areas, especially in the southern portion of the country, are completely without a place to educate the children. Teachers are poorly trained and paid, and schools that do exist lack textbooks, laboratory equipment, and running water.

One of the major hindrances to the country's progress is the tremendous grip that khat chewing has on the people. An average family spends an estimated U.S.$2–3 per day on khat. With an average annual income of only U.S.$499, a family can spend its entire income on khat.

Somalia is one of the world's poorest and least-developed countries. It has few resources, and much of the economy has been devastated by civil war. Some estimate that by the time Somalia's civil war ends, 25 percent of the population will have died and 30 percent—the majority being children—will be permanently damaged because of trauma, malnutrition, and maiming. Over 100,000 deaths were reported in a six-month period following the January 26, 1991, downfall of the Siyaad Barre regime and the subsequent famine. Twenty-five percent of the country's children died from famine and cholera outbreaks.

A few Somali—less than 0.03 percent of the population—are born-again believers. Missionaries were ousted in 1974, and those who remain have suffered persecution and martyrdom. One of the major strongholds in Somalia is disunity and deception. Disunity is described in a Somali proverb: "I and Somalia against the world, I and my clan against Somalia, I and my family against the clan, I and my brother against the family."

The capital city of Mogadishu is very dangerous. Juvenile delinquents, some as young as eight or nine, brandish automatic weapons. There may be as many as 30,000 weapons in the hands of young men and boys who, like Farkan, kill and steal, some simply for fun. Most of the young men chew khat and will do anything to make sure they have a constant supply of the leaf.

Food is power in Somalia. Many times the ships that bring food into the harbor at Mogadishu are shelled and the relief workers shot at because the many clans in the country are each afraid that another will get food and therefore obtain power.

The only hope is for Somalia to open its doors to those who will proclaim the gospel. Many of the citizens have fled to neighboring countries to find food. These refugees can be reached with the gospel while they are away from their homeland.

Who will go and intercede for this devastated land and for the children who will one day hold its future?

Prayer Points

ﹾ· Pray for the safety of relief workers who will go into Somalia and deliver food to the hungry and dying.

ﹾ· Pray for unity in the country. Pray that country, clans, and family will have love for each other.

ﹾ· Pray that the government will open its doors to Christians who respond to the needs of the country for the sake of future generations.

ﹾ· Pray for Somalia to realize that its greatest resource is the minds of its children.

ﹾ· Pray for deliverance from addictions like khat and tobacco chewing. Pray that the young people will be delivered and know that they have hope and a future in the Lord.

ﹾ· Pray for open doors into the refugee camps and schools to teach the children to read and write so that they can understand the Scriptures and go back into their homeland to proclaim the powerful gospel of Jesus Christ.

Quick Reference

Ethnic Breakdown: Somali 85%, Bantu and Arabs 15%
Type of Government: One-party socialist state (no central government)
Economy: Agriculture 59%, Services 31%, Industry 10%
Per capita income: U.S.$499
National debt: U.S.$2.6 billion
Economic conditions: Extremely poor

Education
Quality of education: There has been no central school system for the past 10 years. This is a generation without education.
Gender discrimination against girls: Among the small number of children receiving education, a serious gender gap is emerging, with only about half as many girls enrolled in primary schools as boys.

Religion
Religious concerns: Evangelism is prohibited.
Status of the church: There are less than 3,000 known born-again believers among the Somali. Believers need discipleship and leadership training.
Are Christians being persecuted? Yes

Societal Viewpoint Toward Children
Are they viewed as precious? No

Are there street children? Somalia is a clan-based society, and the clans care for children without a home.

Is there a large population of orphans? There are some orphanages, but it is more likely that the children find homes in the extended family (clan).

Are there child soldiers? Yes. It is very normal for teens to carry guns, and most adults are involved in various militia groups.

Is child labor a problem? Formal employment of children is rare, but youths commonly are employed from an early age in herding, agriculture, and household labor. The lack of educational opportunities and severely depressed economic conditions contribute to child labor.

Sri Lanka

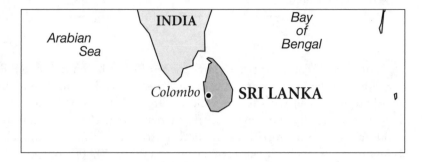

Major Languages: Sinhala, Tamil, English
Total Population: 19,239,000
Population 0–34: 11,979,000
Life Expectancy: 72 years
Religion: Buddhist 71.93%, Hindu 12.00%, Muslim 8.00%, Christian 7.62%,
   nonreligious/other 0.20%, Sikh 0.15%, Baha'i 0.10%
Literacy Rate: male 93%, female 87%

Twelve-year-old Sinaha pushed the soil back and planted a new rubber tree shoot. He was unable to attend school and ever since he was six years old had worked to help support his family. He looked up to see a man in a new automobile drive to the edge of the field, get out, and walk toward him. "Hot day, isn't it?" the man asked.

Sinaha squinted from the bright sunlight and shook his head. He didn't know what to say. He wondered where this man came from. America? Australia? Maybe Germany? What was he doing here?

"Well, son, your daddy and I came to an agreement, and it looks like you will be taking a trip with me. No need for you to be scared. We'll take good care of you. My name is Joe." He smiled. "Everybody's name is Joe where I come from. Come on now, I've got things to do."

Sinaha followed Joe to the edge of the field and climbed into the back of the man's car. He saw his dad as they drove away from the plantation, but he didn't know whether his dad saw him or not.

It seemed like a long journey, and night had fallen before they reached the city. Joe drove down a narrow street and stopped in front of an open doorway. He took Sinaha by the elbow and led him upstairs to a small room. The room was filled with mats, and two boys about his age lay sleeping in the corner.

"Doesn't matter which mat you take to sleep on. Everyone shares around here. There are 24 boys in all." Joe pointed toward the motionless boys lying on the floor. "Those boys don't feel very well, and if I were you, I'd stay away from them. I'll be back for you later on tonight." Joe closed the door behind him.

Sinaha had just been sold into a brothel for young men.

S ri Lanka is renowned throughout the world as a haven for pedophiles. Tour companies in Europe, America, and Australia offer group rates for those men who wish to visit the red light districts of Colombo, Sri Lanka's capital city. The government estimates that there are more than 2,000 active child prostitutes in the country, but private groups claim the number is much higher, estimating 15,000 to 20,000. A 1998 U.N. International Labor Office study placed the total at 30,000. While some children are forced into prostitution, others become prostitutes to escape their dismal home environment.

In the first half of 1999 the police recorded 2,066 cases of crimes against children. Many attribute the problem of child exploitation to the lack of law enforcement rather than inadequate legislation.

The insurgent army, fighting to make the northern section of the country a separate state, has been known to recruit children for use in battlefield support functions and in combat. Some of these children are as young as age 13, and some are recruited forcibly. Young Tamil girls, often orphans, have been systematically recruited. Dubbed "Birds of Freedom," many are reportedly trained as suicide bombers because they may better evade government security.

The government passed the National Child Protection Authority Act to combat the problem of child abuse, including unlawful child labor. However, an estimated 16,500 children are fully employed in the country, with another 50,000 to 100,000 employed in full-time domestic service. Additional thousands of children are believed to be working as house servants, sold by their poverty-stricken parents. Some of these children have been starved, beaten, sexually abused, and forced into prostitution. Although the government does not condone child labor, it does little to stop it. In 1999 there were only between 250 and 300 cases prosecuted for engaging minors in the workforce.

HIV/AIDS is on the rise and is difficult to track in Sri Lanka's mobile society. It is estimated that by the year 2005, Sri Lanka could have over 80,000 cumulative cases of HIV infection. Children like Sinaha are at particular risk and are left without proper medical care.

Sri Lanka was open to the gospel for many years but now is suffering because the government does not grant visas to missionaries. The church has been its own worst enemy in Sri Lanka. Nominalism and lethargy have made the church weak and ineffective.

Prayer Points

∽· Pray for the children who grow up in war not to become hardened to the sanctity of life.
∽· Pray for the children sold to pimps or perverts or into slavery by parents who have no other means of raising money for the needs of the family.
∽· Pray for the apprehension and severe prosecution of national and foreign pedophiles. Also pray for the international networks of prostitution and pedophilia to be exposed and extinguished.
∽· Pray for the supernatural protection of young people in prostitution.
∽· Pray that the church in Sri Lanka will display the love of Christ to their country in ministries of compassion.
∽· Pray for children and young people who are malnourished, live in slums, and have lost their parents by violence.
∽· Pray for effective ministry to impact the lives of young people.

Quick Reference

Ethnic Breakdown: Sinhalese 74%, Tamil 18%, Moor 7%, Burgher, Malay, and Vedda 1%
Type of Government: Parliamentary socialist republic
Economy: Services 60%, Agriculture 21%, Industry 19%
Per capita income: U.S.$700
National debt: U.S.$8.4 billion
Economic conditions: Poor (22 percent below the poverty line)

Education
Quality of education: Civil war has diverted funds from education to support arms.
Gender discrimination against girls: No

Religion
Religious concerns: Evangelical Christians have expressed concern because their efforts at proselytizing often are met with hostility and harassment by the local Buddhist clergy and others opposed to their work.
Status of the church: The Christian church has declined steadily in numbers and influence during this century.
Are Christians being persecuted? Yes. Churches have been bombed.

Societal Viewpoint Toward Children
Are they viewed as precious? No
Are there street children? Yes
Is there a large population of orphans? Yes
Are there child soldiers? Yes
Is child labor a problem? Yes. Children are routinely used in the labor force and as house servants.

Sudan

Major Languages: Arabic, English, over 100 tribal languages
Total Population: 35,080,000
Population 0–34: 27,747,000
Life Expectancy: 57 years
Religion: Muslim 65.00%, Christian 23.19%, traditional ethnic 10.61%, nonreligious/other 1.20%
Literacy Rate: male 58%, female 35%

The gunmen came silently out of the darkness, surrounded the sun-baked mud compound, seized five teenagers, and stole away into the surrounding bush. The youngsters, three boys and two girls, were bound with coarse rope and beaten with rifle butts. On the long march into captivity, one youth tried to escape but was recaptured and slashed to death with heavy axes and machetes. When they reached a base camp, the girls were handed out as slaves to senior guerrillas.

This account, one of many, was given by an eyewitness to the abduction of children in southern Sudan by the Lord's Resistance Army (LRA). The LRA is a guerrilla band that roams the southern portion of Sudan and northern Uganda looking for children on which to prey. They have abducted over 10,000 children for the purpose of taking them into slavery. Besides the LRA, the National Islamic Front (northern Sudan's national army) raids villages and also takes children for the purpose of making them slaves. This, coupled with famine, war, and lack of infrastructure to support education and medical attention, makes Sudanese children some of the most at-risk children in the world today.

Plagued by centuries of tribal conflicts and war, Sudan's present condition is more of the same, only on a grander scale. In 1983 the predominately Christian and animist people of southern Sudan revolted against the northern Islamic government. Wanting to be free from the north's efforts to convert the south to Islam, the south has waged war for over 19 years. Northern Sudan has two goals for subduing the southern portion of the country. First, it wants to obtain dominance over the south's rich grazing lands and vast mineral reserves and thus supplement the lack of farmlands and natural resources in the north. Second, the north desires to convert the south to Islam. The northern army, known as the National Islamic Front (NIF) frequently raids southern villages scattering the people and taking men, women, and children as slaves to be used as domestic help, farmhands, herdsmen, and field workers. The frequent raids keep the people scattered and unable to unify for the purpose of building a strong government that would enable them to defeat the NIF. The southern army, known as the Sudanese People's Liberation Army (SPLA), defends its lands, but the battle has been extremely difficult because of the lack of funds and support from the international community.

Because of the civil war, over five million people have been displaced and over two million killed, many of them children from Christian homes. Over one million of those displaced have fled to the north, where they live in deplorable conditions in settlements and refugee camps without adequate sanitation, water, electricity, or food. The displaced children have few educational opportunities. When state schools are available, they teach the Koran and may require a child to convert to Islam in order to receive an education.

The future for children is dismal. Throughout Sudan a child has less than a 10 percent chance of survival to the age of five and only a 38 percent chance of growing up literate. If the child is a girl who lives in the southern portion of the country, her chances of an education plummet even further. Ninety percent of the girls between the ages of four and seven have been subjected to female genital mutilation by family members as a cultural introduction into womanhood. Adult education is a key in abolishing this barbaric practice.

There are signs of change on the horizon. Recently the northern government invited several leading Christian humanitarian organizations to assist in aiding the children of Sudan. Also, many of the refugees who have fled to other countries are going back into their country, particularly the southern portion, to conduct crusades and open schools and adult literacy centers. There is hope for Sudan. Christians are asking for prayer that the crack in the door will soon turn to a wide-open door that will allow the gospel to be presented to all the people of Sudan.

Prayer Points

⌐· Pray that Christian youth throughout Sudan will get Bibles, teaching, discipleship training, and the encouragement they need to evangelize their country.

⌐· Pray for the families of two million Sudanese who have died in the civil war that is presently taking place in Sudan.

⌐· Pray for Christians internationally to seek what God wants each of us to do to end the horrific atrocities committed against Christians and their families in Sudan. It is a disgrace that the church has not responded to the anguished cries of the believers in Sudan.

⌐· Pray that God will raise up a Cyrus leader full of God's compassionate love to deliver the people from their hell-on-earth existence.

⌐· Pray for Christian groups across the world to become involved in buying back slaves and to begin writing government authorities, the U.N., and the Sudanese government to raise awareness of the abuse of women and children in Sudan.

⌐· Pray for the Lord's Resistance Army to be apprehended quickly and rendered ineffective.

⌐· Pray for adequate food, medical care, and housing for the children and their families and for the endless cycle of war and poverty to be broken.

⌐· Pray for educational opportunities for the children and for churches and Christian teachers to respond to the need to raise the literacy rate.

Quick Reference

Ethnic Breakdown: Black 52%, Arab 39%, Beja 6%, foreigners 2%, other 1%
Type of Government: Military dictatorship
Economy: Services 42%, Agriculture 41%, Industry 17%
Per capita income: U.S.$800
National debt: U.S.$24 billion
Economic conditions: Extremely poor

Education
Quality of education: There is a severe shortage of schools and teachers. Schools for refugees are almost nonexistent. Muslims are Islamizing the entire curriculum.
Gender discrimination against girls: For girls, domestic chores take precedence over education.

Religion
Religious concerns: Evangelism is prohibited. Conversion to Christianity is punishable by death.
Status of the church: The body of Christ is vibrant and growing. Pastors and ministry leaders need training so that they can disciple Christians more effectively.

Are Christians being persecuted? Yes. They are being killed in massive numbers by fundamentalist Muslims.

Societal Viewpoint Toward Children

Are they viewed as precious? No

Are there street children? Children may work in the street markets, but most go home to their families at night.

Is there a large population of orphans? Yes

Are there child soldiers? Yes

Is child labor a problem? Children are routinely used in the labor force.

Syria

Major Languages: Arabic, Kurdish, Armenian
Total Population: 16,306,000
Population 0–34: 12,757,000
Life Expectancy: 69 years
Religion: Muslim 90.32%, Christian 5.12%, nonreligious 2.90%,
    other (Druze, etc.) 1.55%, Baha'i 0.10%, Jewish 0.01%
Literacy Rate: male 86%, female 56%

A visitor who came to Syria on a prayer journey wrote, "We had the opportunity to visit a small village north of Damascus. We found the villagers to be kind and open. While we sat at a local café, the people came up and initiated conversation.

"We befriended a local man, who took us around for a few days and invited us into his home for a meal. After eating a tasty dish of chicken, I watched the younger men and women troop over to the next room to turn on the TV. I cannot imagine the magnitude of culture shock the children suffered as they watched all the new-age philosophy, materialism, and pornography the world can supply over several dozen stations. I'm not sure how valid it is in general, but our guides told us the impression that Syrians have of Christians is based on shows like *Friends*, *Seinfeld*, and *Dharma and Greg*.

"After we left our new friend's apartment, I realized we have a lot of myths to dispel. Wherever we went, many TV antennas were on each street, sprouting over every conceivable type of building from spiffy new apartment buildings to simple, thrown-together shanties. I am told that in many areas where there is no electricity, they rig parabolic antennas and TV sets that run on car batteries, and there is a growing business hauling chargers around the country to recharge ailing batteries used to power the homemade setups."

Sad to say, many people around the world view Christians according to the values that are being exported through TV and the Internet. Children are watching our TV shows and receiving the wrong message about what is right and wrong. It is not uncommon to find a satellite dish mounted on the outside of a Bedouin tent with a TV blaring inside.

A ccording to the U.S. State Department, Syria has been under a state of emergency since 1963. The nation has been involved four times with other Arab countries in wars against Israel. In 1967 Syria suffered a great defeat and in 1973 lost the Golan Heights to Israel. Because of the wars, there has been a great influx of homeless refugees into the country. These refugees, more than half of them children, usually live in makeshift homes and have little or no health care, insufficient food, and contaminated water.

Although the government asserts that girls have the same educational opportunities as boys, this generally is not the case, especially in rural areas. There is a great deal of pressure put on girls to marry early and have children, which is the major reason for their high dropout rate.

In past years children begging from tourists coming to visit the ancient sights in Damascus have been a significant problem. The government passed laws to prohibit the use of children for the purpose of begging. For the most part the practice has been eradicated, but because of the economic downturn, children still sell tissues and "ancient coins" to visitors, and some begging occurs.

Prayer Points

- Pray for Syria's youth to be reached with the gospel in culturally creative ways.
- Pray for this generation to be healed of its hatred for Israel and for God to bring peace in this region.
- Pray for God to give TV producers like SAT-7 and the Bible Channel creative ideas for programming that are anointed and popular among children, teens, and young adults.
- Pray for the local church to be anointed and protected by God.
- Pray for parents to seek God for a better quality of life for their children and country.
- Pray for God to raise up young Joshuas and Deborahs who will have a powerful impact on their nation. Pray that there will be an open-door policy for the gospel to be preached.

↳· Pray for God to give young President Bashar al-Asad wisdom and direction to govern Syria in such a way that God's divine purpose for his life and country will be fulfilled.

Quick Reference

Ethnic Breakdown: Arabs 90.3%, Kurds, Armenians, and other 9.7%
Type of Government: Socialist republic
Economy: Services 49%, Agriculture 29%, Industry 22%
Per capita income: U.S.$1,120
National debt: U.S.$22 billion
Economic conditions: Poor

Education
Quality of education: School system is well organized.
Gender discrimination against girls: No, but for girls early marriage often cuts schooling short.

Religion
Religious concerns: Christians are closely watched, missionaries are not given visas to enter the country, and the government is sensitive to complaints about proselytizing.
Status of the church: Muslims who convert to Christianity must worship underground.
Are Christians being persecuted? No

Societal Views Toward Children
Are they viewed as precious? Yes
Are there street children? The exploitation of children for begging is prohibited.
Is there a large population of orphans? No specific data available.
Are there child soldiers? No specific data available.
Is child labor a problem? The majority of children under 16 who work do so for their parents in the agricultural sector.

Taiwan

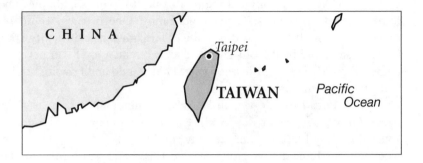

Major Languages: Mandarin Chinese, Taiwanese, Hakka
Total Population: 22,191,000
Population 0–34: 9,702,000
Life Expectancy: 76 years
Religion: Chinese 43.21%, Buddhist 25.00%, nonreligious/other 25.30%,
 Christian 6.06%, Muslim 0.35%, traditional ethnic 0.04%, Baha'i 0.04%
Literacy Rate: male 93%, female 79%

*T*ai Kai, an international student from Taiwan, describes how he came to know Jesus Christ. "When I left my home in Taiwan about a year and a half ago to come to America for graduate study, I knew very little about God. Some of my classmates in undergraduate school were Christians, and once in a while we would talk about Jesus Christ—but not very often.

"I enrolled at the University of Hawaii to get my master's degree in environmental engineering so I could set up and operate a wastewater biological treatment plant back home. My goal was to become extremely wealthy, but God had another plan for my life, and it came about in an unexpected way.

"I was born and raised in a rural area of northeastern Taiwan, a region of fruit and rice plantations, where my father was a farmer. Unlike my seven brothers and sisters, who are all working in businesses in Taipei, I decided to go to school in Taipei and get my undergraduate degree in agricultural engineering. After graduation and service in the army, I worked for two years as a plantation director and then became a lecturer in an agricultural technical school. I realized I wasn't going to make the money I wanted and decided to go to school in the United States to get a master's degree.

"When I arrived in America, everything was so different! I felt lost and inadequate until an American couple, Jim and Nancy, from

211

International Students, Inc., a Christian ministry, became my friends and helped me understand the culture and find my way around. They also took me to church and invited me to a Bible study in their home. There I met two elderly ladies, Gladys and Fanny. One of them could only move around with the help of a walker. The other had difficulty speaking. She stuttered badly. But both had a peace and a joy I had never seen before. From their lives, I learned what God can do and how his strength is made perfect in my weakness.

"Now I realize that we, in ourselves, cannot always do the right thing. Only God is righteous. And we need God in our lives. I knew that I had sin in my life, so I confessed my sins and asked God to forgive me. I believe that Jesus died for my sins, and I have received him as my Lord and Savior.

"Since I have become a Christian, I have peace and joy in my life. My favorite Bible verse is Romans 1:16: 'I am not ashamed of the gospel of Christ, for it is the power of God unto salvation to everyone who believes.'"*

Tai Kai is one of thousands of international students who come to the United States every year to pursue a course of study in universities. Many are open to the gospel and just need someone to befriend them. Two unsuspecting women led Tai Kai to the Lord.

China eyes Taiwan as part of its territory, and the threat of a takeover is always hanging over the tiny island. The U.S. has made public statements in support of Taiwan but at the same time does not recognize Taiwan as a separate country.

Taiwan is one of the most prosperous countries in Asia. It has a high per capita income of over U.S.$12,000. With prosperity often come the problems of greed, gambling, and apathy toward the things of God. There are signs of revival—ministers are going in and holding crusades—but many more strong Christians are needed for church planting and discipleship training.

Prayer Points

⌣· Pray that God will use ministries like International Students, Inc., to impact the lives of the young people who study abroad.

⌣· Pray that materialism won't blind children, teens, and young adults to their need for Christ and that there will be widespread preaching of the gospel in Taiwan.

---

* Adapted from material supplied by International Students, Inc., located in Colorado Springs, Colorado.

⌐· Pray that believers in Taiwan will seek God for powerful strategies to reach this generation.

⌐· Pray that young people going to school and training abroad will become fervent believers in Jesus Christ and take the gospel back to their families, friends, neighbors, and country.

⌐· Pray that China and the international community will peacefully recognize Taiwan as a sovereign nation.

⌐· Pray that culturally relevant Christian materials will be developed and distributed to the young Taiwanese and there will be no compromise in these materials.

⌐· Pray that the long life expectancy of the Taiwanese will be seen as a gift from God. Praise God for the excellent medical care and high literacy rate in Taiwan.

⌐· Pray that Taiwan will use its prosperity to further the gospel of Jesus Christ.

⌐· Pray that the problems of child prostitution and child abuse will be eradicated.

Quick Reference

Ethnic Breakdown: Taiwanese (including Hakka) 84%, Mainland Chinese 14%, Aborigine 2%

Type of Government: Multiparty republic

Economy: Services 62%, Industry 35.3%, Agriculture 2.7%

Per capita income: U.S.$12,399

National debt: U.S.$35 billion

Economic conditions: Stable

Education
Quality of education: Strong commitment to education; extensive higher educational system.
Gender discrimination against girls: No

Religion
Religious concerns: Strong belief in Chinese folk religion.
Status of the church: Stagnation in church growth.
Are Christians being persecuted? No

Societal Viewpoint Toward Children
Are they viewed as precious? Yes
Are there street children? No specific data available.
Is there a large population of orphans? No specific data available.
Are there child soldiers? No
Is child labor a problem? Children may begin working at age 15. Child prostitution is a significant problem.

Tajikistan

Major Languages: Tajik, Russian, Uzbek
Total Population: 6,441,000
Population 0–34: 4,891,000
Life Expectancy: 64 years
Religion: Muslim 89.50%, nonreligious 9.09%, Christian 1.38%, other 0.03%
Literacy Rate: male 100%, female 100%

*P*atrick pulled the heavy blanket up to his chin and tried to ignore the voices of the children outside his window. Although he wasn't sleepy, staying in bed was the best remedy for the extreme cold that seemed to linger everywhere except under his covers. The children's voices became louder. Curious to see what they were up to, he wrapped the covers around him, swung his feet onto the cold cement floor, and walked to the window to watch them.

At 25 he had come to work with the children, his favorite part, and to help their parents start microbusinesses. The children watched his every move. They knew when he went to work, when he slept in, and when he went to the market. Today he was late getting to work, and they had come by to check on him.

Patrick made a mental list of what he had to do that day and decided he couldn't afford the luxury of going back to bed, where he could stay warm with three layers of clothing and the heavy wool blanket that weighed over 10 pounds. Outside his thick covers there was no shelter from the frozen world. He wrapped a wool throw tightly around his shoulders and headed for the kitchen to make some breakfast. He smiled as he overheard the continual chatter, giggles, and laughter of children.

"*Maloko! Maloko!* [Milk! Milk!]," a child selling milk on the street below yelled.

"Eh! Baca, ham in khel na-kuned! [Hey! Boy, don't do that!]" He heard Mathu, the shopkeeper down the street, yell at a child.

Patrick looked at the space heater that began to buzz in the corner of the room. At first he didn't realize what was happening. Then he heard the loud sound of children cheering as if Tajikistan had just won the soccer game of the century. Actually, it was the sound of joy because the electricity had come on. Of course there should be a celebration. No one in the capital city of Dushanbe had had electricity for the past 10 days. This was a day of rejoicing. Patrick tossed the heavy wool throw onto the bed and hurried to plug in the teapot. Today he would have hot tea, and today he would be warm. It would be a great day after all!

Once in the office, Patrick turned his attention to the project at hand—starting microbusinesses for the local people. So far 50 families had received loans for such small businesses as a chicken farm, a flour mill, a grocery store, a macaroni factory, and a bakery. Now many parents could pay the small fees for their children to go to school because they had things to sell. People who once had nothing, not even food on the table, could provide for their immediate and extended families. Patrick was glad he could help.

Tajikistan is an extremely poor country. Since the dissolution of the Soviet Union, the former Soviet republic has not established itself in the commercial market well enough to feed its people. Six years of civil war have also hindered Tajikistan's economy. Most of the food and medical supplies come from nongovernmental organizations or from the governments of countries like Russia and Uzbekistan. A large portion of Tajikistan has no clean drinking water. Much of the country's water is polluted because of toxic chemicals dumped into the lakes and rivers. The water also contains many disease-causing organisms that mainly affect the children.

With well over 70 percent of the population out of work, one of the most pressing needs of the children is for the parents to have productive jobs that will provide money to buy the necessities for their families and support the government funds needed to provide schools and hospitals.

For years Tajikistan has been one of the main producers of illicit opium. While the government says it has forbidden farmers to raise the illegal drug, Russian pastors have made serious accusations that trucks openly transport loads of opium into Russia and sell it on the black market to Russian youth.

Tajikistan needs our prayers. The people are destitute and need to know that God loves them and cares for them.

Prayer Points

- Pray that young people who lived through six years of civil turmoil will find peace and strength in Jesus Christ.
- Pray that believers will be actively involved in educating, providing microbusiness assistance, and offering leadership training so that the young people will be instrumental in developing the infrastructure of their country.
- Pray that the thousands of new mosques will be converted to Esa (Jesus) mosques, that these buildings will be used to further the gospel.
- Pray that the church will rise up in her spiritual responsibility to make sure that children, teens, and young adults will hear the gospel in a clear and culturally sensitive manner. Pray that the Tajiks will give their lives to the Lord and be properly discipled.
- Pray that the young people who are searching for their purpose in life will find and accept Jesus Christ as their Lord and Savior.
- Pray that the Lord will raise up young laborers to serve as pastors, teachers, and evangelists and boldly take the gospel to the remotest areas of their country.

Quick Reference

Ethnic Breakdown: Tajik 64.9%, Uzbek 25%, Russian 3.5%, other 6.6%
Type of Government: Republic
Economy: Services 42%, Agriculture 34%, Industry 24%
Per capita income: U.S.$340
National debt: U.S.$1.3 billion
Economic conditions: Extremely poor

Education
Quality of education: There is a severe shortage of schools and teachers.
Gender discrimination against girls: Girls are being educated.

Religion
Religious concerns: Evangelism is restricted.
Status of the church: There is only a small number of national Christians. The church needs training in leadership, discipleship, and evangelism.
Are Christians being persecuted? Yes, there are reports of churches being bombed.

Societal Viewpoint Toward Children
Are they viewed as precious? No
Are there street children? No specific data available.
Is there a large population of orphans? No specific data available.
Are there child soldiers? No specific data available.
Is child labor a problem? Children may be kept out of school during harvest.

Thailand

Major Languages: Thai, English, ethnic and regional dialects
Total Population: 61,231,000
Population 0–34: 36,944,000
Life Expectancy: 69 years
Religion: Buddhist 92.34%, Muslim 5.24%, Christian 1.62%, Chinese 0.40%, other 0.40%
Literacy Rate: male 96%, female 92%

*B*et Su was only nine years old when she left home. That was over 12 years ago. She came from a poor village in the northern part of the country, where her parents struggled to make a living. One day a man from the city came to them and offered a better life for Bet Su if they would allow him to take her to Bangkok. He said he would find a nice home for her with a childless rich couple who would pay for her education. In return she would be expected to perform simple household chores. She would be the daughter they had never been able to have.

Bet Su's parents were overjoyed that their daughter, who had no chance for an education working the fields, would be given the opportunity to go to school. They made the sacrifice to let her go to the city. Bet Su was taken from her village, sold into a brothel, and forced into a life of prostitution. To make the transaction somewhat legal, the child broker posted a huge debt to the account of Bet Su and her parents, requiring that Bet Su work until the debt was paid in full. The money she receives for servicing 10 to 20 customers a night will never fulfill the debt incurred, and the interest for the loan continues to grow while she wastes away in a house that often gives her a room the size of a bed. Most likely Bet Su will die at an early age of AIDS. With no medical treatment, she is almost sure to die a terrible death away from her family.

*T*oday many missions organizations have set their sights on one of the most neglected segments of society in the world, the young prostitutes of Thailand. Often between the ages of 8 and 15, these children do not set out to become prostitutes. Many are sold into a life of prostitution by their families.

The law in Thailand prohibits trafficking of children, but government officials look the other way as the sex trade grows. Men come from all over the Middle East, the West, and Central Asia to visit the brothels of Thailand. The sex industry has earned Bangkok the title of "the sin capital of Asia."

An estimated 80,000 child prostitutes under the age of 16 work in Bangkok. Between 50 percent and 80 percent of these children are HIV positive. As sex servants in a system that has no regard for their dignity or well-being, these children are living a miserable, shameful existence, completely without hope. Those who have the compassion of Jesus Christ should be compelled to go to the brothels and purchase these boys and girls back so that their dignity can be restored and they can have freedom.

Although literacy rates are high in the country, the recent economic downturn that affected most Asian countries has caused concern in Thailand as children leave school to work and supplement the family income. Most children who work in the labor market serve as gasoline station attendants or helpers in restaurants.

Thailand boasts more statues of Buddha than people. With over 27,000 temples in the country, there is no lack of reminders to the people of the god they are to serve. Christians have been persecuted at the local level, but for the most part, the gospel has been hindered by the ruling spirits that manifest themselves through syncretism, lack of spiritual concern, lax church discipline, immorality of Christian leadership, and misuse of church funds.

Few government restrictions on ministry exist in Thailand, and some reports from recent prayer journeyers and evangelistic outreaches tell of whole villages turning to the Lord because of miraculous healings. Much work remains to be done in this "gospel-ready" country. Christianity entered Thailand over 170 years ago, and currently less than 1 percent of the population have accepted Jesus Christ as their Savior.

Prayer Points

- Pray for the thousands of children who are sold into prostitution each year. Ask God for their release and restoration.
- Pray for more involvement from NGOs (nongovernmental organizations), the United Nations, the church, and relief organizations to work toward ending prostitution in Thailand.

᠆· Pray for the Lord to reveal Himself to everyone practicing Buddhism in the temples. Pray for the Holy Spirit to invade their worship and convict them of their idolatry.

᠆· Pray for God to raise up more laborers to impact the youth culture with high standards of holiness, planting churches in urban and rural areas.

᠆· Pray for the safety of existing missionaries and their families. Pray that their lives will mirror Christ.

᠆· Pray for honest leaders with integrity who will rescue children in the sex industry, drug networks, and crime syndicates. Over two million ungodly people derive their income from the sex industry alone.

᠆· Pray for churches in urban and rural areas to seek God for strategies to reach Thailand and be obedient to carry out His plans.

᠆· Pray for the fear of God to come on those who are full of greed.

᠆· Pray that the parents who give their children up to child brokers will not be so gullible but will recognize the evil that comes from their actions.

᠆· Pray that the sex industry will be exposed for the vile thing it is. Pray for international broadcasting and news networks to air the warped atrocities taking place against children in the sin pits of Thailand.

Quick Reference

Ethnic Breakdown: Thai 75%, Chinese 14%, other 11%
Type of Government: Constitutional monarchy
Economy: Services 49%, Industry 39%, Agriculture 12%
Per capita income: U.S.$2,740
National debt: U.S.$80 billion
Economic conditions: Recovering from economic depression

Education
Quality of education: Instruction includes mandatory Koranic or Buddhist curriculum. A child's family may not be able to afford education after the sixth-grade level. Schools in rural areas are often insufficient.
Gender discrimination against girls: No

Religion
Religious concerns: Evangelism is restricted. The church has not taken the lead to eradicate the sex industry in this country over which God has given it stewardship.
Status of the church: The slow growth rate of the church in Thailand may be a result of corruption and lethargy.
Are Christians being persecuted? No

Societal Viewpoint Toward Children

Are they viewed as precious? No

Are there street children? Yes

Is there a large population of orphans? Yes

Are there child soldiers? No

Is child labor a problem? Thousands of children are sold into prostitution or pedophilia each year. There were reports of employers preventing child workers from leaving the premises. A recent economic downturn has led to children working to supplement their family income.

Tibet

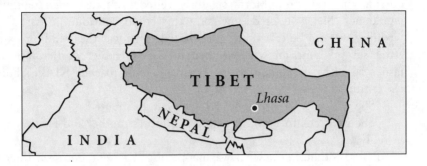

Major Languages: Tibetan, Mandarin Chinese
Total Population: 2,400,000
Population 0–34: No data available
Life Expectancy: 61 years
Religion: Lamaist (Bon) Buddhism 90.0%, traditional religions 6.1%,
    Muslim 2.0%, Christian 0.9%, other 1.0%
Literacy Rate: 22% of ethnic Tibetan population

Altan bowed to the ground in front of a grotesque idol. The angry face stared back at him unchangingly, but still he had to know the answer to his question, and this idol was his only hope. Altan's daughter Methu had just turned 14, and Altan wanted to know whether she should marry the neighbor boy, Ki Lee. There was really no need to wait, and if the idol agreed, arrangements would be made for the marriage ceremony this week.

Methu and Ki Lee had been seen talking together at the village well, and Altan knew that this was a good sign. His visit with Ki Lee's father was short, and the two fathers sealed their agreement with a meal of rice and tea. "Then it is set. When will the presents begin?" Methu's father asked.

"Oh, I think tomorrow Ki Lee will deliver the first gift of some bright-colored ribbons to Methu. Shall we say about the time the sun sets? Then we will proceed with the gifts about the same time every day for the next three days. Okay?"

When the wedding day came, the sky was a beautiful clear blue. Methu got up early in the morning to dress for her special occasion, the day she had waited for all of her life. At midmorning she heard the sound of horses. Her heart skipped a beat because she knew it was Ki Lee and his family coming to get her. Father would tell her when to go outside to meet them, but until then she would sit quietly on the floor of her hut.

She strained to hear what was being said outside. Both families yelled and screamed back and forth. Ki Lee insisted that Methu come outside and join him. Methu's family yelled back that their daughter would not. She wondered how long this could continue. What if the wedding were to be called off? She waited. This was the wedding game. After several bouts of what seemed like irresolvable conflict, Methu's father called her to come outside. Even as she approached Ki Lee's horse, the families still yelled at each other.

"She will go with our son," Ki Lee's family shouted.

"She will remain with her family," Methu's mother and father yelled in reply.

Before Methu knew what was happening, Ki Lee rode toward her on his horse and scooped her up. Together they rode off to begin their new life. This was the marriage ceremony for her tribe. Everyone rejoiced because it had been a good screaming match. Of course, love had prevailed, and the happy couple eventually were able to live on their own.

*K*nown as the "Rooftop of the World," Tibet rests on a high plateau in the mountains. The predominant religion is a form of shamanism called Bon, which was mixed with Buddhism and eventually became known as Tibetan Buddhism. When the Tibetans were overrun in the 1950s by China, their leader, the Dalai Lama, was forced to flee to India.

Tibetans remain one of the hardest peoples in the world to reach with the gospel. They have suffered much persecution from the Chinese, who have attempted to crush their religion, and as a result they have become resistant to any religion other than their own.

The people live in filth and poverty and are plagued with disease, hopelessness, and death. They have poor sanitation, and there have been reports of malnutrition, especially among the children. Stunted growth because of improper diet has also been a problem among children.

Parents are often reluctant to send their children to school for fear they will become absorbed into the Chinese culture and language and lose their values and Tibetan identity.

There are a few reports of Tibetan believers, but the country remains unreached and not open to the gospel.

Prayer Points

- Pray that this generation of young people will have a supernatural encounter with Jesus Christ.
- Pray that God will release strategies to reach the Tibetans with the gospel, as there are only 200 known Tibetan believers.

- Pray that God will raise up Christians who speak the Tibetan language to teach the people to read and write.
- Pray that this generation of young people will be trained for well-paying jobs. The annual income of the Chinese living in Tibet is five times greater than that of Tibetans.
- Pray that during Tibetans' times of demon worship, God will break through the darkness and supernaturally reveal the love of Christ and His redemption for all mankind.
- Pray that the Panchen Lama and Karmapa Lama, young Tibetan spiritual leaders, will be reached with the gospel while they are in exile and will be instrumental in bringing the gospel to their people.
- Pray that Tibetans living abroad will be reached with the gospel and God will raise up apostles, prophets, pastors, teachers, evangelists, missionaries, and church planters among ethnic Tibetans.
- Pray that God will grant favor to churches and ministries working in Tibet.
- Pray that the Han Chinese in Tibet will be reached with the gospel and that house churches will be planted among them.
- Pray that the international community will respond with food for malnourished pregnant and nursing mothers. The children's growth has been stunted from a lack of proper nutrition.
- Pray that the young women who were brutally raped and jailed by the Chinese government while trying to escape to India to become Buddhist nuns will be emotionally and spiritually healed, that they will be supernaturally protected by angels of God, and that Jesus will reveal Himself to them as the one true God.

Quick Reference

Ethnic Breakdown: Chinese 60%, Tibetan 40%
Type of Government: Chinese Communist Party
Economy: Agriculture and Animal Husbandry 59%, Tourism 29%,
Manufacturing 12%
Per capita income: U.S.$400 for Chinese, U.S.$80 for Tibetans
National debt: No specific data available.
Economic conditions: Extremely poor

Education
Quality of education: There is a severe shortage of schools and teachers who can teach the ethnic Tibetans in their own language. The educational system teaches Chinese language and culture. Most Tibetans will allow their children to be taught only in the Tibetan language.
Gender discrimination against girls: Not much importance is placed on education for girls.

Religion

Religious concerns: Due to their persecution by the Chinese and the attempt to crush their religion, Tibetans are resistant to outside influence and afraid of losing their identity as Tibetans. Because of this and their nomadic lifestyles and hard-to-learn languages, Tibetans remain one of the hardest peoples in the world to reach with the gospel.

Status of the church: Nationals must worship underground.

Are Christians being persecuted? Yes, especially by their families.

Societal Viewpoint Toward Children

Are they viewed as precious? Yes

Are there street children? Yes

Is there a large population of orphans? No specific data available.

Are there child soldiers? No specific data available.

Is child labor a problem? No specific data available.

Tunisia

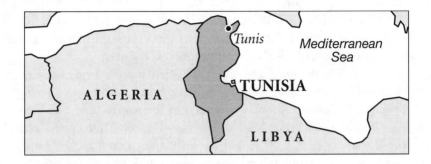

Major Languages: Arabic, French
Total Population: 9,593,000
Population 0–34: 6,494,000
Life Expectancy: 74 years
Religion: Muslim 99.66%, Christian 0.22%, nonreligious/other 0.10%,
  Jewish 0.02%
Literacy Rate: male 79%, female 55%

*F*atima's parents own a tourist resort on the Mediterranean Sea near
the coastal town of Tunis. Each summer during her childhood,
Fatima enjoyed lounging on the beach and sitting by the pool at her
father's hotel. Some of her fondest memories are of playing with the children of the guests who came to the hotel from France, Germany, Saudi
Arabia, and neighboring Algeria. Many of the children she met were
from wealthy oil families of different religious backgrounds. Although
her family was not extremely wealthy, they enjoyed a good standard of
life. Fatima thought the world was a perfect place, and she often dreamed
of traveling to new countries and perhaps even someday visiting America.

Her Muslim parents were quiet, peaceable people. Her father attended
the mosque every Friday evening, and Fatima frequently watched as he
laid out his prayer rug during a call to prayer and knelt toward Mecca to
pray. She thought nothing could shatter her peaceful life.

Fatima attended the finest schools in Tunis. She enjoyed privileges
not allowed girls in most Muslim households. She learned to drive a car.
She could dress in Western clothes and go to movies that met with her
father's approval. Although there were many men her father could have
chosen for her to marry, he postponed her marriage until she had earned
her college degree. After much discussion between her father and her
grandfather, it was decided that she should attend the University of

Paris. Since Fatima had spoken French all her life, Paris sounded like the perfect place. Fatima looked forward to visiting the museums and decided to major in art history.

When Fatima turned 18, her brother accompanied her to Paris to see that she was properly enrolled in her freshman classes. Even with his help, she was unprepared for the loneliness she experienced.

"I was totally alone and so afraid. Paris is such a huge place. Even though I had met many French families while I was growing up, once in France, I felt like I didn't have a friend in the world," Fatima explained.

"That's when I met Marice. He was also from Tunisia and attended the University of Paris. We met at one of the gatherings for Islamic students. At first we just talked about politics and how things were back in Tunisia, but then we moved on to more controversial topics, like how to make the government more radical. I had no idea that Marice was a member of the Hizb Nahda [Renaissance Party].

"At first, the ideas Marice presented to me were strange, and I was totally unwilling to submit to Allah. Then I realized they were true. It would be better for Tunisia to come under *sharia*. We must change our country back to true Islam and follow the Koran. That is the only way we will succeed as a people. Our numbers are growing, and many of us are willing to lay down our lives for the cause of Islam."

Fatima's appearance certainly reflected the change in her political beliefs. Dressed in a black *burqa,* she spoke through a woven screen that covered her eyes and allowed her only partial vision. Even though the temperature outside was close to a hundred degrees, Fatima's hands were gloved and her feet were shod with black boots.

"I have returned home and will live with my parents until I marry a cousin or close relative. My parents do not believe the way that I do, but they understand and are very compassionate."

M any of the elite youth of Tunisia are finding a cause to fight for in becoming members of the Hizb Nahda. The government of Tunisia keeps a close watch on this group as well as its neighbor, Algeria, which harbors many militant Muslim groups. If Algeria succumbs to the Shiite Muslim faction, Tunisia may not be able to stand against the strong anti-Western influence. The government of Tunisia has been able to keep the radical youth of the Hizb Nahda at bay, but there is no telling how long it can withstand the pressure from this new elite group.

Prayer Points

~· Pray for the disillusioned youth in Tunisia to find the answers they are seeking in the gospel of Jesus Christ rather than in fundamentalist Islam.

~· Pray for God to bless Christians with creative ways to reach the children in Tunisia. Pray that God will draw the children to Himself and speak to them through dreams and visions.

~· Pray for the more than 350,000 Tunisian students studying abroad. Pray that they will form relationships with mature Christians and come to know Jesus Christ as their personal Savior.

~· Pray for an increasing Christian witness in Tunisia. Many consider Tunisia to be the gateway to the Islamic nations of North Africa and the Middle East.

~· Pray that the children of Christian families will become friends with Muslim children and will speak to them about God's love.

~· Pray for the believers in Tunisia. Ask God to raise up wise Christian leadership to disciple the people, unite them, and encourage them to share their faith with others.

~· Pray that job opportunities will open up for young people.

~· Pray that the more than 500,000 Tunisians working abroad will encounter Jesus Christ in a life-changing way and return home to tell their friends and family about Him.

Quick Reference

Ethnic Breakdown: Tunisian Arab 67.1%, Sahel Bedouin 21.4%, Hamama Bedouin 3.5%, Algerian Arab 2.4%, Levantine Arab 2.0%, other 3.6%

Type of Government: Republic

Economy: Services 55%, Industry 23%, Agriculture 22%

Per capita income: U.S.$1,820

National debt: U.S.$12.1 billion

Economic conditions: Poor

Education

Quality of education: School system is well organized.

Gender discrimination against girls: Girls are being educated.

Religion

Religious concerns: Evangelism is prohibited.

Status of the church: Believers must worship in secret.

Are Christians being persecuted? No

Societal Viewpoint Toward Children

Are they viewed as precious? Yes

Are there street children? No specific data available.

Is there a large population of orphans? No specific data available.

Are there child soldiers? No specific data available.

Is child labor a problem? The law protects children who work, and records are examined to ensure that employers comply with the minimum age law and that children are not exploited.

Turkey

Major Languages: Turkish, Kurdish, Arabic
Total Population: 66,667,000
Population 0–34: 43,477,000
Life Expectancy: 72 years
Religion: Muslim 99.64%, Christian 0.32%, Jewish 0.04%
Literacy Rate: male 92%, female 72%

R od looked at the long line of children winding among the tents like a giant snake. "Is there a circus coming to town? What in the world are all these children waiting for?" he asked his translator. Rod had come to Turkey with a team of disaster-relief workers to minister to children while the doctors and nurses tended to the wounds and mental stress that the people had endured during the recent earthquakes. The government of Turkey had set up tent cities to provide temporary housing for the thousands of citizens who had lost their homes. Never had Rod seen so many children stand for so long in such an orderly line without adult supervision.

"Today we promised the children we would do face painting while their parents were being treated at the clinic, and they are lined up in anticipation," Saffen said. Downcast, he added, "It's a sad thing, too."

"Why?" Rod asked.

"Sir, we have no face paint. I thought I could secure some theater makeup, but I was unable to find any. The children will be disappointed." He shook his head.

Not a man to give up easily, Rod suggested, "Let's find some tempera paint and use that. That would work, wouldn't it?"

Saffen's eyes lit up. "But of course. I will send for some now!"

Within the hour the team of face painters had set up shop. They kept busy for the rest of the day painting flowers and rainbows on little faces and hands. The medical clinic was able to tend to patients without interruption.

One woman who accompanied her children to get their faces painted said to Rod, "Thank you so very much for caring enough about our children to come all the way from America to touch their lives." Tears rolled down her cheeks as she talked of their losses and their appreciation, not only for the medical help but also for the ministry to the children.

*I*n Turkey it is against the law to distribute Christian material to a minor, and anyone caught giving a Bible or other Christian literature to a child may be arrested. While freedom of religion is part of Turkey's constitution, in reality many Christians are harassed and regularly arrested for proselytizing adults. Islamic forces see Christianity as a threat to their freedom. They try desperately to hold back the tide of Western influence that has flooded their country and to establish strict *sharia* (Islamic law). Christianity is categorized with immoral Western TV shows, video games, movies, and printed matter. In their zeal to hold a strong Muslim line, the fundamentalist Islamic forces threaten and harass people and hold Turkish women in complete subjection to men.

Young people who pour into Turkey's urban areas are continually subjected to Western thought, and as literacy rises (upward of 80 percent), many are questioning the ways of their ancestors. Women and young people who can read and write are able to enter college and join the workforce and are consequently exposed to new ideas. Pray for the tide of thought to be changed in Turkey. Pray that the immorality spread by Western media and the Internet will not close the door for Christianity to enter the country.

Many Christian leaders feel that Turkey is the key to bringing the gospel to the Muslim world. As Christians we have a huge task. Some groups have made inroads with the gospel through friendship evangelism, as most of the country's population is open to prayer and this type of "soft witness."

Prayer Points

- Pray that God will heal the children's nightmares that resulted from the 1999 earthquake.
- Pray that God will give the young people dreams and visions of Jesus Christ, the true Son of the living God.

- Pray that young people will start questioning the practices of Islam and begin to hunger for the love of God in their lives.
- Pray that powerful churches and ministries will receive God-given revelations of how to reach this generation.
- Pray that God's purpose and destiny for Turkey will be fulfilled in this generation.
- Pray that the gospel can be brought to this nation.
- Pray that a vast army of young people will be saved, discipled, and trained to take the gospel to every person in Turkey.

Quick Reference

Ethnic Breakdown: Turk 64.5%, Northern Kurd 8.9%, Turkish Kurd 8.0%, Crimean Tatar 7.0%, Levantine Arab 1.8%, other 9.8%

Type of Government: Multiparty republic

Economy: Agriculture 46%, Services 34%, Industry 20%

Per capita income: U.S.$2,780

National debt: U.S.$104 billion

Economic conditions: Poor

Education

Quality of education: There is a shortage of schools and teachers.

Gender discrimination against girls: Not much importance is placed on education for girls.

Religion

Religious concerns: Evangelism is restricted.

Status of the church: The church is growing in the midst of persecution and needs training in discipleship and leadership.

Are Christians being persecuted? Yes. Secular Muslims who convert to Christianity are severely harassed. Practicing Muslims who convert to Christianity could be martyred.

Societal Viewpoint Toward Children

Are they viewed as precious? No

Are there street children? Yes

Is there a large population of orphans? Yes, especially children with disabilities.

Are there child soldiers? No specific data available.

Is child labor a problem? Children are routinely used in the labor force.

Turkmenistan

Major Languages: Turkmen, Russian, Uzbek
Total Population: 4,518,000
Population 0–34: 3,303,000
Life Expectancy: 61 years
Religion: Muslim 91.84%, nonreligious/other 5.47%, Christian 2.66%,
  Jewish 0.03%
Literacy Rate: male 99%, female 97%

Natisha's heart sank when she realized she was going to have a baby. At 18 she had been married less than three months, and although the baby would be welcome in their home, she wanted to protect herself emotionally in case it did not live. Because of the lack of nutritious food and proper sanitation in her country, there was a good chance the baby would be stillborn or die shortly after birth. Where was the joy and expectancy Natisha wanted to have?

"Not to worry," Natisha had tried to assure her mother when she told her family the news of her pregnancy. "Some babies do live."

Her baby would probably be underweight, just like everyone else's. Then there would be the crucial year, waiting to see whether it would live. There would be no celebration until the child's first birthday. Then the family would have a big party and invite everyone to celebrate.

When Natisha visited the UNICEF clinic three months into her pregnancy, the nurse lectured her sternly about the importance of eating as much protein as possible. "You must gain weight. You are much too thin," the nurse said, but meat and cheese were almost impossible to buy in Ashgabat, the capital of Turkmenistan. Even if there were meat to buy, Natisha had no money to purchase such an extravagant item. The nurse wrote down the name of some vitamins, but when Natisha went to the pharmacy to check on them, it had no supplements for sale. One man told her where to find the vitamins, but they were much too expensive.

All her life Natisha had worked hard in the fields after spending the day at school. She always thought that someday the economy would turn around. Then she would be able to get a job in the city in a nice office with other young girls like her. However, since the Soviet government had fallen and no support had come to Turkmenistan, jobs were nowhere to be found. Two of her friends attempted to commit suicide because of the bleak prospects for young people in the country.

It's probably a good thing we don't know anything different in Turkmenistan, Natisha thought. *We have our families and our heritage. At least we enjoy being around each other.* She resigned herself to the fate of her unborn child. *If my child dies, I will have another.*

According to the U.S. State Department, the government of Turkmenistan has not taken effective steps to address its environmental and health problems. Consequently infant and maternal mortality rates are high. In a society where great emphasis is placed on childbearing after marriage, Natisha is caught in a catch-22 situation. The situation is so bad that a child is not considered a part of the family until its first birthday.

Health care is almost nonexistent, especially in the rural areas. Medicines must be purchased with hard currency, making it extremely difficult for those who are without work and live on government incomes. Only 15 percent of the maternity clinics in the republic have running water, which contributes to the high mortality rate among newborns. Doctors, often undertrained and badly equipped, must deal with shortages in medicines and supplies, as well as the chronic sanitation problems.

Because of the lack of opportunity for youths in Turkmenistan, many have emigrated to other countries. The government is trying hard to adjust to a free market economy, but without the trade and subsidies given by the former Soviet Union, it is extremely difficult. Turkmenistan's promise is in its oil and natural gas reserves, ranked fifth in the world. If this prospect is properly developed, the income could provide significant help for the fledgling country.

Turkmenistan commits the worst violations of religious freedom of all the former Soviet republics. Only communities of the Sunni Muslim Board and the Russian Orthodox Church have been given state permission to function. Today there are approximately 500 born-again Turkmen believers. The support the government has given the Afghanistan Taliban shows the extent to which it leans toward the enforcement of *sharia* (Islamic law).

Prayer Points

- Pray that health conditions will improve for young mothers and their babies.
- Pray that there will be enough nutritious food to feed children, teens, and young adults and that the supply of good water will be greatly augmented.
- Pray that the young people will be healed of the emotional scars left from the civil unrest and turmoil that have been taking place since the 1990s.
- Pray that the environment will be cleaned up for the sake of the young people and their future.
- Pray for better relationships between Turkmenistan and other former Soviet nations.
- Pray that the rich resources God placed in the land will be cultivated and used to benefit the masses of people.
- Pray that there will be an increase in the number of Turkmen believers and that God will give them strategies to reach this generation. Pray for their protection.

Quick Reference

Ethnic Breakdown: Turkmen 77%, Uzbek 9.2%, Russian 6.7%, Kazakh 2%, other 5.1%
Type of Government: Republic
Economy: Industry 62%, Services 28%, Agriculture 10%
Per capita income: U.S.$920
National debt: U.S.$2.1 billion
Economic conditions: Poor

Education
Quality of education: There is a severe shortage of schools and teachers because of increased class sizes and low salaries, already in arrears.
Gender discrimination against girls: There is little difference between the education provided to girls and boys.

Religion
Religious concerns: Evangelism is restricted. There is a small number of Turkmen believers.
Status of the church: Nationals must worship underground. They need discipleship and leadership training. Turkmen believers are becoming more interested in reaching their nation as well as people in Afghanistan and Iran with the gospel.
Are Christians being persecuted? Yes

Societal Viewpoint Toward Children

Are they viewed as precious? Yes, after birth; however, a large number of abortions are performed each year.

Are there street children? No specific data available.

Is there a large population of orphans? No

Are there child soldiers? No specific data available.

Is child labor a problem? The government prohibits forced and bonded labor of children.

United Arab Emirates

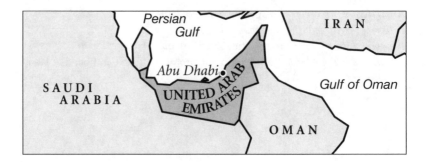

Major Languages: Arabic, Persian, English
Total Population: 2,369,000
Population 0–34: 1,338,000
Life Expectancy: 74 years
Religion: Muslim 65.45%, Hindu 17.00%, Christian 9.25%, Buddhist 4.00%,
    other 2.50%, nonreligious 1.30%, Baha'i 0.50%
Literacy Rate: male 79%, female 80%

Oil was discovered in the United Arab Emirates (UAE) in 1962, and since that time the country has made great strides economically, socially, and materially. The UAE holds 10 percent of the world's oil and natural gas reserves. These reserves are predicted to last another 100 years. The UAE can boast that it is one of the most developed countries in the Middle East, although this prosperity has not come without a price. With so much money, the society now has discretionary income for drugs, prostitution, and pornography.

A sociologist from the UAE noted that the young people are being spoiled with so much money. He said that they can afford to either visit foreign prostitutes locally or go abroad regularly on sex tours. The result of engaging in prostitution has been an increase in AIDS cases. One nurse in a women's hospital said, "We have seen whole families that tested positive. The women here are ignorant of these matters, and the men have such totally separate lives that their wives have no idea what they are doing." The sex traffic between Thailand and the UAE is being blamed for the high incidence of AIDS among the Arab population in the Arabian Peninsula. Packaged tours to Bangkok's brothels and night-clubs are a regular attraction, where 30 percent to 50 percent of the prostitutes are known to be infected with AIDS. Medical personnel describe the Emirates as the AIDS capital of the Gulf.

The children of the UAE have been dubbed as having "wealthy neglect syndrome." Many mothers spend their days watching TV and allow their children to be raised by foreign maids who do not speak Arabic and therefore cannot communicate with them. The youths have little to do and become bored. Their idleness and abundance of money become a disastrous combination.

One of the advantages of this wealth is that women have more educational opportunities, although they may suffer for delaying marriage until their education is complete. One young woman, Helhal, lent insight into the thinking of many young professional women. "I wanted very much to marry. I love children, and I wanted my own," Helhal said, "but in my family, we are permitted to marry only cousins. Since I delayed marriage to get an education, there are no unmarried cousins left, so I will remain single." She talks freely about her decision. "If I had chosen to marry against my family's wishes, I would have had to be prepared to separate myself from them because they would disown me. I am emotionally tied to my family, and they are very important to me. I would not risk my closeness to them because of a marriage of which they do not approve."

With a per capita income of over U.S.$17,400, the United Arab Emirates enjoys a standard of living experienced by only a few other countries in the world. BMWs, Ferraris, and Mercedes, along with Jeeps and Land Cruisers, make up the bulk of automobiles on the streets of the capital city of Abu Dhabi. UAE telecommunication ranks with some of the best in the world. The UAE has more multistory air-conditioned malls than the population warrants, and many more are under construction. The number of banks and jewelry stores per capita is the highest in the world.

Eighty-five percent of the population is expatriate. Europeans and Americans come mainly to work in the petroleum industry. Almost every home has at least one servant of Filipino, Indian, Sri Lankan, or Pakistani descent. The expatriate community is allowed to worship as it pleases without government interference, and Christians may advertise openly for special meetings. This is due in part to favor the church has with the government because of providing services for the people prior to their increase in wealth. In the past Protestants provided hospitals and health clinics for the people.

Christians are not allowed to proselytize, and a Muslim who converts to Christianity is considered apostate and may be killed for renouncing his or her faith.

Prayer Points

⌐· Pray that the local church will seek God for strategic ways to minister to children, teens, and young adults.

⌐· Pray that Christian videos, radio broadcasts, SAT-7 TV broadcasts, and literature distribution will be effective in reaching this generation.

⌐· Pray that the people of UAE will not allow their riches to spiritually lull them to sleep.

⌐· Pray that the people of UAE will have a longing to have a personal relationship with Esa (Jesus Christ), whom the Koran mentions more times than Muhammad.

⌐· Pray that the church will have a heart for missions locally and abroad, especially in other needy 10/40 Window countries.

⌐· Pray that as this generation seeks God for its purpose in life, it will have a hunger to know more about Jesus Christ and His plan for people's lives.

⌐· Pray that alcohol, other drugs, and the growing problem of prostitution will not ensnare the young people.

Quick Reference

Ethnic Breakdown: Emiri 19%, other Arab and Iranian 23%, South Asian 50%, other 8%
Type of Government: Confederation of six monarchies
Economy: Industry 52%, Services 45%, Agriculture 3%
Per capita income: U.S.$17,400
National debt: U.S.$15.5 billion
Economic conditions: Prosperous, stable economy

Education
Quality of education: School system is well organized. Instruction includes mandatory Koranic curriculum.
Gender discrimination against girls: Girls are being educated equally with boys.

Religion
Religious concerns: Evangelism is prohibited. The conversion of a Muslim to Christianity is punishable by death. Christian education and witnessing to nationals are severely restricted.
Status of the church: No national church exists. Only foreign Christians have freedom to worship and witness. The expatriate church needs more leadership, discipleship, and evangelism training.
Are Christians being persecuted? No

Societal Viewpoint Toward Children
Are they viewed as precious? Yes
Are there street children? No significant data available.

Is there a large population of orphans? No significant data available.

Are there child soldiers? No significant data available.

Is child labor a problem? A significant number of camel jockeys are children under the minimum employment age of 15.

Uzbekistan

Major Languages: Uzbek, Russian, Tajik
Total Population: 24,756,000
Population 0–34: 17,905,000
Life Expectancy: 64 years
Religion: Muslim 83.50%, nonreligious 14.52%, Christian 1.28%,
  Buddhist 0.30%, traditional ethnic 0.20%, Jewish 0.20%
Literacy Rate: male 100%, female 100%

Sasha put the little brown book under her coat and held it close to her body. She purposed to look at it when she got home. She would read it over and over again and even memorize the sayings. The man who gave her the book told her there were only a few of these books published in all of Uzbekistan and each one was precious.

Once at home Sasha took off her coat and laid the book on the table. "Mama, look at what the man from the Bible Society gave me."

Nadia turned from tending to her baby chickens near the warm stove in the kitchen to look at Sasha's new book. "Oh, Sasha, I never thought I would see the day we would get a Bible in the Uzbek language." She turned the pages carefully. "Look at what this says, 'To fear the Lord is to hate evil.' Sounds like a very wise saying to me."

"It is filled with wise sayings. The man called it 'The Proverbs of Solomon' and said that Solomon was the wisest man who ever lived. Mama, can we read the Proverbs tonight before we eat dinner?"

"Of course. Your father and your sisters will also enjoy hearing them."

The people of Uzbekistan love proverbs and wise sayings. On March 30, 2001, the first edition of Proverbs was released in the country. Ten thousand books were printed for distribution. Compass Direct, a news-reporting agency based in Istanbul, Turkey, reported that an official ceremony was held in Uzbekistan's capital city of Tashkent. At the ceremony, the Deputy Chairman for Religious Affairs congratulated the Bible Society of Uzbekistan and its partnering translators on the historic release of the book.

U zbekistan proclaimed its independence from the Soviet Union on September 1, 1991, and became an independent republic four months later when the Soviet Union disbanded. It remains one of the poorest areas in the former Soviet states, and its mixture of over 30 different ethnic groups sometimes causes tension. More than 60 percent of its people live in densely populated rural communities, where many of the schools are outdated and poorly maintained. In recent years, school enrollment has dropped because children are leaving the classroom to work in the cotton fields and in the service industry to provide extra income for their families. Poverty is extreme, but the people are warm and friendly and willing to share what they have with others.

Environmental pollution is a major problem for the Uzbeks, especially those persons living in the polluted Aral Sea area, where it is estimated that 69 out of 100 adults are terminally ill. The health-care system is unable to care for the needs of all these people. Children are in desperate need of better health care and protection from pollution-related illnesses.

Several prayer journeys have been conducted into the country, and believers were found. One church located in the capital city has over 3,000 members and has planted over 55 churches in neighboring communities. The majority of the population is Muslim. The government remains resistant to the gospel, and it is against the law to preach the gospel. Believers face persecution from authorities and ostracism from their families.

Prayer Points

- Pray that God will raise up Christian organizations to eradicate environmental pollution, which is taking a toll on the population, especially children, teens, and young adults.
- Pray that children, teens, and young adults will have visions and dreams of Jesus Christ and know the great love He has for them.
- Pray that God will draw entire Uzbek families to Himself through dreams and visions.
- Pray that the future young leaders will know Christ and will govern their nations by His principles.
- Pray that believers will develop culturally relevant Christian reading materials, since Uzbekistan is blessed with such a high literacy rate.

↩· Pray that the Aral Sea will be cleaned up. Many illnesses and deaths of children are caused by poor sanitation and pollution.

Quick Reference

Ethnic Breakdown: Uzbek 71%, Russian 8%, Tajik 5%, Kazak 4%, Karakalpak 2%, Tatar 2%, other 8%
Type of Government: Republic, with executive power concentrated in the presidency
Economy: Services 46%, Agriculture 27%, Industry 27%
Per capita income: U.S.$970
National debt: U.S.$3.2 billion
Economic conditions: Poor

Education
Quality of education: Budget constraints are causing a decline. There is great need for more schools and teachers.
Gender discrimination against girls: For girls, domestic chores take precedence over education.

Religion
Religious concerns: Evangelism is restricted. Proselytizing and conversion are illegal.
Status of the church: The few national believers need discipleship and leadership training.
Are Christians being persecuted? Yes.

Societal Viewpoint Toward Children
Are they viewed as precious? Yes
Are there street children? No specific data available.
Is there a large population of orphans? No
Are there child soldiers? No specific data available.
Is child labor a problem? Children are kept out of school to harvest and to work in the service industry.

Viet Nam

Major Languages: Vietnamese, English, French

Total Population: 78,774,000

Population 0–34: 60,623,000

Life Expectancy: 69 years

Religion: Buddhist 54.14%, nonreligious 21.80%, Christian 8.16%, traditional ethnic 8.10%, Cao Dai/Hoa Hao 5.60%, Chinese 1.10%, Muslim 0.70%, Baha'i 0.40%

Literacy Rate: male 97%, female 91%

*L*ai Li placed the crutch under her arm and headed to market. With her crutch she could walk quickly, especially during the first part of the day before her arm got tired. She adjusted her eyes to the bright sun as she walked toward the busy street where she would buy rice and vegetables for herself and her three-year-old son.

One day at the market she met a man who asked to speak with her. "What's your name?" the tall American asked through an interpreter.

"Lai Li," she replied.

"My name is Jeff. I am here to work on a project in Viet Nam. May I ask what happened to your foot?" He pointed to the missing limb.

"I stepped on a land mine," she answered.

"Maybe I can help you. First I'd like to show you a magic trick," Jeff said and smiled.

"Yes, yes," she said. She liked to be entertained. She watched as the interpreter knelt down before Jeff, took the heel of Jeff's shoe in his palms, and began to twist Jeff's foot in a complete circle. She put her hand on her face in horror as Jeff yelped as if in excruciating pain. Surely this was a trick!

Jeff pulled up his pants to reveal an artificial leg. "You see, I have the same problem as you. I lost my leg on a land mine in this very country

30 years ago. I have help now, so I don't use crutches like you do. Would you like a foot like mine to help you walk without a crutch?"

"Could it be possible to walk without my crutch?" Lai Li exclaimed.

"Yes, it is. My brother and I have come to Saigon to fit people like you with new limbs. Here is our card. Will you come and visit us at the clinic so we can get you a new leg?"

The next day Lai Li asked her neighbor to take her on his motorcycle to the clinic to meet Jeff. Over the space of two weeks, she received a new leg and began following instructions on how to care for her new limb and walk properly so that she would not be in pain.

*L*ai Li is one of many who as children lost limbs to land mines planted during past wars. Jeff received a grant from the U.S. government to set up a clinic in Viet Nam to help those who have had their limbs amputated. He trained Vietnamese workers to run the clinic and fit artificial limbs so that the project could continue long after he returned to the United States.

Extreme poverty has taken its toll on Viet Nam. Beggars, some of them children, roam the streets, asking for money to feed themselves and their families. Although the production of rice has gone up in recent years, approximately 40 percent to 50 percent of children under 12 years of age are malnourished. Families simply cannot afford to feed their children.

As in many countries, extreme poverty leads parents to sell their children into prostitution and bonded labor. Many children are "economic orphans," given over to orphanages because their parents cannot afford to take care of them or have been displaced and have decided to leave them because of the uncertainty of their future.

Believers in Viet Nam are beaten, harassed, and imprisoned for their faith. Even though persecuted, the church is growing as people meet in house churches.

The children of Viet Nam need our prayers.

Prayer Points

⌇· Pray that God will raise up effective ministries to impact children, teens, and young adults with the gospel. Pray also for the safety of the large number of street children who often fall prey to prostitution, commercial sex, drugs, and harsh labor.

⌇· Pray that there will be enough food produced to feed the children.

⌇· Pray that parents' economic situations will improve so that they will not have to sell their children into prostitution and bonded labor.

Foreign investments have fallen drastically from U.S.$8.3 billion in 1996 to approximately U.S.$1.6 billion in 1999.

⌣· Pray that the poverty cycle of economic orphans will be broken.

⌣· Pray that the trafficking of children will stop and that predators will find other ways to make a living.

⌣· Pray that Christian organizations will open schools for children, teens, and young adults living in poverty-stricken areas.

⌣· Pray that God will use Vietnamese Christians to impact children, teens, and young adults with the gospel.

Quick Reference

Ethnic Breakdown: Vietnamese 90%, Chinese 3%, Muong, Tai, Meo, Khmer, Man, and Cham 7%

Type of Government: Communist State Party–dominated constitutional republic

Economy: Services 41%, Industry 33%, Agriculture 26%

Per capita income: U.S.$240

National debt: U.S.$7.3 billion

Economic conditions: Extremely poor

Education

Quality of education: A shortage of schools and teachers is currently developing. Schooling is not free. There may be no school within walking distance.

Gender discrimination against girls: Domestic chores take precedence over education.

Religion

Religious concerns: Evangelism is prohibited.

Status of the church: The church needs discipleship and leadership training as it evangelizes in Viet Nam's hostile environment. Christians make up a rapidly growing 10 percent of the population.

Are Christians being persecuted? Yes.

Societal Viewpoint Toward Children

Are they viewed as precious? No

Are there street children? There are approximately 19,000 street children in Viet Nam. Children may be forced out of their homes because their families do not have enough money to care for them.

Is there a large population of orphans? Yes

Are there child soldiers? No specific data available.

Is child labor a problem? Thousands of children are exploited in labor. Widespread poverty continues to contribute to child prostitution in major cities, especially among girls but also among boys.

Western Sahara

Major Languages: Hassaniyah Arabic, Moroccan Arabic
Total Population: 245,000
Population 0–34: No data available
Life Expectancy: 66 years
Religion: Muslim 100%
Literacy Rate: male 57%, female 31%

I've never seen this much water in all my life," Mariam exclaimed as she looked at a swimming pool for the first time. Slowly she ventured into the cool blue water, coaxed by her new American host family, the Armstrongs. To most American children, swimming pools and summertime fun go together, but Mariam is a Sahrawi refugee child from Western Sahara who lives in the Sahara Desert region of western Algeria. Sahrawi children never see water in larger quantities than what a small bucket will hold. One child who visited Spain drank copious amounts of water in an effort to store up enough in his body to last him through the remainder of the summer when he returned home to the desert.

Each summer approximately 10,500 children are placed with host families in Europe (Spain receives the most) and the United States. Families in the U.S. received their first children in 1999, when nine children were hosted, and the number has increased in subsequent years. These children gain exposure to Western culture, learn English, and establish ties that link them forever with loving host families. They also gain a reprieve from the 130-degree desert heat with no electricity or running water. Extremely intelligent, the children want to learn and experience everything they can about Western and European cultures and people.

These children serve as a bridge between two cultures, often replete with misconceptions on both sides. One Sahrawi mother repeatedly asked, "Are you going to take my daughter to the United States and put her in an institution?"

The mandate of Matthew 25:40 to invite strangers into our homes rests on us all. Jesus Christ said, "I tell you the truth, whatever you did for one of the least of these brothers of mine, you did for me."

*T*he country of Western Sahara was once a Spanish protectorate. When the Spanish withdrew in 1976, Moroccan troops invaded the country and forced a large portion of the inhabitants to flee for their lives into the desert under a fiery hail of napalm. The majority of people from this land still live in the desert of Western Algeria. They have not been able to return to their homeland even to visit their relatives who remain in Western Sahara. Large sand berms, complete with barbed-wire fences and land mines, deter any of those who live in the desert from visiting relatives.

While the Sahrawi Republic, the government formed by the refugees living in Western Algeria, is recognized by over 70 nations and has diplomatic standing at the United Nations, Moroccans govern the Sahrawi's homeland of Western Sahara in matters such as government, spending, infrastructure, and health care. The United Nations–sponsored referendum on self-determination for Western Sahara and whether the Sahrawi can return to their homeland has repeatedly been postponed. Meanwhile the Sahrawi still exist in tents. Will Christians respond in their time of need?

Recently UNICEF published the results of a study that showed today's Sahrawi children to be approximately two inches shorter than their parents were at the same age. This is attributable to nutritional deficiencies (fruits and vegetables are in short supply in the desert) and harsh environmental elements. Some of the refugee camps have gardens of approximately 10 acres, but these supply only a meager amount of the fruits and vegetables a child needs to ensure proper growth.

Sahrawi family units have strong ties, and the Sahrawi Republic government encourages large families and promotes education. Ambassador Moulud Said, the representative of the Sahrawi Republic in the United States, said, "Our children are the future, and they must be educated. We will not fight for our cause unless we have to. If we must fight, we will do so for an educated society. We will not shed one drop of blood for an uneducated nation." This philosophy has served the Sahrawi refugees well. They have a 95 percent literacy rate, with boys and girls receiving equal education.

The country of Western Sahara is closed to the gospel, and there are no known media outreaches to the children and youth.

Prayer Points

～• Pray that the Sahrawi children and their families will be able to leave the refugee camps peacefully and return to their homeland.

～• Pray that the international community will bring pressure on Morocco to agree to the desires of the Sahrawi people as to whether they want to be under Moroccan rule or be self-governed so that this generation will be able to build a future in its homeland.

～• Pray for the young adults living in the refugee camps who have never seen their relatives in the occupied territory of Western Sahara to be united with their families.

～• Pray for children who don't have proper food to eat or enough safe water to drink.

～• Pray that Christians internationally will be able to impact the lives of the Sahrawis with the gospel.

～• Pray for the babies who are born and raised under poor medical conditions to receive adequate health care, including eye gear to protect them from harsh weather.

～• Pray that the children will have adequate blankets to protect them from the extremely cold desert nights.

～• Pray that God will use leaders to properly train up the nation for the time when He opens the door for the people to return to their homeland.

～• Pray for President Mohammed Abdelaziz, Ambassador Moulud Said, and other leaders of the Sahrawi Republic to find Jesus Christ as they are seeking to preserve their nation.

～• Pray that we as Christians will do all we can to provide help for their poor.

～• Pray that young adults will be used mightily by God to help build the infrastructure of a nation when the people return to their homeland.

Quick Reference

Ethnic Breakdown: Sahrawi, Berber, Arab (percentages unavailable)
Type of Government: De facto control by Morocco of Western Sahara. The United Nations oversees the refugees in Western Algeria.

Economy: Trade 48%, Industry 34%, Agriculture 18%
Per capita income: No specific data available.
National debt: No specific data available.
Economic conditions: Extremely poor

Education

Quality of education: Education in the Sahrawi refugee camps is free and
   compulsory through primary school. It does not have much value in
   the occupied territory of Western Sahara.

Gender discrimination against girls: Females in the Sahrawi refugee camps have
   equal opportunities with boys. Education is not as important to the families
   living in the occupied territory.

Religion

Religious concerns: Evangelism is prohibited.
Status of the church: No national church exists.
Are Christians being persecuted? No

Societal Viewpoint Toward Children

Are they viewed as precious? Yes
Are there street children? No
Is there a large population of orphans? No
Are there child soldiers? No
Is child labor a problem? No specific data available.

Yemen

Major Languages: Arabic, Mahri, Malay, Farsi (Western)
Total Population: 17,479,000
Population 0–34: 13,977,000
Life Expectancy: 60 years
Religion: Muslim 99.94%, Christian 0.05%, Jewish 0.01%
Literacy Rate: male 62%, female 18%

On July 5, 2000, a Yemeni court sentenced 25-year-old Muhammad Omer Haji to death. Muhammad was allowed one week to reconsider his conversion from Islam to Christianity. If he failed to come before the court and recant his newfound religion three times, he faced execution for apostasy, as prescribed by Islamic law.

"His situation is very serious and dangerous," the convert's defense lawyer, Muhammad Abdul Karmi Omarawi, told a Compass Direct news reporter.

Muhammad Haji described his imprisonment in Yemen, with its constant beatings, threats, and interrogation. For weeks he was harshly beaten every night by police officers who warned him that they would kill him if he did not repent and turn back to Islam. Haji had fled Somalia in 1994 and come to Yemen as a refugee, and the officers wanted to know names of other Somali Christians he knew. Haji said, "Every night they beat and punished me. I was not able to stand, walk, or even talk." On what he described as his worst night, three security officers and three policemen masked him and took him up a high mountain at midnight. After giving him a severe beating, they vowed to throw him off the mountain if he refused to recant. "To save my life that night," Haji admitted, "I said I believed in Islam. Otherwise I would have died."

Later Muhammad Haji's wife was also arrested and beaten. Even her pleas for milk for their baby were denied.

Haji's lawyer said his client's choice was clear cut: He would live if he chose to return to Islam, and he would die if he chose to remain a Christian.

Yemen is reported to be one of the poorest countries in the Arab world, with well over 40 percent of the country living in abject poverty. For almost 20 years the people of Yemen lived in the grip of civil war. In 1967 the southern portion of the country adopted a strict Marxist orientation. Hundreds of citizens fled to the northern sector. Only as recently as 1990 was the country united as the Republic of Yemen.

The children suffer as a result of the war. Lack of infrastructure and diversion of money to purchase arms and maintain troops siphoned money away from educational programs, college grants, and development of health-care programs to prevent childhood diseases.

Even though the law states that everyone is to be educated for at least nine years, this provision is not enforced. Because of poverty, many children are required to work in subsistence farming. Even in urban areas children work in stores and workshops, sell goods on the streets, and beg. According to a recent UNICEF report, many girls do not attend school at all. The female literacy rate in Yemen is 18 percent, and in most of the rural areas, female literacy is nonexistent.

Disease is one of Yemen's worst enemies. Diarrhea, typhoid, and malaria constantly plague the children. Officials in the capital plead for foreign workers to bring simple, life-giving health principles to their people.

Addiction to *khat* is also a national cause for concern. Up to a third of the available resources of land and water go toward the growing of khat, a plant that works as an amphetamine when chewed. Yemeni adults typically chew khat leaves each afternoon for at least five hours. People spend as much as a quarter to a third of their cash income on the plant, even forgoing food for themselves and their families.

Even in the midst of disease and poverty, the Yemeni people consider children to be their greatest asset. Sons are valued as heirs, and daughters are valued because they bear children. Girls are taught to be patient, loving, modest, and helpful. Boys learn that they must protect the women in their family and uphold the family honor.

The young boys love to play soccer. Often there is no soccer ball available, so they use whatever is handy—from empty bottles to rag balls. Girls seldom have time to play as they are engaged in cooking, tending to the younger children, and doing household chores.

Not only treasured by their families, the children are also treasured by God. In Isaiah 45:3, God says, "I will give you the treasures of darkness, riches stored in secret places." We have a right before the Father to claim the precious "treasures" of Yemen for the kingdom of God.

Prayer Points

～· Pray for the female children of Yemen. They are poorly educated, and many do not attend school at all.

～· Pray for Christian organizations to respond to the pleas of the government to teach simple principles of hygiene and sanitation.

～· Pray for an end to the addiction of the Yemeni people to khat.

～· Pray for God's ideas to reach this country through the children, teens, and young adults of Yemen.

～· Pray for innovative strategies in presenting the gospel that are relevant to the youth culture.

～· Pray for the continued protection and strength of the Yemeni believers. Pray for good discipleship materials for young believers.

～· Pray for improvements in the health-care system.

～· Pray for an end to FGM. Praise God that the government is working to eliminate this inhumane practice.

Quick Reference

Ethnic Breakdown: Yemeni Arab 89.3%, Somali 3.7%, Sudanese Arab 1.7%, Arabized Black 1.1%, Indo-Pakistani 1.0%, other 3.2%

Type of Government: Republic

Economy: Industry 42%, Services 38%, Agriculture 20%

Per capita income: U.S.$260

National debt: U.S.$4.5 billion

Economic conditions: Extreme poverty. Over 40 percent of the population lives below the poverty line.

Education

Quality of education: An estimated 45 percent of children between the ages of 6 and 15 do not attend school.

Gender discrimination against girls: Not much importance is placed on education for girls.

Religion

Religious concerns: Evangelism is prohibited.

Status of the church: Yemen is one of the world's least evangelized countries, and the government will not allow the few resident Christians to witness. The few Christians need encouragement, discipleship, and leadership training.

Are Christians being persecuted? Yes

Societal Viewpoint Toward Children

Are they viewed as precious? Yes

Are there street children? Children may work or beg in the street markets, but they go home to their families at night.

Is there a large population of orphans? No specific data available.

Are there child soldiers? No specific data available.

Is child labor a problem? Children are routinely used in the labor force. Many children are required to work in subsistence farming because of the poverty of their families.

Glossary of Terms

Abaya: a long robe-style outer garment worn by Muslim women.

Animism: worship of nature and inanimate objects with the belief that spirits inhabit them.

Believer: a person who has placed his or her faith in Jesus Christ as Lord and Savior.

Bonded labor: work under an obligation or according to a prearranged written agreement.

Burqa: a tentlike garment Muslim women may be required to wear in public that covers women from head to toe with only a small embroidered grill at eye level through which they can see.

Chinese: where found in the religion statistics provided for each nation, "Chinese" refers to a blend of folk religions, Daoism, and Buddhism.

Conscription: compulsory enrollment, especially in the armed forces.

Culturally sensitive: presenting the gospel to people in their own language and cultural context.

Dalai Lama: a Tibetan Buddhist leader of the Yellow Hat sect (ruling in exile in India). Ethnic Tibetans carry and post his picture, even though many have been killed, imprisoned, or tortured for this "crime."

Ethnolinguistic: an ethnic or racial group whose identity is distinguished by traditions of common descent, history, customs, and language.

Ethnoreligionist: follower of a non-Christian or pre-Christian religion tied closely to a specific ethnic group.

Fatwa: an order issued by one of the *ulama,* the body of religious scholars recognized as experts in Muslim religion and law. A fatwa might or might not be enforced by a government, depending in part on the government's degree of adherence to Islamic law and the relationship between a particular government and the scholars in their midst.

FGM: female genital mutilation is the term used to refer to the removal of part or all of the female genitalia.

Forced labor: being forced to work, often for low wages or no wages at all.

Ger: a strong, practical tent used by nomadic herders living on the Asian steppes in Mongolia.

Hijab: a veil that covers all of a Muslim woman's hair.

Imam: a Muslim who serves as a spiritual leader of a mosque.

Indigenous religions: a set of beliefs in a supernatural power or powers originating and growing in or from a particular environment. In some areas, the indigenous religions are ethnic or tribal, each group having its own particular tradition.

Intercessor: one who prays for the needs of others.

Islam: literally means "submission to the will of Allah (god)."

Islamic republic or state: a government that bases its laws on the Koran.

Jihad: an Islamic concept often defined as "holy war," in defense of Islam in militant opposition to any other religion.

Karmapa Lama: a boy thought to be the 17th reincarnation of the great living Buddha. He is of the Black Hat sect of Tibetan Buddhism and secretly left Tibet as a young man in December of 1998 seeking religious teaching in India.

Khat (or *myrrha* in Swahili): a leafy addictive plant grown in the highlands of Kenya and Ethiopia; also *qat* or *kat*.

Khmer Rouge: Communist movement, headed by Pol Pot, that ruled Cambodia from 1975 to 1979 and murdered, worked to death, or starved close to 1.7 million Cambodians. Still active today as a guerrilla force, the Khmer Rouge recruits many children as soldiers.

Koran: book of sacred writings accepted by Muslims as revelations made to Muhammad by Allah through the angel Gabriel.

Lama: a Buddhist priest believed to be reincarnated. Lamas are divided into several sects distinguished by the color of their hats.

Lost boys of Sudan: a group of approximately 4,300 Sudanese boys who fled in the early 1990s from their wartorn home in southern Sudan. They walked 1,200 miles to a refugee camp in Kenya and are now in the process of relocating to the United States.

Muhammad: a man who felt God had called him to be a prophet. During the 600s he wrote the Koran, which contains the basis of the doctrines and teachings of Islam. Muhammad is known as the father of Islam.

Mullah: an educated Muslim teacher, trained in traditional religious law and doctrine, who usually holds an official post.

Muslim-background believer (MBB): a former Muslim who has placed his or her faith in Jesus Christ as Lord and Savior.

Nationals: peoples or ethnic groups of a particular country having a common origin, tradition, and language; indigenous birth or origin in a place or region; people who have always lived in a place, as distinguished from a visitor, temporary resident, or foreigner.

Nonreligious: persons professing no religion and having no interest in religion.

Panchen Lama: the 11-year-old Yellow Hat, recognized by the Dalai Lama as his successor, who is being held captive, along with his family, by the Chinese.

Prayer journeyer: one who travels along strategically developed routes for the purpose of waging spiritual warfare and establishing the blessing of God throughout the designated area.

Prayerwalk: walking through a neighborhood, city, or country and praying for the area.

Praying Through the Window I: global prayer initiative in October 1993 that focused on 62 countries located in the 10/40 Window as part of the AD2000 Movement.

Praying Through the Window II: global prayer initiative in October 1995 that focused prayer on the 100 Gateway Cities of the 10/40 Window as part of the AD2000 Movement.

Praying Through the Window III: global prayer initiative in October 1997 that focused prayer on the 10/40 Window unreached people groups, most of whom have never heard the gospel in their own language and in a culturally sensitive way, as part of the AD2000 Movement.

Praying Through the Window IV: global prayer initiative in October 1999 that focused prayer once again on the countries of the 10/40 Window. This was the last prayer initiative of the AD2000 Movement.

Praying Through the Window V: global prayer initiative in October 2001 that focused prayer on the children, teens, and young adults in the 10/40 Window. The prayer initiative was continued under WINDOW INTERNATIONAL NETWORK.

Ramadan: the month-long fast during the ninth month of the Muslim year in which one abstains from food, drink, and sexual intercourse from sunup to sundown.

Sharia: a legal system based on the teachings of the Koran. As Islamic fundamentalist movements gain more power, there is growing pressure to adopt *sharia* in many Muslim nations.

Shiite Islam: the minority branch of Islam that traces its lineage to Ali, the first cousin and son-in-law of Muhammad. The Shiites have traditionally represented the underclass and the disenfranchised in Islam.

Soft witness: witnessing by prayer and good deeds.

Syncretism: the belief and practice of fusing together two or more religions.

Taliban: the ruling party of Afghanistan until the U.S.-led coalition against terrorism caused its collapse following the terrorist attacks of September 11, 2001. Never internationally recognized as Afghanistan's legitimate government except by Pakistan, Saudi Arabia, and the United Arab Emirates, the Taliban emerged in Kandahar in 1994 as a militant group of Islamic religious students. It took the capital, Kabul, in 1996 and eventually controlled around 95 percent of the country under its strict interpretation of Islamic law.

Three-Self Patriotic Movement: one of two official "churches" in China, headed by government-appointed leaders and consistent with Communist ideology. It was founded in 1954 by Chairman Mao.

UNICEF: United Nations Children's Fund.

Unreached people groups: those who have yet to hear the gospel in their own language or within a cultural context they can understand.

Videmegon: the practice of selling young girls to a family as a servant or laborer; also a girl sold in this way. Often the girls are promised an education, or their family is promised wages in exchange for their services.

Zoroastrianism: a religion founded around 600 B.C. by Zoroaster. Zoroastrians believe in the dualism of good and evil as either a cosmic dualism between the supreme god and an evil spirit of death or as an ethical dualism within the human consciousness.

Bibliography

The 10/40 Window Reporter Newsletter. Christian Information Network. <www.win1040.com>

Africa Inter-Mennonite Mission. <www.aimmintl.org>

Africa Policy Electronic Distribution List. <www.africapolicy.org>

Ahmed, Nafeez. "Algeria and the Paradox of Democracy." *Algeria Watch International*, November 1, 2000. <www.pmwatch.org>

Algeria Information. <www.reach4algeria.com>

Ali, Sharifah Enayat. *Cultures of the World: Afghanistan*. New York: Benchmark Books, 1995.

Amnesty International Human Rights Page. *Annual Report 1999*. <www.amnesty.org>

Amnesty International News Service. <www.amnestyusa.org>

Arab Net. <www.arabnet.com>

Arnot, Dr. Bob. "The Children of Sudan, Innocent Victims of War and Famine." *Save the Children*. <www.savethechildren.org/press/pr>

Ashagrie, Kebebew. "Statistics on Working Children and Hazardous Child Labor in Brief." International Labor Organization. Geneva: International Labor Office, revised April 1998.

Asia Society. "Video Letter from Japan: My Family." 1988. <www.askasia.org>

Asianinfo.org. <www.asiainfo.org>

Augustin, Byron. *Enchantment of the World: Qatar*. Chicago: Children's Press, 1997.

Badjan, Isatou. *The Independent Column*. February 16, 2001. <www.allafrica.com>

BBC News. "Country Profiles." <http://news6.thdo.bbc.co.uk/hi/english/world/africa/country_profiles/newsid_1054000/1054396.stm>

Beaton, Margaret. *Enchantment of the World: Senegal*. Chicago: Children's Press, 1997.

Berg, Elizabeth. *Countries of the World: Ethiopia*. Philadelphia: Gareth Stevens Publishing, 2000.

Bethany World Prayer Center. "Unreached Peoples Prayer Profiles."
  <www.bethany-wpc.org/profiles/home.html>

Boko, Michee. "High Levels of Air Pollution Spur Respiratory Ailments."
  IPS News Reports. <www.ips.org/index.htm>

Branigin, William. "Health Care Woes Burden Vietnam." *Washington Post
  Foreign Service*. <www.vinsight.org/0494/health.htm>

Britannica Book of the Year 2000. Encyclopedia Britannica, Inc., 2000.

Britannica Book of the Year 2001. Encyclopedia Britannica, Inc., 2001.

Britannica.com. <www.britannica.com>

Britton, Dolly. *The People of Thailand*. New York: Rosen Publishing Group,
  1997.

Cahill, Mary Jane. *Major World Nations: Israel*. Philadelphia: Chelsea House
  Publishing, 2000.

Caleb Project. <www.calebproject.org>

Cambodian Outreach Project. <www.cambodiaoutreach.org>

CATO Institute. <www.cato.org>

Central Intelligence Agency World Factbook 2000. <www.cia.gov>

The Consultative Group on Early Childhood Care and Development.
  "Childrearing Practices in Sub-Saharan Africa." <www.ecdgroup.com>

Cooper, Robert. *Cultures of the World: Bahrain*. New York: Benchmark
  Books, 2000.

Countries of the World and Their Leaders. Detroit: The Gale Group, Thomsen
  Learning, 2001.

Countrywatch.com. <www.countrywatch.com>

Cox, Christopher. "Cambodian Kids Roam the Streets." *Boston Herald*,
  April 27, 2000.

CultureGrams. <www.culturegrams.com>

Development Programme. <www.meltingpot.fortunecity.com/lebanon/
  254/undp.htm>

Docherty, J. P. *Major World Nations: Iraq*. Philadelphia: Chelsea House
  Publishing, 1999.

Ebert, Michael, ed. *WindoWatchman.*Colorado Springs: Christian
  Information Network, 1994.

E-Conflict World Encyclopedia. <www.emulateme.com>

Education International. <www.ei-ie.org>

Encarta 2000. <www.encarta.com>

Every Home For Christ Newsletter. January/February 2001.

Fisher, Frederick. *Countries of the World: Indonesia.* Milwaukee: Gareth Stevens Publishing, 2000.

Foster, Leila Merrell. *Enchantment of the World: Afghanistan.* Chicago: Children's Press, 1996.

———. *Enchantment of the World: Iraq.* Chicago: Children's Press, 1991.

———. *Enchantment of the World: Oman.* Chicago: Children's Press, 1999.

Frank, Nicole. *Welcome to Egypt.* Milwaukee: Gareth Stevens Incorporated, 1999.

Geographic.org. *Taiwan Economy Report.* <www.photius.com/wfb2000/countries/taiwan/taiwan_economy.html>

Global March Against Child Labour. *Child Labour News Service.* <www.globalmarch.org>

Goodman, James. *Cultures of the World: Thailand.* New York: Benchmark Books, 1991/1994.

Goodwin, Jan. *Price of Honour—Muslim Women Lift the Veil of Silence on the Islamic World.* London: Warner Books, 1994.

Goodwin, William. *India: Modern Nations of the World.* San Diego: Lucent Books, 2000.

Guinea Development Foundation, Inc. <www.guineadev.com>

Hassall, S, and PJ Hassall. *Brunei.* New York: Chelsea House, 1988.

Hassig, Susan M. *Countries of the World: Iraq.* New York: Gareth Stevens Publishing, 1993.

———. *Cultures of the World: Somalia.* New York: Benchmark Books, 1997.

Heinrichs, Ann. *Enchantment of the World: Nepal.* Chicago: Children's Press, 1996.

———. *Enchantment of the World: Tibet.* Chicago: Children's Press, 1996.

Hestler, Anna. *Cultures of the World: Yemen.* New York: Benchmark Books, 1999.

Hopkins, Michael, and Jawahir Yusuf Adam. *Somalia 1999 Human Development.* United Nations.

Human Rights Internet. <www.hri.ca>

Human Rights Watch. *World Report 1999, 2000.* Human Rights Development. <www.hrw.org>

The Institute on Religion and Democracy Report, "Brutal Facts About Life and Death in Sudan." <www.angelsinsudan.com>

International Christian Concern. <www.persecution.org>

International Monetary Fund. "Poverty Reduction Strategy Paper—Burkina Faso." <www.imf.org>

International Rescue Committee. <www.intrescom.org>

International Women's Rights Action Watch. *Country Report: Algeria*, September 1, 1998. <www.igc.org/iwraw/publications/algeria>

Japan Information Network. <www.jinjapan.org>

Japan Mission. <www.japanmission.org>

Johnson, Julia. *United Arab Emirates: Major World Nations*. New York: Chelsea House Publishing, 1987.

Johnson, Marcia L., and Jeffrey R. Johnson. *Daily Life in Japanese High Schools*. Indiana University, October 1996. <www.indiana.edu~japan/digest9.htm>

Johnstone, Patrick. *Operation World*. Grand Rapids, Mich.: Zondervan Publishing, 1993.

Joint United Nations Programme on HIV/AIDS. "UNAIDS/WHO Working Group on Global HIV/AIDS and STI Surveillance." <www.unaids.org>

Joshua Project 2000. <www.ad2000.org>

Just Grieve for Sudan. <www.jg4.com>

Kagda, Falaq. *Cultures of the World: Algeria*. New York: Benchmark Books, 1997.

Kaplan, Robert D. *The Ends of the Earth—A Journey at the Dawn of the 21st Century*. New York: Random House, 1996.

———. *The Ends of the Earth—A Journey to the Frontiers of Anarchy*. New York: Peter Smith Publisher, 2000.

Kemp, Charles. *Cambodian Health*. Baylor University. <www.baylor.edu/~Charles Kemp/ cambodian_health.html>

Kendra, Judith. *Threatened Cultures: Tibetans*. New York: Thomson Learning, 1994.

Kondansha's Encyclopedia of Japan. "Christianity in Japan." <www.baobab.or.jp/stranger/mypage/chrinjpa.htm>

Kowalczuk, Magda. "Japan: Homeless Sleep in Shadow of First-World Wealth." *IPS-Inter Press Service*, 1997. <www.oneworld.org/ips2/mar/japan.htm>

Lands and Peoples. Danbury: Groiler Educational Corp., 2001.

Lerner Geography Department Staff. *Uzbekistan*. (Then & Now Series). Minneapolis: Lerner Publications Company, 1993.

Levy, Patricia. *Cultures of the World: Sudan*. New York: Benchmark Books, 1997.

———. *Cultures of the World: Tibet*. New York: Benchmark Books, 1996.

Lies, Elaine. "Japan Suicide Rate Clings Near Record High." *Reuters,* June

30, 1999. <www.mentalhealth.about.com/health/mentalhealth/library/archives.htm>

Lyle, Garry. *Major World Nations: Iran.* Philadelphia: Chelsea House Publishing, 2000.

Martin, Alice. "Djibouti Drug Culture Leaves Dying Women High and Dry; The Social Fabric Is Unravelling." *The Guardian* (London), October 28, 1996.

McClung, Floyd, ed. *Light the Window.* Seattle: Youth With A Mission (YWAM) Publishing, 1999.

Medecins Sans Frontieres. *Activity Report—Project Profile.* <www.msf.org>

Milich, Leonard, and Mohammed Al-Sabbry. *The "Rational Peasant" vs. Sustainable Livelihoods: The Case of Qat in Yemen.* Society for International Development, 1995. <www.ag.arizona.edu/~lmilich/yemen.htm>

Mulloy, Martin. *Major World Nations: Syria.* Philadelphia: Chelsea House Publishing, 1999.

Munan, Heidi. *Cultures of the World: Malaysia.* New York: Benchmark Books, 1990.

Nation by Nation Almanac. <www.nationbynation.com>

National Geographic. Washington, D.C.: National Geographic Society.

Naylor, Kim. *Mali (People and Places of the World).* New York: Chelsea House Publishing, 1987.

Net Africa.com. <www.netafrica.com>

NgCheong-Lum, Roseline. *Cultures of the World: Maldives.* New York: Benchmark Books, 2000.

Nomachi, Kazuyoshi, and Robert Thurman. *Tibet.* Boston: Shambhala Publishing, 1997.

OC International. <www.oci.org>

"Old Cambodia War Zones Face Dire Poverty." U.N. <www.phnompenhdaily.com/02-10-99a.htm>

O'Shea, Maria. *Countries of the World: Iran.* Milwaukee: Gareth Stevens Publishing, 2000.

———. *Cultures of the World: Kuwait.* New York: Benchmark Books, 1999.

Otis, Jr., George. *Strongholds of the 10/40 Window.* Seattle: Youth With A Mission (YWAM) Publishing, 1995.

Panafrican News Agency. "Infant Mortality Rate in Nigeria Still High." January 28, 2001. <www.allafrica.com>

PeaceNet Prison Issues Desk. <www.prisonactivist.org>

Pegues, Beverly, ed. *WindoWatchman II.* Colorado Springs: Christian Information Network, 1997.

Pioneer Bible Translators. <www.pioneerbible.org>

Qatar Info. <www.qatar-info.com>

Raemy, Mylaene. "Ghana Today." *The World Book Encyclopedia.* Edition J.A. Chicago, 1977.

Relief Web. "The Use of Children as Soldiers in Africa." United Nations Office for the Coordination of Humanitarian Affairs (OCHA). <www.reliefweb.int/library/documents/chilsold>

Sachs, Susan. "Saudi Arabia Bridles as Rights Group Charges Widespread Abuses." *New York Times,* March 28, 2000. <www.library.cornell.edu/colldev/mideast/saudhr.htm>

Saigon Children's Charity. <www.saigonchildren.com>

SAO Cambodia. <www.sao-cambodia.org>

Seah, Audrey. *Cultures of the World: Vietnam.* New York: Benchmark Books, 1994.

Seffal, Rabah. *Cultures of the World: Niger.* New York: Benchmark Books, 2000.

Shapiro, Wendy. "The Problems of the Videmegons in Benin." <www.saisjhu.edu/depts/mideast/scnd/news/vol10>

Sheehan, Sean. *Cultures of the World: Lebanon.* New York: Benchmark Books, 1997.

South, Coleman. *Cultures of the World: Jordan.* New York: Benchmark Books, 1997.

———. *Cultures of the World: Syria.* New York: Benchmark Books, 1995.

Sunandini, Arora Lal. *Countries of the World: India.* Philadelphia: Gareth Stevens Publishing, 1999.

Tales of Asia. <www.talesofasia.com>

Target the Nations (compact disk). Galcom International, 1997. <www.galcom.org>

Thoennes, Kristin. *Countries of the World: Israel.* Mankato: Gareth Stevens Publishing, 1999.

———. *Countries of the World: Nigeria.* Mankato: Gareth Stevens Publishing, 1999.

———. *Thailand.* Mankato: Bridgestone Books, Capstone Press, 1999.

Tunisia Online. <www.tunisiaonline.com>

UNICEF. <www.unicef.org>

United Arab Emirates News. <www.worldskip.com/uae>

United Nations. <www.un.org>

United Nations High Commissioner for Refugees. Statistics, 1998. <www.unhcr.ch/refworld/refbib/refstat/1998/98tab01.htm>

United Nations Office of Drug Control and Crime Prevention Country Profile Reports. <www.odccp.org>

United States Agency for International Development Intra-Agency Working Group on Female Genital Cutting (FGC). "40% Nigerian Women Are Victims of Genital Cutting." As reported by *Vanguard Daily* (Lagos, Nigeria), March 2, 2001. <www.allafrica.com/stories/200103020233.html>

United States Census Bureau. <www.census.com>

United States Department of State. *2000 Annual Report on International Religious Freedom*. September 5, 2000. <www.state.gov/www/global/human_rights/>

United States Department of State. *Background Notes*. <www.state.gov/www/background notes/>

United States Department of State. *Country Reports on Human Rights Practices*. <www.state.gov/www/global/human_rights/>

United States Department of State. *Country Reports on International Religious Practices*. <www.state.gov/www/global/human_rights>

United States Department of State. *International Narcotics Control Strategy Report*. <www.state.gov/www/global/narcotics_law/>

United States Embassy in Conakry, Guinea. <www.eti-bull.net/usembassy/>

United States Library of Congress. "Country Studies." <www.loc.gov>

University of Minnesota. "United Nations Committee on Economic, Social and Cultural Rights." <www1.umn.edu/humanrts/un-orgs.htm>

University of Pennsylvania, School of Arts and Sciences. *Facts About the Republic of Benin: Official Document*. <www.sas.upenn.edu>

Vietnam: Sector Update/Health. <www.worldbank.org.vn/secup/navpl4.htm>

The White House Fact Sheet Released by the Office of the Press Secretary. "The United States and Nigeria: Joining Forces to Fight AIDS and Infectious Diseases." August 27, 2000. <www.state.gov/www/regions/africa/fswh_000827_aids.htm>

The Voice of the Martyrs. <www.persecution.com>

The Voice of the Martyrs. *Country Summaries: Special Issue 2001*.

Wagner, C. Peter, Stephen Peters, and Mark Wilson, eds. *Praying Through the 100 Gateway Cities of the 10/40 Window*. Seattle: Youth With A Mission (YWAM) Publishing, 1994.

Waseda University Library. "Abortion in Japan." August 16, 1999. <www.prochoice.about.com/newsissues prochoice/library/weekly/aa081699.htm>

Whitaker, Brian. "Weaning Yemen off Qat." *Middle East International*, 18 June 1999. <www.al-bab.com/yemen/artic/mei49.htm>

Whitehead, Susan. *Major World Nations: Jordan.* Philadelphia: Chelsea House Publishing, 1999.

Wilkins, Francis. *Let's Visit Thailand.* London: Burk Books, 1985.

Window Ministries for the 10/40 Window. <www.windowministries.org>

Women of Vision Newsletter. <www.AD2000.org>

World Bank Group Press Release. "World Bank Approves $11.7 Million Loan for National Health Program in Guinea-Bissau." November 26, 1997. <www.worldbank.org/html/extdr/extme/indexpr97.htm>

World Book Encyclopedia. Chicago: Scott Fetzer Co., 1993.

World Christian Encyclopedia. 2d ed., vol. 1. David B. Barrett, George T. Kurian, Todd M. Johnson, eds. Oxford University Press, 2001.

World Health Organization. *Epidemiological Fact Sheet on HIV/AIDS and Sexually Transmitted Diseases.* <www.who.int/emc-hiv/fact_sheets/index.htm>

World Organisation Against Torture. <www.omct.org>

Worldmark Encyclopedia of the Nations. Moshe Y. Sachs, ed. New York: John Wiley & Sons, 1997.

Wright, David K. *Enchantment of the World: Albania.* Chicago: Children's Press, 1997.

—————. *Enchantment of the World: Brunei.* Chicago: Children's Press, 1991.

Nancy Huff

A former teacher in public and private schools for 13 years, Nancy has a B.S. in mathematics and a master's degree in English as a second language.

She is founder and president of Teach the Children International (TCI), a nonprofit organization that reaches out to children at risk in the United States and abroad.

Overseas, TCI provides humanitarian relief, school supplies, and outreach programs for refugees. TCI has sponsored refugee programs for the Kosovar in Macedonia and Albania, the Sudanese in Egypt and Sudan, and the Sahrawi in Algeria.

Each year TCI sponsors a citywide call to the people of Tulsa, Oklahoma, where Nancy lives, to pray for schools. The purpose of this call is to encourage individuals, churches, and organizations to intercede for specific schools.

Nancy writes magazine articles and books about education and children's issues to raise awareness and promote public involvement in the needs of children. She hosts a daily radio program, "Transformation Time," that encourages people to take their place in prayer.

Nancy may be contacted at

Teach the Children, International, Inc.
PO Box 700832
Tulsa, OK 74170-0832
Email: TCI@Transformation.org
Website: www.TransformationTime.org

Beverly Pegues

A career paralegal turned mission agency administrator, Beverly Pegues is president of WINDOW INTERNATIONAL NETWORK, founded by her and her late husband, Leonard, and former executive director of the Christian Information Network. She has coordinated prayer in the 10/40 Window since October 1993. Beverly is also actively involved in training and outreach to the 10/40 Window nations.

Beverly speaks at conferences, churches, and retreats nationally and internationally. She has spoken in many countries, including Cyprus, Indonesia, Germany, Jordan, Egypt, Sudan, Sweden, Lebanon, and Canada. She also leads prayer journey teams into the 10/40 Window. Her delightful personality reflects the warmth and love of Jesus Christ as she ministers on subjects of prayer, praise, worship, and maturing in our faith.

Beverly is the principal author of *WindoWatchman I* and is the editor of *WindoWatchman II*. These books document the signs, wonders, and miracles the Lord performed in the lives of people in the 10/40 Window nations, prayer journeyers, and the home-based intercessors during the worldwide Praying Through the Window initiatives. In 1999 Beverly and Luis Bush co-authored *The Move of the Holy Spirit in the 10/40 Window.*

WINDOW INTERNATIONAL NETWORK coordinated millions of intercessors to pray during the 2001 Praying Through the Window V: Children, Teens, and Young Adults.

You can contact Beverly at

WINDOW INTERNATIONAL NETWORK
PO Box 49127
Colorado Springs, CO 80949-9127
Phone: (719) 522-1040
Fax: (719) 277-7148
Email: win@win1040.com
Website: www.win1040.com